Policing, Race and Racism

Michael Rowe

Routledge
Taylor & Francis Group

LONDON AND NEW YORK

First published by Willan Publishing 2004
This edition published by Routledge 2012
2 Park Square, Milton Park, Abingdon, Oxon OX14 4RN
711 Third Avenue, New York, NY 10017

Routledge is an imprint of the Taylor & Francis Group, an informa business

Paperback
ISBN-13: 978-1-84392-044-1

Hardback
ISBN-13: 978-1-84392-045-8

British Library Cataloguing-in-Publication Data

A catalogue record for this book is available from the British Library

Typeset by TW Typesetting, Plymouth, Devon
Project managed by Deer Park Productions, Tavistock, Devon

Policing, Race and Racism

Policing and Society Series

Series editors: Les Johnston, Frank Leishman, Tim Newburn

Published titles

Policing, Ethics and Human Rights, by Peter Neyroud and Alan Beckley
Policing: a short history, by Philip Rawlings
Policing: an introduction to concepts and practice, by Alan Wright
Psychology and Policing, by Peter B. Ainsworth
Private Policing, by Mark Button
Policing and the Media, by Frank Leishman and Paul Mason
Policing, Race and Racism, by Michael Rowe

Contents

List of tables and figures   vii
Acknowledgements   viii

1 **Introduction**   1
   The murder of Stephen Lawrence: another instalment in a
      tale of failure   4
   The Macpherson Report: an overview   7
   Institutional racism: origins and controversies   9
   About the book   13

2 **Recruitment, retention and promotion**   20
   The historical context   22
   Recruitment initiatives   24
   The experience of minority ethnic officers   31
   Legal and regulatory factors   33
   Pragmatic factors   37
   Police legitimacy   40

3 **Racism and the role of police culture**   43
   Stereotyping and 'cop culture'   46
   Police culture as an obstacle to reform   54
   Rank-and-file culture as an obstacle to reform: the case of
      the Black Police Association   58

4 **Community and race relations training**   61
   A brief history of police CRR training   63
   Challenges in contemporary CRR training   66
   Approaches to police CRR training: the challenge of the
      'affective domain'   72
   Reform through training: reconsidering the nature of police
      culture   74

5 **Stop and search**   78
   Suspicious minds: stop and search before the 1984 Police and
      Criminal Evidence Act   80
   The PACE framework   83

Post-Macpherson developments   89
Discretion, street crime and measuring police performance   93
Section 60: a return to 'sus'?   95

6 **Racist incidents, policing and 'hate crimes'**   **99**
The conceptual ambiguities of hate crime   102
Applying hate crime law in practice   107
Concluding comments: reconsidering hate   117

7 **Accountability and complaints**   **120**
The principle of police accountability   122
Complaints against the police   129
Police–community relations: centralisation vs. devolved
    policing   134

8 **Policing diversity**   **137**
The impact of the Lawrence Inquiry   140
Policing diversity: conceptual framework and implications   144

9 **Conclusion**   **153**
The complexities of change   156
Dynamics of police reform   160
The social context of policing   161
The individuation of institutional racism   167

References   **170**

Index   **180**

List of tables and figures

Table 2.1: Representation by grade band of Police Service, 2002   22
Table 2.2: Minority ethnic representation, as percentage of each
    rank, 1992 and 2002   31
Table 2.3: Number of minority ethnic officers, resident population
    and future targets, selected police service areas, 1999 and 2002   35
Table 5.1: Stop and searches per 1,000 population 1994/95,
    selected forces   85
Table 5.2: Stop and searches of persons under Section 1 of
    PACE 1984 and other legislation, by ethnicity, 1997–2002, per
    1,000 of population and total number.   87
Table 6.1: Victim perceptions of the seriousness of racially
    motivated and non-racially motivated crime   105
Table 6.2: Racially aggravated offences, 1999–2000, by police
    service area   110
Table 6.3: Identification of racist incidents by police service and
    CPS, 1999–2000, per cent   111
Table 8.1: Models of police–community relations   142

Figure 2.1a: Police recruitment poster   26
Figure 2.1b: Police recruitment poster   27
Figure 5.1: Section 60 stop and searches by ethnicity, England
    and Wales, 1998–2002   96
Figure 6.1: Breakdown of racially aggravated offences recorded
    by the police in England and Wales, 1999–2000   113
Figure 6.2: Detection rates of racially aggravated and non-racially
    aggravated offences, 1999–2000   114
Figure 8.1: Policing diversity: recent official publications   143

Acknowledgements

I am happy to acknowledge the very many people who have helped to shape the ideas that underpin this book. Much of the primary material that is incorporated into the following chapters has been gathered as part of various research projects conducted for police services in England and Wales between 1999 and 2003. More than 200 police officers, police support staff and members of the public engaged in police training gave their time generously and shared their perspectives on the impact of the Lawrence Report, and I am very grateful for their cooperation. I am also indebted to Sam Johnson who, as a research assistant, conducted many of these interviews, and to Rob Pugsley who was project administrator. Jon Garland was also heavily involved in these research projects and read draft versions of several of the chapters that follow and I owe him a huge debt for the many years of discussion and debate that have helped me shape half-baked ideas into something resembling a systematic and rational analysis.

Over several years students enrolled in postgraduate courses at the Scarman Centre at the University of Leicester have provided an excellent forum in which I have been able to develop understanding of policing, race and racism. It is a paradox of the educational process that the person ostensibly delivering teaching may learn more about the subject matter at hand than the students who might expect to profit from their lectures and seminars. I hope that the postgraduate students who have attended my classes in recent years have learnt from them and I am pleased to record my sincere thanks to them for their generous support.

As always, the biggest debt is owed to Anna, Derry, Maggie and Niall, without whom – as someone else once said – this book would have been written in half the time. I wouldn't have had it any other way, though.

Michael Rowe

Chapter 1

Introduction

Two significant anniversaries passed during the period in which this book has been written, both of which led the media to reassess the state of race, racism and the British police service. April 2003 saw the tenth anniversary of the murder of Stephen Lawrence marked with a memorial service that was attended by many high-profile figures alongside his family and friends. Eight months later the media devoted many column-inches to reviewing the extent to which progress had been made in the five years since publication of the Macpherson Report in January 1999. In many respects this book seeks to add to this debate by taking as a recurring theme the question: 'What has changed since Macpherson?'. While what is outlined in the following chapters is intended to provide a thorough analysis of the myriad of policies and initiatives that have been generated in the half decade since the Lawrence Report appeared, it is emphasised at the outset that a definitive answer to that question remains elusive. As much as can be stated with any certainty is that those responsible for managing and leading the police service have developed a raft of measures in response to the Lawrence Report that have covered a very wide range of police activity. The extent to which these have improved the quality of service that minority ethnic communities receive from the police is, however, much more difficult to discern and it is certain that the gulf in public trust and confidence in the police that Macpherson identified has not been fully bridged.

While milestones such as these invite debate and discussion, some of the themes reviewed in the chapters that follow are subject to recurring media scrutiny, as racist and deviant police officers have entered public discourse about law and order. In October 2003 a BBC documentary, *The Secret Policeman*, revealed extreme racist attitudes expressed by a number of police officers undergoing basic training at Bruche, near Warrington (BBC, 2003). The programme contained secretly filmed footage of an officer donning a Ku Klux Klan-style white hood, improvised out of a pillowcase, and boasting that he would like to kill Asians and 'bury them under the train tracks' if he could get away with it. Another officer boasted that he would issue minority ethnic motorists with fixed penalties in circumstances where he would let white people escape with an informal caution. A third officer claimed that he joined the police service because he knew it was a racist organisation and it would allow him to 'look after his own'. As the journalist who had gone undercover to make the programme noted, the clandestine footage, recorded with poor lighting, focus and soundtrack, was reminiscent of the earlier surveillance material of the suspects in the Lawrence murder case, which showed them practising their knifing techniques and boasting of their racism.

Both the programme itself and the huge public outcry that it occasioned revealed some interesting wider dimensions about policing, race and racism in contemporary British society. First, condemnation of the officers' views emanated from across the police establishment. Several forces were implicated in the programme, since the probationer officers were serving in North Wales, Cheshire and Greater Manchester Police, and senior officers were quick to condemn the racist attitudes the programme had revealed. The documentary itself contrasted the official prohibition of racist language with earlier footage, recorded in the 1980s, of an interview with the then chairman of the Police Federation, Les Curtis, who defended police officers' use of the term 'black bastard' on the grounds that such expressions were commonly used in society at large. In response to the 2003 documentary no senior officer, Federation spokesperson, or government official sought to defend the racist attitudes that had been revealed on the grounds that these were privately expressed or that these could be distinguished from the professional standards of behaviour to which officers were expected to adhere. Neither did the police seek consolation in an oft-cited claim that the police service reflects the worst elements of the wider society that it serves as well as the best. As is outlined later in this book, these attitudes towards racism in the police – that crude stereotyping is unfortunate but does not impact on behaviour, or that it reflects broader problems in society – have been advanced in the past by those seeking to marginalise or downplay the issue.

The Secret Policeman raised other factors of huge relevance to consideration of institutional racism and the impact of the Macpherson Report, but which did not receive such widespread attention following the broadcast. Early in the documentary it was noted that the new recruits were advised that racist language was not allowed in the training room, and might lead to disciplinary proceedings. However, the journalist also recorded that the Police Federation advised that officers facing such sanctions would be defended. Later in the documentary, footage showed one of the police trainers informing the class that one of their colleagues – the only from a minority ethnic background – would no longer be attending. The tone in which the announcement was delivered caused amusement among the trainees, some of whom had expressed reservations about an Asian being among them, giving the impression that the trainer was colluding in the ostracism of a minority ethnic recruit. Neither of these aspects of the BBC documentary elicited significant comment in the media furore that surrounded its broadcast and yet both raise questions about institutionalised racism, given that they relate to organisational features of the police service. Instead the media focus was on the dramatic and abhorrent footage of officers proudly discussing their prejudice, a serious problem that needs attention but not clear examples of institutional racism, which was the key finding of the Macpherson Report. The manner in which the concept of institutional racism has been understood and much misrepresented in the aftermath of the Lawrence Report is discussed later in this chapter.

Within a few days of broadcast of *The Secret Policeman* the media reported other examples of racism experienced by black and Asian police officers. One example was the case of PC Ishfaq Hussain, who resigned from the West Midlands Police alleging that the force had failed to protect him against racism from his colleagues and from the public. In his letter of resignation, Hussain claimed that 'rather than tackling racist incidents [the police] perpetuate them and anyone who challenges this conduct is persecuted' (*Guardian*, 2003a). These cases followed quickly in the wake of the case of Supt. Ali Dizaei, who had been suspended from his job with the Metropolitan Police while subject to charges of corruption. Following the collapse of the case against him, in September 2003, it was claimed that racists opposed to him had made spurious allegations in an effort to undermine him and the investigation into these complaints had been described as a 'racist witch-hunt' (*Guardian*, 2003b). The case of Supt. Dizaei is discussed at greater length in Chapter 2 of this book. Instances such as these suggest that there is now a broad consensus that racism is a continuing and serious problem in contemporary policing, and that it must be tackled. To that extent, the establishment of images of racist police officers as 'folk devils' suggests that the Macpherson Report has had an important effect in sensitising mainstream white society to the realities of racism and has helped to create an agenda for reform. However, as is demonstrated in the chapters that follow, and argued at length in the conclusion, this agenda has established a relatively narrow – even if extensive – programme of activity and one that undermines the concept of institutionalised racism, which was the distinctive contribution of the Macpherson Report. Before outlining the conceptual debates surrounding institutional racism, a brief overview of the Lawrence case and the subsequent Macpherson Inquiry is given.

The murder of Stephen Lawrence: another instalment in a tale of failure

Shocking though they are, the bare details of the racist murder of Stephen Lawrence in April 1993 on a street in Eltham, south London, do little to explain the enormous ramifications to which they would give rise. As Lawrence, an 18-year-old student who wanted to become an architect, and his friend, Duwayne Brooks, made their way home at around 10.30 on the evening of 22 April they were suddenly and without provocation attacked by a gang of white youths, one of whom shouted 'what, what nigger' as he approached. Even after the assailants had fled down a nearby side street it was not clear to Brooks, or the few other witnesses, that Lawrence was seriously hurt. Brooks ran from the scene, fearful that the attackers would return, and urged his friend to follow: which Stephen tried to do. However, his wounds, it turned out, were extensive and it was noted with surprise by the coroner that Stephen managed to cover approximately 130 yards up Well Hall Road before collapsing on the pavement. While Brooks phoned for an ambulance, Lawrence was comforted by a couple who happened to be passing, during which time two police officers arrived at the scene, but did not provide any first aid treatment. By the time the ambulance arrived Lawrence's condition appeared – to the untrained eyes of the others present – to be deteriorating. Such was the loss of blood from the two serious stab wounds inflicted on Stephen that it seems likely that he was dead even before the ambulance arrived, within 25 minutes or so of the attack.

When considering the actual sequence of events surrounding what has become one of the most renowned crimes of recent decades in British society, it is remarkable how ordinary many of the details of the case were. The above summary is intended simply to establish the bare facts of the murder; the details outlined in the paragraphs below are gleaned from the Macpherson Report, Cathcart's (2000) account and from contemporaneous newspaper reports. What stands out from these more detailed reports is how routine much of the context of the case was. For example, Lawrence and Brooks were at the bus stop where the attack occurred as they were hurrying so that Lawrence could get home before a curfew laid down by his father. The actual attack lasted no more than 10 seconds or so and some of those who saw it had little idea that it was serious until they read subsequent newspaper coverage appealing for witnesses to come forward (Cathcart, 2000: 65). The two police officers who arrived at the scene before the ambulance speculated that it may have been stuck in traffic, and one officer left to investigate the whereabouts of the paramedics. What became one of the most widely discussed and extensively analysed crimes of recent times combined a mixture of the tragic and mundane in much the same way as so many other offences.

It is also clear that the violent assault that killed Stephen Lawrence was not an isolated event at that time in that part of south London. Two earlier racist murders had occurred in the area: in February 1991 Rolan Adams was stabbed to death, and the following year 15-year-old Rohit Duggal was the victim of a racist murder in Eltham. The investigation of the Lawrence case involved re-examining other knife attacks that had occurred in the previous weeks and months as the police considered that those responsible for stabbing Stacey Benefield, Gurdeep Bhangal, Darren Whitham and Lee Pearson in separate incidents might also be implicated in Stephen's murder (Cathcart, 2000: 80–6). Added to this local history of violence and racism was the presence, in nearby Welling, of the headquarters of the far-right British National Party, which would win a council seat in Millwall a few months after the Lawrence murder. Against this context the killing of Stephen Lawrence quickly became a high-profile crime. A few weeks after the murder, Doreen and Neville Lawrence, Stephen's parents, were supported by South African President Nelson Mandela, who met them during a visit to London. In June 1993 some 700 people, including two local MPs, attended a memorial service.

During the first few days following the murder several independent sources suggested to the police the names of five white youths who may have been involved in the attack. Each had a reputation for violence and for the use of knives. Although Macpherson's Report (1999: 13.9) argued that the failure to arrest these suspects quickly was a fundamental mistake early in the police investigation, since it may have allowed forensic evidence to be destroyed, the five youths – Jamie Acourt, Neil Acourt, Gary Dobson, Luke Knight and David Norris – were eventually taken into custody early in May 1993. From this point onwards a series of legal controversies developed that have surrounded the police investigation of the murder and are outlined in greater detail in the Macpherson Report. The first of these was the announcement in July 1993 that the Crown Prosecution Service (CPS) had dropped charges against two of the five suspects on the grounds of insufficient evidence. Two years after the murder, as the CPS and the police investigation ran out of steam, the Lawrence family – in an extremely rare legal move – brought a private prosecution against the same five suspects. Early in the proceedings, the judge indicated that the eye-witness evidence that was the primary basis of the prosecution case would not be admitted, which meant that the case was withdrawn and the defendants acquitted.

Once the CPS had decided not to bring prosecutions and the private case brought by the Lawrence family had come to nothing, the final possibility of establishing in law who had committed the murder rested in the coroner's inquiry into Stephen's death. The inquest had been postponed on several occasions, as other legal matters were pending, and was not held until February 1997. In a statement to the coroner's court, Doreen Lawrence outlined her anger that the police had not been more systematic in collecting evidence in the hours and days following the murder, and suggested that it was this lack of evidence that was at the root of the failure to secure convictions in the case. Her perspective on the role and attitude of the police is summed up in a few sentences from her statement (cited in Cathcart, 2000: 276):

> My son was murdered nearly four years ago. His killers are still walking the streets. When my son was murdered the police said my son was a criminal belonging to a gang. My son was stereotyped by the police – he was black then he must be a criminal – and they set about investigating him and us. The investigation lasted two weeks. That allowed vital evidence to be lost.

Perhaps the most dramatic element of the coroner's court proceedings, however, was that it provided the first occasion on which the five suspects in the case, who had been acquitted at the Old Bailey and so could not face subsequent prosecution, spoke in public about the case. The five were summoned to appear at the hearing, they did not attend voluntarily, and were advised by the coroner at the outset that they were not on trial and had the right not to answer questions if to do so would be self-incriminating. This option was keenly pursued by all five, each of whom refused to answer even the most basic questions about themselves, their whereabouts on the night of the murder, any knowledge that they had of events; even, in one case, refusing to confirm their name on the grounds that to do so might be incriminating. While this tactic meant that nothing was revealed about their involvement, or non-involvement, in the crime it proved a turning point in the history of the Lawrence murder. Although the jury at the coroner's court returned the verdict that Lawrence had been unlawfully killed in a racially motivated attack, they were forbidden by law from naming suspects. However, an unlikely source was to break this legal restriction, in response, it claimed to the outraged public response to the lack of cooperation and the silence of the five youths. Thus the *Daily Mail* front-page headline on 14 February 1997 proclaimed in huge letters 'MURDERERS: The Mail accuses these men of killing. If we are wrong, let them sue us', below which were individual photographs of the five suspects along with their names.

Following the coroner's verdict the head of the Commission for Racial Equality, Herman Ousely, requested that the Home Secretary establish a public inquiry into the crime and subsequent policing and legal developments. Such calls had emanated from various sources over the years since Stephen's murder but had been consistently refused by Conservative government ministers. It may have been fortuitous that public concern about the murder and subsequent investigation was rising in the weeks immediately before the general election that saw a Labour government in power for the first time in eighteen years. Within weeks of taking office, the new Home Secretary, Jack Straw, announced the establishment of a public inquiry into the affair, under the direction of Sir William Macpherson, a former High Court judge. The Macpherson Inquiry first sat in March 1998, took evidence for six months, and its final report was published in January of the following year.

The Macpherson Report: an overview

The public inquiry into the Lawrence case took evidence from officers and witnesses directly involved at the scene of the murder, from those engaged in the subsequent investigation, senior officers responsible for the general direction of enquiries, and from chief officers, including the commissioner of the Metropolitan Police, Sir Paul Condon. In addition, civil servants, expert witnesses and academics provided evidence. The breadth of the final report, referred to interchangeably in this book as the Macpherson Report or the Lawrence Report, is readily apparent, covering the precise details of the investigation as well as broad contextual matters such as concerns about police use of stop and search powers and the deaths of minority ethnic people while in custody. Many of these issues are reviewed in subsequent chapters of this book. Emerging from all of these matters are three broad themes relating to the police investigation: the incompetence of the police, suggestions of corruption, and the role of racism. Underpinning all of these recommendations was the central thrust of the Report, that a ministerial priority be established ensuring that the police service 'increased trust and confidence in policing amongst minority ethnic communities' (Macpherson, 1999: 327). The Report's findings in relation to the first two of the three themes – relating to incompetence and corruption – will be briefly outlined below, before a more detailed discussion of institutional racism.

Instances of police incompetence are given at many stages in the Lawrence Report. Even a cursory reading of the contents page, with subentries including 'training inadequate', 'lack of command and organisation', 'lack of documents', 'disarray', 'absence of logs', 'lack of information', 'lack of directions and control' and 'fundamental error', reveals a catalogue of mistakes in the early stages of the investigation. Among these was a failure to seal the scene of the incident or to carry out house-to-house enquiries. Some of these errors seem to be the responsibility of officers involved in the investigation while others appear to have arisen due to a lack of resources or institutional shortcomings. In the latter category were the problems that arose from the investigation using HOLMES (Home Office Large Major Enquiry System), intended to provide a computerised means of ensuring that information is effectively processed, cross-referenced, actioned and followed up. Since the technology and training to operate the system were both lacking, the investigation was hampered to such an extent that leads were not followed speedily and information was not shared among the investigating officers (Cathcart, 2000: 45–6). The lack of sensitivity with which the Lawrence family were treated by officers working on the case, the failure to keep them properly informed of developments surrounding the investigation, and the lack of first aid training of officers at the scene all provided evidence that the Lawrence case was flawed by police incompetence. The Macpherson Report made clear that the errors that marred the investigation of the Lawrence murder were not confined to particular mistakes made by junior officers responsible for day-to-day inquiries but extended up the ranks of the police service. In contrast to previous official reviews of policing, most notably the 1981 Scarman Report into the Brixton disorders, Macpherson did not exonerate senior officers for the mistakes of their subordinates. One of the main findings contained in the Lawrence Report was that 'the investigation was marred by a combination of professional incompetence, institutional racism and a failure of leadership by senior officers' (Macpherson, 1999: 46.1).

A serious allegation surrounding the Lawrence case was that the murder investigation had been hampered by police corruption. Much of this concern centred on the role played by an established member of the criminal network operating in the area at the time, Clifford Norris, father of one the main suspects, David Norris. Macpherson records that Clifford Norris had, it emerged in 1994, bribed witnesses in the Stacey Benefield stabbing, with which David was charged, against giving evidence, and the Lawrence family suggested to the Inquiry that it could be inferred that something similar had happened with regard to Stephen's case. Both Cathcart's (2000) and Macpherson's (1999) accounts of the early stages of the murder investigation note that people who may have been witnesses to the crime or possessed other information were reluctant to speak to the police – which explained why the police received various anonymous notes outlining local rumour about who was responsible. Macpherson (1999: 8.18) is clear, though, that no collusion or corruption could be proved to have influenced the investigation of the Lawrence murder.

By far the most significant finding of the Lawrence Report, however, was that the police service is institutionally racist. Consideration of this matter had been extensive during the Inquiry, a number of expert witnesses had given evidence outlining different perspectives on the nature of the problem of racism in the police service and Sir Paul Condon, Commissioner of the Metropolitan Police, had been questioned by Macpherson on the subject. During his appearance before the Inquiry, Condon rejected claims that the police service was institutionally racist, arguing that a lack of clarity concerning the precise definition of the term made it impossible for him to do otherwise. He also claimed that '[by] describing the challenge and issues as "institutional racism" you are ascribing the notion to all officers, that they are walking around just waiting to do something' (*PA News*, 1998). Somewhat surprisingly, Condon went on to claim the police service had 'always challenged racism'. Having denied the problem of institutional racism, Condon, along with other senior officers, negotiated a sharp reverse of this position once the Macpherson Report was published containing a stark declaration that the police service was institutionally racist. The Lawrence Report (1999: 6.34) defined the concept in the following terms, which quickly became predominant:

> The collective failure of an organisation to provide an appropriate and professional service to people because of their colour, culture or ethnic origin. It can be seen or detected in processes, attitudes and behaviour which amount to discrimination through unwitting prejudice, ignorance, thoughtlessness and racist stereotyping which disadvantages minority ethnic people.

Institutional racism: origins and controversies

While Paul Condon's initial refusal to accept that the police service is institutionally racist on the grounds that the term suggests that individual officers are overt and deliberate racists seems incongruous, given that the concept has rarely been used in this way, another aspect of his position is defensible. Condon argued that he could not be expected to accept that the police service is institutionally racist when there is no consensus on what the term itself means. The lack of conceptual rigour that has surrounded the term is readily apparent from even a brief review of the literature and against such confusion it seems reasonable for a senior police officer to reserve judgement. The contours of the debate about the nature of institutional racism are reviewed in this section and it is argued that the definition that Macpherson arrived at does not resolve these ambiguities. A number of ways in which the concept has been misinterpreted and misapplied in the post-Lawrence era are also identified.

As Singh (2000) outlined, the concept of institutional racism developed alongside the Black Power movement in the United States in the late 1960s and the 1970s. The term was introduced by Carmichael and Hamilton (1967), who contrasted institutional racism with individual racism. Essentially the concept denoted a break with prevailing understandings of racism that located the problem with the pathologies of individuals who were conceived either as deviants subscribing to illiberal and outmoded pseudo-scientific notions of racial supremacy or, more commonly, as misguided people afraid of groups unknown to them and perceived as threatening. Whichever model of racism may have been applied in various circumstances, the analytical focus remained on the values, attitudes and social practices that reinforced prejudice and discrimination among individuals. The sociology of 'race relations' in Britain during the 1950s and 1960s reflected this focus. Many studies during this period examined the social context of poor housing, competition for employment and other social pressures deemed to create a climate in which stereotyping and prejudice flourished (Banton, 1967; Glass, 1960). In contrast to such analysis, the notion of institutional racism developed in order that broader power relations and structural dimensions of society were included in analysis of the production and reproduction of racism, and the relation of this to other forms of marginalisation.

Perhaps the key distinction between individual and institutional racism is that the latter places greater emphasis on outcomes and effects, rather than intent. Practices and procedures that result in inequality may be regarded as institutionally racist, whatever their expressed purpose. As is outlined in the chapters that follow, many aspects of policing that have disadvantaged black and Asian people in Britain have been conceived of and implemented in terms that do not explicitly relate to race or ethnicity. For example, stop and search powers have not been devised in order to encourage or allow police officers to focus undue attention on certain minority ethnic groups, but in practice this is what they are alleged to encourage, even if the individual officers concerned are not motivated by personal prejudice. Institutional racism, as Oakley's evidence to the Lawrence Inquiry outlined (Macpherson, 1999: 6.31), describes the position that arises from the broader social position of the police, such that:

> ... if the predominantly white staff of the police organisation have their experience of visible minorities largely restricted to interactions with such groups, then negative racial stereotypes will tend to develop accordingly.

While the Macpherson Report's finding that the British police service is institutionally racist created considerable controversy, in many respects it actually offered little that was qualitatively new in terms of its underlying analysis of the problem. As Solomos (1999) pointed out, the definition contained in the report is broadly similar to 'indirect racial discrimination' that was outlawed by the 1976 Race Relations Act, which – as with Macpherson's definition – refers to the unintended consequences of actions that might not have been designed to discriminate. Since the publication of the Macpherson Report was so widely contrasted with the earlier Scarman Report into the Brixton disorders of 1981, it was not surprising that the former's identification of institutional racism was compared with the latter's insistence that this was a charge that could not be upheld. Macpherson, it was argued, had overturned Scarman's perspective. Although it is certainly the case that the Scarman Report did not accept that institutional racism existed in the police service whereas the Lawrence Report came to the opposite conclusion, there is actually little between the two documents in terms of their broader analysis of racism. The surface differences between a report that endorses a finding of institutional racism and another that does not disappear on closer inspection since Scarman's (1981) rejection is largely explained by his peculiar definition of the concept, which suggested that it only existed if, as a matter of deliberate policy, institutions intended to discriminate on the basis of race. As Keith (1993) argued, Scarman's very narrow definition of institutional racism suggests that he failed to understand the history of the concept.

Nonetheless, much of the language and conceptualisation with which the Scarman and Macpherson Reports discuss racism in the police are broadly the same, a point that the latter notes (Macpherson, 1999: 22). For instance, Scarman (1981: 6.35) noted that 'racialism and discrimination against black people – often hidden, sometimes unconscious – remain a major source of social tension and conflict', phraseology echoed in Macpherson's reference to unwitting prejudice. One difference that does stand out between the two relates to the culpability attached to senior ranks for the racism identified in the police service. In Scarman's account it is apparently axiomatic that senior police officers operate in good faith and are not associated with the prejudice and discrimination that their juniors sometimes exhibit. Scarman (1981: 4.63) argued that while 'racial prejudice' might on occasion cloud the judgement of junior officers on the street faced with rising levels of crime, 'such . . . bias is not to be found amongst senior police officers'. As was noted earlier, Macpherson clearly implicates higher ranks in the failure to properly investigate the murder of Stephen Lawrence. That senior officers might share the racist attitudes of the subordinates does not, in itself, point to institutional racism, however, since it continues to be a problem associated with individuals.

Since the Macpherson Report does not provide an innovative restatement of institutional racism, it is inevitable that some of the ambiguities surrounding the term continue to apply in the post-Lawrence era. Chief among these is the problem of 'conceptual inflation' (Miles, 1989), whereby any discrimination or disadvantage experienced by minority ethnic communities is explained in terms of racism. It might be that more complex processes of exclusion, not all of which are related simply to racism, explain the difficulties faced by minority ethnic groups. If the concept of institutional racism is used as a default means of explaining almost anything that leads to exclusion and marginalisation, then there is a danger, as Keith (1993: 199–200) noted, that it becomes little more than an 'all-embracing term of abuse, a rhetorical accusation of guilt'. Concerns have been expressed that the term 'institutional racism' has had a perverse outcome in terms of recent debates about policing in Britain in that it has allowed for individual officers to absolve themselves of responsibility for their actions and behaviours, on the basis that the problem is beyond any individual, and, relatedly, it allows the police service in general to seek refuge from criticism by highlighting the political, economic and cultural aspects of wider society that explain the unfortunate shortcomings of any particular organisation.

Much of the media coverage of racism in policing that followed in the wake of the 2003 TV documentary *The Secret Policeman*, referred to earlier, has tended to use the phrase institutional racism in ways Keith warned about. The concept seems to have been misapplied along two lines. First, the charge of institutional racism is used to denote a racism that is enduring and has been resistant to change. That the problem has not been resolved is taken as evidence that it is of an institutional nature, when in fact the types of behaviours concerned seem to have little to do with institutional racism in the sense outlined here, but to be more closely related to individual overt witting racism. The second way in which the concept of institutional racism seems to have been misapplied in media discourse is by using it to indicate that the issue is widespread, as though the presence of a significant number of individual racists means that the problem becomes, by a process of aggregation, institutional in nature.

In short, it seems that the Macpherson Report's finding that the police service is institutionally racist helped to establish a political climate in which many of the policies and initiatives that are outlined in the following chapters of this book could be devised and implemented. As is clear from what follows, the five years since the Lawrence Report appeared have seen very considerable activity with the express intention of improving minority ethnic communities' trust and confidence in the police service. The extent to which these have led to an improvement in these relations is difficult to gauge: that there is still progress to be made does not mean that none has been forthcoming during the period since the Report was published. In reviewing the changing contours of police relations with minority ethnic communities it is important to recognise the broader social and political context in which these develop. It is argued in the conclusion that continuing processes of racialisation and criminalisation, surrounding ongoing debates about, for example, drugs and gun-related crime, mean that the police service is likely to continue to face strained relations with sections of the community. While the argument that racism within the police service is a reflection of racism in society more generally has often been used as a complacent excuse for inaction, it remains the case that attempts to address problems discreetly within individual organisations without addressing the broader social context surrounding them cannot hope to achieve anything more than provisional successes.

About the book

Much of the primary research that underpins the discussion that follows has been undertaken as part of a series of studies carried out for the British Home Office and various police services intended to gauge the effectiveness of community and race relations or diversity training provided to police officers. Discussion of these findings is contained in Chapter 4, which explores the impact of training at greater length. Conducting these interviews provided an excellent opportunity to ask officers and civilian staff a wide range of questions about the nature of race and racism within the police service, their attitudes towards minority ethnic groups and the impact that the Lawrence Inquiry had made on policing in contemporary Britain. These interviews were conducted between 1999 and 2003 and involved some 218 individuals drawn from three of the major metropolitan police services in England and Wales as well as two smaller, more mixed constabularies. Those interviewed ranged from senior officers, up to and including Association of Chief Police Officers (ACPO) ranks, and civilian managers, to junior constables and administrative staff. Alongside these interviews, formal discussions were carried out with those with specialist knowledge of these subjects, such as, for example, various members of the Black Police Association. The qualitative information gathered from these interviews has been supplemented with secondary data from a variety of sources, as outlined in the following chapters.

The book is structured around the key issues that emerged directly from the Lawrence Report and that have featured in the ongoing debates about policing, race and racism. In no way does the book claim to be an exhaustive review of all that has been done in the five years or so since publication of Macpherson's findings: several important topics, such as the role of family liaison or crime scene management or the extent to which the police disclose information about investigations, are mentioned only in passing. Instead the focus of the book is on matters that have greatest relevance in terms of broader relations between the police, minority ethnic communities and the public at large.

Chapter 2 examines the long-standing efforts that the police service has made to increase recruitment from minority ethnic communities. While the Lawrence Report made clear recommendations about how the recruitment and retention of minority ethnic staff should be encouraged and monitored, it is clear that the various attempts that have been implemented since the 1970s have generally met with little success. Not only does the overall proportion of black and Asian officers remain stubbornly low, at around 3.5 per cent in 2002, it continues to be the case that this figure is lower among senior ranks and that most minority ethnic officers are concentrated in more junior posts. A frequent technique used to try to attract more minority ethnic applicants to the police service has been to use existing staff with such backgrounds as 'ambassadors' who can encourage others to seek a career in the police service. Not only may this prove problematic since the assumption that minority ethnic officers will have an empathy with others of a similar ethnic background might prove simplistic, it can also backfire if, as happened in September 2003, minority ethnic officers withdraw their support on the grounds that the service has not done enough to confront racism. Such approaches reflect a more general trend in recruitment campaigns that assume that minority ethnic communities do not pursue careers in the police service because they erroneously believe they will experience racism from colleagues. In many interviews carried out by the author, white police staff have maintained that such problems, which may once have existed, are no longer a feature of the police service. Similarly, recruitment posters and the like tend to portray an inclusive harmonious multi-racial police service. One reason why recruitment campaigns have not been more successful, it is argued in Chapter 2, is that potential minority ethnic recruits have perceptions of the police service that are not misplaced or outdated, but are based on real experience of fraught relations between the police and minority ethnic communities. The chapter concludes by critically examining three broad reasons why the police service has sought to increase the proportion of minority ethnic officers. Legal and regulatory factors, pragmatic benefits, and concerns relating to the legitimacy of the service have all driven efforts to increase recruitment and retention of minority ethnic staff. It is argued in the chapter that increasing the numbers of officers from such backgrounds will not, in and of itself, necessarily lead to improved relations with minority communities. It is simplistic to assume that the ethnicity of officers is the overriding factor shaping relations with the community, and the structural and institutional roles of the police are vital to the future dynamics of these relations.

While the Lawrence Report's emphasis on institutional racism focused attention on broader structural factors, it is clear that many of the developments instigated in its wake have sought to address police culture, which has long been identified as a source of racism within the service. Moreover, police culture has also been used to explain the apparent ability of junior officers to resist reforms introduced from the top that do not coincide with their conceptualisation of the police role. Chapter 3 considers how the notion of police culture has been used to explain various dysfunctional and deviant aspects of policing. The chapter explores the relationship between racism and broader aspects of police culture that have been noted in various studies of the service. In particular, the sense of mission, cynicism, and the social isolation of police officers from wider society are outlined and the role that these have played in the development of racism is discussed. While such analysis relates racism within the police to the experiences of doing police work, others have suggested that the service is attractive as a career to those who hold certain values and beliefs, and that racism is related to the characteristics of those who join the service. Efforts to encourage a more diverse range of recruits would, it is argued, help to overcome cultures of racism within the service.

Chapter 3 continues by exploring some of the conceptual weaknesses surrounding arguments about police culture, drawing in particular on the work of Chan (1996, 1997) and Waddington (1999a). Among these are the lack of a clear link between the attitudes and values of police officers and the way in which they actually behave while on duty, and the need to consider police culture against the broader structural and institutional position of the police service in wider society. The chapter concludes by outlining the ways in which the occupational culture of the police service, which stresses loyalty to colleagues and team membership, can inhibit efforts to challenge racism. The extent to which minority ethnic officers have felt the need to tolerate racism from colleagues in order to fit in and be accepted is noted. It was against this background that in the mid-1990s the Black Police Association (BPA) was developed, initially in the Metropolitan Police, to provide a supportive network for minority ethnic staff. The obstacles that the BPA has faced in its efforts to tackle racism within the service, not least the series of allegations of misconduct and impropriety falsely made against a number of high-profile members of the organisation, are outlined in the final section of the chapter.

Chapter 4 evaluates various training programmes in 'community and race relations' or 'policing diversity' that have been developed in the wake of the Lawrence Report. While much police training has tradition-ally been based on an instructional model whereby officers are guided on how to act and behave in a range of circumstances, their legal powers and responsibilities, organisational procedures and the like, there have been aspects of social and interpersonal skills included in the training curriculum for many years. The chapter outlines distinct approaches to police training on issues relating to ethnicity and racism, contrasting those that adopt a broadly behavioural approach intended to guide officers on how to act professionally and those intended to affect their values, beliefs and attitudes. It is suggested that much of the recent in-service training is based on the latter model. The chapter provides a summary of a three-year evaluation of these training programmes, paying particular attention to the training of civilian support staff alongside police officers, the contribution of community representatives brought into sessions to provide insight into attitudes towards the police service, and the impact that the programmes had in terms of the ongoing working practices of those who attended them. In broad terms it is argued there was a general failure to transfer the training to the workplace and that more needs to be done to ensure that such programmes are embedded into police work. While the training programmes reviewed offer a positive opportunity for officers and civilian staff to reflect upon their own values and attitudes, there is little evidence that the broader institutional aspects of racism are addressed. A recurring theme of this book, as outlined in the conclusion, is that many of the initiatives devised to tackle racism in the police service in the post-Lawrence Report era have not addressed the institutional dimensions of the problem. Training programmes such as those evaluated in Chapter 4 continue to focus upon individuals by encouraging critical reflection on attitudes and behaviour. Worthy though this may be, the chapter argues, it does not address structural dimensions of the problem or the broader social context within which the police operate.

Allegations that the police in Britain pay disproportionate attention to minority ethnic groups when it comes to stop and search have been a recurring theme for several decades. As Chapter 5 outlines, suggestions that various minority ethnic groups have been over-involved in street crime can be traced back to eighteenth-century concerns that the Irish were largely responsible for 'footpad robbery'. The chapter explores recent concerns that black people are over-policed in terms of stop and search as the strategy developed in the early 1980s amid broader criticisms over aggressive policing tactics. Against this background, and the experience of urban unrest in the early 1980s that was linked, in part, to confrontational police operations, the 1984 Police and Criminal Evidence Act (PACE) restricted the powers of officers by requiring them to have 'reasonable suspicion' of criminal activity or intent prior to stopping any individual. As the chapter outlines, the various codes of practice issued under the rubric of the Act specifically stipulate that an individual's ethnicity is not, in and of itself, grounds for reasonable suspicion that can justify a police stop. PACE also led to improvements in the recording of stop and searches so that there is now a considerable body of evidence that suggests that minority ethnic groups are over-represented in terms of stop and search compared with the resident population. Several possible reasons for this over-representation are reviewed in the chapter, including that it might reflect disproportionate levels of criminality, be it as a result of racist policing, or due to the demographic characteristics of those areas where stop and search is most likely to be conducted.

While the Lawrence Report considered the issue of stop and search, many of its recommendations in this area called for further research, and Chapter 5 provides an overview of some of the key findings of the Home Office-sponsored programme of research that has been conducted since 1999. A key finding of this research has been that the over-representation of minority groups is largely related to their being resident in areas with higher levels of street crime. While this finding might suggest that the problem of the over-representation of minority ethnic groups in stop and search is not due to individual officers acting on the basis of stereotypes or prejudices, it does suggest that an institutional problem continues to exist if, for whatever reason, these groups continue to be over-policed. It is argued in Chapter 5 that increasing media and political concern about street crime and the widespread powers available to the police under Section 60 of the 1994 Criminal Justice and Public Order Act mean that controversies about stop and search are unlikely to decline.

Chapter 6 explores concerns about the inadequacy of the police response to racist violence as they have emerged since the late 1970s. As is outlined, a key complaint emanating from campaigning groups and as expressed in various official reports into the problem is that police officers often denied or marginalised the racist dimension to incidents. In this way, a defining feature of the experience of victimisation was often overlooked and the police failed to recognise the additional impact of racism on what would otherwise often be considered low-level criminal incidents. Another problem frequently identified during the 1980s was that a lack of coordinated response from local agencies, including the police, meant that racist violence and harassment often 'fell through the net'. It is argued in the chapter that these two weaknesses in the response to racist violence – the denial of a racist component to offences and the lack of a coordinated response – have been addressed since the mid-1990s. Following a review of the measures that have been taken, in particular the provisions contained in the 1998 Crime and Disorder Act that established a series of 'racially aggravated offences', the chapter examines data indicating that there is considerable discrep-ancy among the 43 police services of England and Wales in terms of the number of offences that are recorded in this way. In addition, it seems that there is considerable variation in the extent to which the police identify racially aggravated offences to the Crown Prosecution Service.

Following on from this review of policy and empirical evidence relating to racist crime, the chapter considers wider debates about 'hate crime', a legal concept that has developed in the United States. The discussion of hate crime begins by consideration of some of the conceptual controversies that have surrounded the term. Among these is the issue of whether the introduction of stiffer penalties for perpetrators of hate crime amounts to punishment of the thoughts and motivations of offenders, rather than concentrating, as it is argued that most criminal law does, on the actions of perpetrators. Finally, the chapter considers some practical problems that might arise should hate crime legislation be passed in Britain, in particular the difficulties of effectively policing incidents labelled as 'hate crime'. In general terms the chapter concludes that, for conceptual and practical reasons, there is little to be gained from enacting hate crime laws in Britain.

Chapter 7 examines debates relating to police accountability. Although these have been affected by the Lawrence Report, which made several recommendations in this area, it is clear that these are also of general significance. The chapter outlines the development of police accountability in the form of local police authorities and police community consultative groups that were introduced in the wake of the 1981 Scarman Report, and suggests that neither sets of arrangements have effectively represented diverse communities. Partly in the light of these limitations, the 1998 Crime and Disorder Act has required greater levels of consultation with local communities about policing priorities. The chapter outlines and endorses a distinction made by authors such as Keith (1988) and McLaughlin (1991) between mechanisms for formal accountability and those for consultation, which have much less scope for controlling or directing the police. It is also simplistic to assume that the difficult relations that have existed between the police and some minority ethnic communities can be resolved simply by improved dialogue, since problems arising from structural dimensions of policing are unlikely to be resolved as a result of consultation, although some benefits might arise.

The chapter continues by considering the systems for dealing with complaints made against the police, outlines the role of the Police Complaints Authority and the reasons why this was replaced in 2004 by an Independent Police Complaints Commission, which has a wider remit and additional powers of investigation. The extent to which this will lead to a decrease in private civil action being brought against the police, which has been increasing in recent years, remains to be seen. Chapter 7 concludes by outlining the implications of the recent centralisation of police governance, which has seen the power of the Home Secretary to direct police activity increase. At the same time, but in the opposite direction, there has been a process of devolution, ostensibly to ensure that police priorities are determined at a level closer to local communities. The impact of these countervailing tendencies on accountability is reviewed in the chapter.

The much-cited concept of policing diversity is examined in Chapter 8, which investigates the implications of social fragmentation on a policing system supposedly based on a tradition of consent. It is argued that developments in the post-Lawrence period amount to a significant repositioning of the police role in relation to racism and a move away from a situation in which the police provide a broadly similar service to all of the public to one that recognises that different sections of the community have legitimate needs that the service ought to meet, but that these are not consistent across all sections of society. While the chapter generally supports the need for the police to be responsive, it argues that, in practical terms, the complexities of diverse communities are such that effectively accounting for differences and reflecting these in policy becomes increasingly difficult. It is argued that this problem reflects a more fundamental problem in that the concept of community that continues to underpin developments in policing remains very simplistically defined in territorial terms. That different types of communities exist above and beyond those conceived in geographical terms poses important challenges to the notion of policing by consent, as the chapter outlines.

The concluding chapter provides a summary of the key themes of the book, and pays particular attention to ways in which the distinctive promise that the Lawrence Report seemed to offer in advocating the concept of institutional racism has been lost. Chapter 9 argues that while it is not possible to finally decide whether the Lawrence Report has brought about substantial reform of the police service, two things are clear. On the one hand, there have been countless policy formulations and initiatives designed to change the way in which police officers individually and collectively think and behave. As outlined throughout the book, some of these have been more successful than others, but it is apparent that much effort and resource have been expended. On the other hand, though, it is equally apparent that the fundamental aim spelled out by Macpherson, 'to improve public trust and confidence in policing amongst minority ethnic communities', has not been fully realised. In conclusion, the book suggests that this has not been achieved because the institutional and structural role of the police in society has not been addressed and the continuing racialisation of debates about gun crime, street crime and drug crime means that for some minority ethnic communities there are little grounds for optimism about the future direction of relations with the police.

Chapter 2

Recruitment, retention and promotion

The Macpherson Report made 70 recommendations regarding a wide range of issues affecting the policing of minority ethnic communities and the police response to victims of serious crimes in general. Among these were three relating to recruitment and retention, the fulfilment of which – it was held – would be an important end in itself and contribute to the fundamental objective spelled out by Macpherson: to improve the 'trust and confidence' of minority communities in the police. The three particular recommendations were:

Rec'n. 64. That the Home Secretary and Police Authorities' policing plans should include targets for recruitment, progression and retention of minority ethnic staff. Police Authorities to report progress to the Home Secretary annually. Such reports to be published.

65. That the Home Office and Police Services should facilitate the development of initiatives to increase the number of qualified minority ethnic recruits.

66. That Her Majesty's Inspectorate of Constabulary (HMIC) include in any regular inspection or in a thematic inspection a report on the progress made by Police Services in recruitment, progression and retention of minority ethnic staff.

In addition, recommendation 2 (ix) was that the Home Office establish performance indicators relating to the recruitment, retention and progression of minority ethnic staff. While the manner in which these recommendations have been implemented and the extent to which they have been achieved is considered in some detail later in this chapter, it is important to emphasise that these proposals restate shortcomings within the police service that have been noted very frequently and subject to considerable debate. In the mid-1990s two reports, one produced by the Commission for Racial Equality (CRE, 1996) and one by (HMIC, 1996), urged that steps be taken to ensure that the ethnic diversity of British society was more closely reflected within the police service. Both of these studies noted that demands to improve equal opportunities had been made in earlier documents produced by powerful police bodies. The CRE report, for example, pointed out that a 1990 policy document issued by the Association of Chief Police Officers (ACPO), *Setting the Standards for Policing: Meeting Community Expectations*, had argued 'forces should strive to improve equal opportunities within the organisation'. It also referred to a 1992 HMIC report, *Equal Opportunities in the Police Service*, and one from the late 1980s (CRE, 1988), *Employment in Police Forces: a Survey of Equal Opportunities*. Additionally, the CRE report noted that the 1981 Scarman Inquiry had emphasised that (Scarman, 1981: 5.12): 'A police force which fails to reflect the ethnic diversity of our society will never succeed in securing the full support of all its sections.'

Turning to the Scarman Report itself, it too noted that the under-representation of black and Asian people within the police had been a fairly long-standing matter of concern and that various attempts to rectify the problem had been made since the mid-1970s. Scarman (1981: 5.6) pointed out that while the service had made efforts to recruit minority officers, there was clearly some reluctance among the black community to seek careers within the police service. The precise findings and recommendations of these various reports will be explored below, but the apparent intractability of the issue is worth noting at this stage. Report upon report, and those mentioned above are but a few of the total, have expressed concern and dismay at the situation, suggested broadly similar solutions, and then joined the litany of documents to be cited in subsequent investigations. It is not being suggested that the police service has done nothing to address the problems so frequently identified, and some details of the measures taken are included below. However, despite decades of recruitment drives and associated activity, the number of minority ethnic police officers remains low, with 3.5 per cent being of a minority ethnic background in 2002 (Home Office, 2003). The percentages for special constables and support staff were 3.6 per cent and 5.3 per cent respectively. These figures have risen slightly each year since 1999. Given that results of the 2001 Census suggest that the minority ethnic population of England and Wales was 8.7 per cent, the police service is clearly unrepresentative. The position is compounded by the fact that minority ethnic officers are less represented in higher ranks, as Table 2.1 shows.

In addition, the figures for the police service compare badly when judged against many other agencies within the criminal justice system.

Table 2.1 Representation by grade band of Police Service, 2002

	White	Minority ethnic	% Minority ethnic
Constable	97,616	2,865	2.9
Sergeant	18,474	372	2.0
Inspector	6,195	99	1.6
Chief Inspector	1,584	24	1.5
Superintendent	1,266	23	1.8
Assistant CC	155	2	1.3
Chief Constable	54	1	1.9

Source: Home Office, 2003: 19

Home Office data reveal, for example, that 4.9 per cent of Prison Service staff, 9.7 per cent of those in the Probation Service, 10.5 per cent of the Forensic Science Service and 14.2 per cent of the Immigration Service were of a minority ethnic background in 2002.

This chapter explores the historical background of minority ethnic recruitment policies and campaigns in recent decades, illustrates some of the key efforts made by the service in this direction, and explores reasons why relatively little progress has been made, these efforts notwithstanding. One of the recurring arguments put forward to explain this situation is that minority ethnic individuals who might otherwise be attracted to a police service career are deterred from doing so because of their perception that they will encounter racism and fail to progress. The views of officers of a minority background will be outlined here in an effort to establish the validity of these perceptions, and some of the initiatives introduced to change the internal culture of the organisation will be examined. In conclusion the chapter critically reviews the various reasons why the establishment of a more representative police service is regarded as a priority.

The historical context

The lack of non-white applicants to the police service was identified as a problem as early as 1962 in evidence presented to the Royal Commission on Police by the National Council for Civil Liberties, which raised a series of concerns about the nature of police relations with the black community. The first 'non-white' applicant to the Metropolitan Police Service was interviewed in 1964 but rejected on the grounds that he was 'voluble, excitable and of a volatile temperament' (HMIC, 1997: 65). The lack of applicants was recognised by the service during this period – and a lack of recruits of any ethnic background was cause for concern in the mid-1960s. The Assistant Commissioner at the Met reflected that:

> What puzzles me is why they don't apply. We have no objection to coloured applicants and will take them if they are of a suitable standard. But the pioneers in London have got to be of quite high quality because they are going to be under some pressures.
>
> (*The Times*, 25 May 1966: 14)

It was not until 1966 that Mohamed Yusuf Daar began work as a constable for Coventry City Police, and so became the first Asian officer in Britain. The following year Norwell Roberts became the first black officer employed by the Met. The recruitment of these officers was treated as a human-interest story in much of the media, an item in the *Times* diary, for example, noted that:

> On the first morning that he has walked a beat by himself, Britain's 'coloured' police constable had no ambitions to 'start off with a bang'. There was plenty of goodwill in the air. At times it seemed to the new policeman that somebody wished him 'good morning' every 10 paces . . . Since his appointment in March, Police Constable Daar has met little or no hostility.
>
> (*The Times*, 27 September 1966: 11)

While the public in Coventry may have welcomed PC Daar, other press reports from the period suggest that the potential recruitment of minority ethnic recruits drew racist abuse in other cases. Within a fortnight of *The Times* reporting that Ralph Ramadhar was to become Britain's first 'West Indian' policeman, in Birmingham City Police, the same newspaper reported that he had received a letter from Colin Jordan, leader of the National Socialist Movement, suggesting that he 'think again' about his prospective career (*The Times*, 5 August 1966: 10). The following year it was reported that a swastika had been daubed on the wall of a police training college following the arrival of a black recruit.

Even during this early period the recruitment of minority ethnic officers was regarded as problematic. A Home Office circular issued to police forces in 1967 urged the appointment of liaison officers to encourage recruitment from 'immigrant' communities and arguing that the police had an important role to play in promoting 'good race relations' more generally. It was reported that the circular also suggested that police forces ought to invite community leaders to give talks to officers on the customs and attitudes of the 'immigrant groups'.

Following accusations of police violence against black people in Manchester, the local force appointed such a liaison officer in November 1967, *The Times* reported. Difficulties with such posts were recognised by the 1971/2 Select Committee on Race Relations and Immigration, which recommended that the police service needed to ensure that such posts were not considered to be 'dead end' work. The Committee also urged the Home Office to review recruitment procedures to see why minority ethnic applicants were not forthcoming. As a more recent HMIC (1997: 66) report notes:

> Progress was slow, despite some targeted campaigns to attract recruits from the visible minority population, and by 1974 there were only about eighty non-white officers serving nationally.

While official sources seem to have been unclear about why minority ethnic individuals were not attracted to a career in the police service, members of those communities seemed to express other views. David Michael, who completed a 30-year career in the Met in 2002, reflected in an interview with the author on the circumstances in which he joined the service in the early 1970s:

> Before Norwell Roberts joined the Met there was an implicit colour bar and in fact, when I joined the Metropolitan Police in December 1972 and then I went out on the streets of Lewisham in early 1973, I met many black people of Caribbean origin who, as well as telling me they were proud to see me wearing a Metropolitan Police uniform on the streets of Lewisham, which was a big compliment at that time, were telling me at first hand either they had applied to join the Metropolitan Police or the British Police Service, being well educated, some of them actually having held senior rank in police services in the Caribbean and they were just turned down outright for the simple reason that they were black people.

Recruitment initiatives

Recruitment drives via minority ethnic media have been a mainstay of efforts to increase numbers. Such posters and adverts tend to portray a career in the police service in terms of a rewarding profession and to stress the desire of forces to more closely represent the diversity of the population. Several examples of these posters are included in Figure 2.1a,b. Other efforts to promote a police career among minority ethnic communities are made less explicitly, through attempts to promote a positive impression of the service in routine contexts. A series of 'multicultural evenings' held by Leicestershire Constabulary to promote dialogue between the police and minority ethnic communities was singled out as an example of 'good practice' by HMIC (1997: 73).

Some of the measures that might be taken, as suggested by HMIC (1997: 75), include using black and Asian officers in recruitment drives, if they are willing, and 'recognising the importance of family influences ... and try to use existing networks more successfully'. Such steps run a risk of marginalising the issue of minority ethnic representation by marking it out as the concern of black and Asian officers, although HMIC is not suggesting this is the sole strategy to be adopted. One police officer with considerable experience of diversity issues interviewed by the author reported that 'I've got a colleague who is an ethnic minority member of the group and unfortunately he still feels as if he's under-represented and on display'.

Furthermore, relying on black and Asian officers to act as recruiting officers simply by virtue of their ethnicity may prove ineffective. A point returned to later in greater detail is that it is simplistic to assume that minority ethnic officers will have an empathy with others of a similar ethnic background, as so many other aspects of an individual's identity must also be considered. A further problem might be, as the author has witnessed, that they advise black or Asian potential candidates *not* to apply to the service since the extent of racism they might encounter may be so considerable. The role of minority ethnic officers in recruitment drives became a matter of controversy in 2003 in the aftermath of the case of Ali Dizaei, the Met police superintendent who was cleared of charges of corruption amidst accusations that the officer had been subject to a prolonged racist campaign. The Met's Black Police Association advised black and Asian people not to join the police service since Dizaei's case indicated a lack of commitment to tackling racism within the service (*Guardian*, 2003f).

The ethical dilemma facing black and Asian officers who are asked to act as 'ambassadors' points to a more fundamental conundrum surrounding recruitment adverts and the like. As the examples reproduced in Figure 2.1 illustrate, adverts replete with black, Asian and white officers present an image of policing without any mention of racism. This might be understandable in the narrow terms of an advertising campaign, but seems unlikely to coincide with the perception of the audience to which they are targeted. That there is lack of credibility at the heart of such campaigns was illustrated by the poet Benjamin Zephaniah's refusal to allow the Metropolitan Police to use lines from his poem 'The London Breed' ('I love this concrete jungle still, with all its sirens and its speed, the people here united will create a kind of London breed') on a recruitment poster. Zephaniah explained that his refusal was due to his having 'been a victim of them on too many a night driving home ... The

Figure 2.1a   Police recruitment poster

London Breed is a real celebration of multicultural Britain, but the police do not reflect that' (*Guardian*, 2001). The solution to this problem is difficult to determine but this might be one reason why the extensive recruitment campaigns run for several decades have not been more successful.

In addition to advertising campaigns to boost recruitment, a range of positive steps have been taken to boost the possibility of minority ethnic

Figure 2.1b   Police recruitment poster

applicants succeeding. Under the 1976 Race Relations Act, the more far-reaching step of introducing forms of positive discrimination in favour of minority ethnic applicants has been ruled out. Such a step was seen as a key component to increasing the number of African American officers in the United States during the period since the urban unrest of the mid-1960s (Leinen, 1984; Holdaway, 1996). Measures such as lowering the entry requirements for such candidates, for example, have been rejected for legal, moral and pragmatic reasons, since it was considered that they would marginalise such officers once they were in the workplace. While not going so far as this, a range of lesser initiatives have been developed, such as pre-application access courses run to improve the chances of minority ethnic (and other) candidates reaching the required standard. Greater Manchester Police, for example, ran a ten-week course in 2002 for minority ethnic students from Oldham to give them insight into a career in policing and advice on how to join the service (*Police Review*, 2002b). West Yorkshire Police were commended by HMIC for a police–schools liaison unit, designed to promote insight and mutual support between the police and education authorities (HMIC, 1997: 33). Some forces run mentoring schemes designed to provide support for individuals as they move through the recruitment, selection and training process before becoming full constables. At the same time as launching a diversity strategy in 2001, the Metropolitan Police began allowing Muslim women officers to wear the Hijab headdress as part of their uniform and reviewed policy on hairstyles, which may have previously deterred Rastafarian applicants. In 2003 it was reported that plans by the Metropolitan Police Authority to run a 'refer a friend' scheme, whereby minority ethnic officers who recruited others would be awarded £350, were dropped following objections by independent advisors and staff groups. Concerns were expressed that the scheme was replete with associations with slavery, offering as it proposed, financial rewards for the 'delivery' of black staff. Additionally, it was suggested that the payments would lead to suggestions that individuals had been attracted purely due to the financial incentive and would lead to allegations of tokenism (*Guardian*, 2003c).

Many of these recruitment initiatives rely on an assumption that minority ethnic individuals who might otherwise consider policing as a career are not persuaded to apply because they lack information about what the job might entail or because they fail to understand the real nature of policing. The history of poor relations between minority communities and the police and the mutual suspicion that has surrounded them means, the argument implies, that minority ethnic individuals who might otherwise apply do not appreciate the 'real' nature of policing as a career. Repeatedly those, usually white, police officers and civilian staff interviewed recognised that there is a public perception that minority officers might expect to experience racist 'banter' or abuse in the workplace. Almost without exception, though, they were emphatic that such perceptions were erroneous since, even if such behaviour was once tolerated, it was no longer a routine part of working life. The impact of such misconceptions – the argument held – was compounded by an historical legacy of the failure to recruit minority ethnic staff, which meant that those who might consider a career in the police service did not have older family members or friends who had been an officer and who would encourage them along a similar career path.

The informal recruitment opportunities that kinship networks offer have not operated within minority ethnic communities. Nonetheless, the argument that the police environment no longer tolerates racist language or behaviour, as put forward by white staff interviewed by the author, cannot be reconciled with the perceptions of black officers who repeatedly and consistently noted that such problems continue to be a feature of police culture, an issue discussed at greater length in Chapter 3. Consistent with the tone of interviews with black officers conducted by the author were Cashmore's (2000: 10–12) findings that suggested that black and Asian officers were subjected to racist abuse by their colleagues as the latter sought to 'test' their loyalty and belonging. Similarly, an earlier study by Holdaway and Barron (1997) found that three-quarters of the black officers they interviewed who had resigned from the service had experienced racist language. Holdaway and Barron (1997: 138) noted that many white officers who had resigned also stated that they had heard such language. However, they tended to downplay 'the acceptability and effects of derogatory language on their black and Asian colleagues'.

Other reasons cited by interviewees related to the isolation that minority ethnic officers could be expected to experience from their own communities once they joined the police service. As is noted below, the history of poor relations between the police and minority ethnic communities has meant that officers who are of such a background themselves are seen to be symbolically betraying their 'own kind'. Other interviewees noted that female Muslim officers found great difficulty reconciling their cultural and professional roles, and that this deterred them from becoming officers in the first place. Smith (1994: 1096) describes the combination of factors that dissuaded black and Asian applicants in the following terms:

> Because of antagonism between the police and Afro-Caribbeans, many black people see joining the police as going over to the enemy. Many south Asians regard policing as a low-status job. Ethnic minority officers face at best continual racist banter and at worst abuse and harassment from their white colleagues; they also have to cope with racist responses from white members of the public, and with disapproval from members of their own group.

While the prospect of racism from colleagues and pressure from sections of the public have been widely cited as reasons that dissuade black and Asian people from joining the police service, a notable feature of a recent

29

study was that these groups shared many perceptions of a career in the police service of a more general nature. Stone and Tuffin (2000) reported that minority ethnic communities were concerned about issues such as antisocial working hours, the perceived dangers associated with policing, poor levels of pay relative to other occupations, and a host of factors that might apply to individuals of any ethnic origin. Conversely, similarities of this sort were found in earlier studies of the potential attraction of police work that suggested that black, Asian and white youths ranked job security, variety of work, pay and prospects in the same order (Holdaway, 1996: 142). Nonetheless, Stone and Tuffin's (2000: vi–vii) findings clearly demonstrated that minority ethnic people regarded racism as a major disincentive to joining the police service, citing the following factors:

- The thought of having to work in a racist environment, having to face prejudice from both colleagues and the general public on a daily basis.

- The isolation of minority ethnic police officers in a predominantly white male culture, leading to them having to deny their cultural identity in order to fit in.

- The danger of the job and having to deal with unpleasant situations coupled with a lack of confidence in (racist) colleagues assisting them in circumstances where their life or physical safety were at risk.

- The anticipated reactions of friends or family, who they thought might be disappointed, fearful for their safety, and perhaps hostile; they also felt that minority ethnic police officers might be put under unreasonable pressure to reveal sensitive and confidential information.

- Concerns over pressure from the local community to decide where their loyalties were and, for Asian Muslim women with strong religious beliefs, whether the job was appropriate for a woman.

- Black and Asian women were anxious about being subjected to both sexism and racism if they joined the police.

- A perception that minority ethnic police officers have little or no promotion prospects, which in turn would limit their chances of getting the financial rewards associated with the higher ranks of the police service.

It was noted earlier that many of the white police officers and support staff interviewed were adamant that their workplace was not tolerant of racist language or behaviour, although it was sometimes acknowledged that this had been evident in the past. Frequently interviewees stressed that they understood that minority ethnic communities perceived there to be a problem of racism, but that this sincere view was erroneous as racism was no longer a significant issue in the workplace. However, Stone and Tuffin's (2000) report notes that the perceptions of minority ethnic communities are based on their own experiences of contact with officers or derived from reports of cases in which black or Asian officers have discussed racism and discrimination to which they have been subjected. In other words, the perceptions of racism within the police service that deter minorities from applying are the consequence of their own experience, not simply an outdated artefact from an earlier period in which problems may have existed. The culture of policing and the denial of racism are discussed at greater length in the following chapter.

The experience of minority ethnic officers

The treatment and experience of black and Asian officers once in post has also come under increasing scrutiny since the Lawrence Report was published, not least because of evidence suggesting that such officers face discrimination in terms of promotion and are likely to leave the police service more quickly than their white counterparts. While an HMIC (1996) report found that systems of appraisal intended to underpin promotion were ineffective and inefficient for all staff, regardless of their ethnicity, there is evidence that the position is especially difficult for those of a minority ethnic background. Table 2.2 represents some of the data from Table 2.1, but compares it with the position from a decade earlier to show that there has been some progress of minority ethnic officers into more senior ranks, but that this has been very slow.

As the table indicates, the proportion of minority ethnic officers has risen at every rank over the decade, and some of the increase above the

Table 2.2 Minority ethnic representation, as percentage of each rank, 1992 and 2002

	% Minority ethnic 1992	% Minority ethnic 2002
Constable	1.43	2.9
Sergeant	0.45	2.0
Inspector	0.30	1.6
Chief Inspector	0.06	1.5
Superintendent	0.20	1.8
Assistant CC	0.00	1.3
Chief Constable	0.00	1.9

Source: ACPO, 1995: 37 and Home Office, 2003: 19

rank of sergeant is due to promotions as the constables of 1992 have advanced in their careers. Despite this modest progress, concern remains that the career development prospects for minority officers are worse than those of whites. A series of employment tribunal cases in which police services have discriminated against black and Asian officers have received considerable media attention in recent years. The first of these was brought by PC William Halliday against the Met in 1990, and the following year Constable Surinder Singh and sergeants Satinda Sharma and Anil Patani successfully sued the Chief Constable of Nottingham-shire for racial discrimination (Holdaway, 1996: 150). More recently, in 1999, one of the Met's longest-serving black officers, PC Bowie, was awarded £7,000 by an employment tribunal after he had been dis-criminated against by being overlooked for promotion and had endured more than two decades of racist abuse. At the time that Bowie's case was settled, it was reported that there were 31 cases of racial discrimination outstanding against the Metropolitan Police.

Many senior officers and commentators on policing have shared concern that minority ethnic staff are not promoted to senior ranks to the extent expected. Although the first black chief constable, Mike Fuller, was appointed in Kent Constabulary in 2003, it is clear that progress has continued to be slow. A radio documentary broadcast in 2000 explored the nature of the training offered to future police leaders on the Senior Command Course run by National Police Training. It noted that those on the course failed to reflect the diversity of broader society:

> It's been said that the training here merely turns out clones, from our observation over six months this is clearly not the case. The problem we have seen though is deep-rooted: not that they end up the same but that they start out representing such a narrow section of modern Britain, predominantly white, male, aged 38–48. In that respect the new chief police officers for the new millennium look depressingly like the old.
>
> (BBC, 2000)

One response to this has been the development, jointly by the National Black Police Association and Centrex (as National Police Training became known after April 2002), of a leadership course intended to help retain minority ethnic officers and to boost their chances of promotion. While the programme's aim to help 10,000 officers by 2009 may be laudable, it appears to be predicated on an assumption that the failure of black and Asian officers to progress up the career ladder has been a consequence of their own shortcomings, rather than a result of an institutional 'glass ceiling'. The president of the National Black Police Association reportedly saw the benefits of the course in the following terms:

The programme will encourage officers to apply for promotion where they had previously ruled themselves out. It encourages other ways of thinking, taking responsibility and not playing the victim.

(Police Review, 2002c)

Given the raft of employment tribunal rulings that have shown that minority ethnic officers have been subjected to racial discrimination, it seems incongruous to imply that additional training in personal leadership development is required for them to make progress in circumstances where the problem to be tackled is an institutional one. The manner in which the notion of institutional racism has been misapplied in ways that shift the focus onto the properties of individuals recurs throughout this book. In the context of training and stop and search, discussed in Chapters 4 and 5 respectively, there are similar processes whereby the notion of institutional racism is misapplied by a focus on the attitudes and behaviour of individuals.

Much of the debate and discussion surrounding the recruitment and retention of minority ethnic police officers treat the reasons for demanding a more representative service as axiomatic. Reviewing key studies in this field suggests that a range of advantages is perceived to follow if the number of minority ethnic recruits is increased. Essentially these fall into three broad categories: legal and regulatory, pragmatic, and those relating to legitimacy. An HMIC review of these issues published in 1996 identified similar reasons for addressing the issues of recruitment, arguing that increasing the number of minority ethnic officers would lead to greater efficiency, better value for money, better service to the community, and greater credibility for the service as a whole (HMIC, 1996: 11).

Legal and regulatory factors

In this section the various legal and regulatory processes that require police services to ensure that they recruit minority ethnic staff, and treat them equally once employed, will be explored. Although the legal context of policing was altered significantly by the 2000 Race Relations (Amendment) Act, this legislation reinforced and codified a series of requirements that were already in place at the behest of the Home Office.

While the 1976 Race Relations Act prohibited discrimination in the provision of goods, facilities and services, the extent to which this, the primary piece of legislation in terms of tackling racial discrimination, applied to the police service was limited. The 1976 Act did not apply to operational aspects of policing, such as the use and abuse of stop and search powers that are discussed elsewhere in this book. They did, however, apply to some aspects of policing that might be construed as service provision; for example, the manner in which crime-prevention advice is given to the public. In terms of the impact of the 1976 Act on issues relating to the employment of staff, it is clear that the legislation against racial discrimination contained in section 4 apply equally to the police service as to any other organisation.

However, it is also apparent that, as with the public services more generally, the 2000 Race Relations (Amendment) Act significantly changes the legal context against which the recruitment, retention and promotion of minority ethnic police staff takes place. In keeping with Macpherson's demand that 'the full force of the race relations legislation should apply to all police officers, and that Chief Officers of Police should be made vicariously liable for the acts and omissions of their officers' (Macpherson, 1999: 328), the 2000 Act fully includes the police service. Under the terms of the Act, the police service now has a proactive legal duty to tackle racial discrimination and promote 'race equality'. The Commission for Racial Equality suggests that if a police service is fulfilling its legal duties, the following features will be among those apparent (CRE, 2002):

- The workforce will be representative of the population from which the force and the police authority fill their posts.

- There will be no significant differences between ethnic groups in terms of complaints about unfair treatment.

- Ethnic minority staff will be as likely as other staff to remain in the service.

- Employment practices will attract good candidates from all ethnic groups.

- The police service will have a good reputation in the area as a fair employer.

While the 2000 Act made the recruitment and retention of minority staff within the police service the focus of particular legislation, and one that also applies to health services, schools and universities, and the public sector as a whole, other steps had also been taken in the post-Macpherson era. In particular, responding to the recommendations outlined at the beginning of the chapter, the Home Office had directed police services to meet targets intended to match the ethnic profile of the workforce with that of the local population. In addition, various other agencies, such as the Association of Police Authorities and the Association of Chief Police Officers, were tasked with a wholesale review of recruitment and selection processes and policies designed to ensure an end to institutional racism. A series of milestones were established against which the progress of each police service could be measured after three, five, eight and ten years. Table 2.3 provides an overview of the numbers of minority ethnic officers in 1999 and 2002, the proportion of the overall population from a minority ethnic background, and the number of minority ethnic officers to be recruited for the ten-year plan to be realised, for selected police service areas.

Progress is assessed against these targets by the annual inspection procedure conducted by HMIC, with the results published annually by the Home Office. Table 2.3 incorporates information gleaned from the first 'milestone' report published in 2003. It is apparent from the table that these measures introduced by the Home Office, which do not stem from primary legislation but do have a regulatory impact on the police service, have had a positive effect. The percentage of minority ethnic officers has risen in each of the police service areas listed above, and a review of the figures for all 43 services in England and Wales indicates that the percentage rose in all but three areas (Cambridgeshire, Norfolk and Northamptonshire). However, it remains the case that much faster progress will be required if the ten-year target, whereby the ethnic make-up of the police service will match that of the overall population, is to be achieved.

Table 2.3 Number of minority ethnic officers, resident population and future targets, selected police service areas, 1999 and 2002

Force	Size in 1999	% of popn. minority ethnic	Number of ethnic minority officers		% of ethnic minority officers		Increase needed to achieve 2009 target
			1999	2002	1999	2002	
Bedfordshire	1,050	10.00	36	49	3.4	4.5	69
Greater Manchester	6,890	7.58	166	213	2.4	3.0	356
Hertfordshire	1,706	4.71	20	31	1.2	1.7	60
Lancashire	3,245	5.00	39	59	1.2	1.8	123
Leicestershire	1,974	11.00	88	97	4.5	4.6	129
Metropolitan Police	26,106	25.00	865	1,286	3.3	4.9	5,661
Nottinghamshire	2,269	3.52	60	72	2.6	3.1	20
Thames Valley	3,789	5.35	80	106	2.1	2.8	122
West Midlands	7,215	16.11	300	369	4.2	4.8	862
West Yorkshire	5,065	9.45	134	152	2.6	3.1	345

Source: Home Office (1999a: 3; 2003: 38)

The 2003 milestone report applied the 'representativeness' test to all police services, to establish whether the services employed minority ethnic staff in the same proportion that they were present in the local resident population. Seven forces met this criterion but they were all relatively small forces that tended to operate in areas with minority ethnic populations that were much smaller than the national average. In Gloucestershire, for example, the sixteen minority ethnic officers constituted 1.4 per cent of the force total, which compared favourably with the 1.0 per cent of the local population of a minority ethnic background. The distribution of minority ethnic communities within counties that combine rural and urban areas may mean that an average figure is somewhat misleading. While Leicestershire, for example, might contain a minority ethnic community that amounts to 11.0 per cent, this figure obscures very considerable differences between rural areas that are predominantly white and some urban areas where a majority of the community are of a 'minority' ethnic background. Achieving a representative workforce in which 11.0 per cent are of a minority ethnic background will still mean disproportionality at the more local level. Merseyside was the force that met the test that had the largest minority ethnic population: in that case the 81 officers amounted to 2.0 per cent of the total, which exactly mirrored the overall population. This pattern seems to suggest that forces in such circumstances find it easier to achieve a relatively small target than do larger forces that have to recruit much greater numbers. For example, Gloucestershire was set a target of five in 1999, whereas the Metropolitan Police had to bring in 5,661 additional minority ethnic officers.

One set of reasons that has driven police service attempts to improve the recruitment and retention of minority ethnic officers has been the increasing legal and regulatory framework that has focused attention on these matters. The 2000 Race Relations (Amendment) Act has given additional impetus to developments that had been ongoing in the police service (but maybe not elsewhere in the public sector) for several years and codified in law a range of measures already introduced by central government. The Act requires that the police service be proactive in terms of pursuing equality, rather than the narrower focus of previous legislation that was concerned with ensuring that practices did not directly or indirectly discriminate. The extent to which the law and systems of formal regulation can be used to bring about change within the police service, or any other organisation, is a matter of considerable debate. Following the introduction of the 1984 Police and Criminal Evidence Act, there has been substantial analysis of the degree to which police officers, faced with a new system of controlling well-established patterns and principles of conduct, have been able to circumvent regulations imposed upon them (Dixon, 1997). Clearly it would be naïve to assume that the legal requirements briefly detailed here will lead to a wholesale reform of the recruitment and retention of minority ethnic officers and support staff. However, the need to comply with these places more urgent demands upon the police service than earlier exhortations and pleas for progress appear to have done.

Pragmatic factors

A further set of reasons can be identified in arguments about recruiting and retaining a police service that is broadly representative of the population. Alongside the legal and regulatory frameworks that serve as an impetus for change in this area are a series of arguments that suggest various pragmatic benefits to be had from increasing the minority ethnic personnel within the service. Essentially these fall into two categories: those that foresee increased operational effectiveness and those that emphasise human resource advantages. The latter perspective was advanced during the launch of a Metropolitan Police initiative, 'Protect and Respect', intended to promote diversity within the service. Arguing that there was a 'business case' to pursue recruitment of minority ethnic officers, Sir Ian Blair, Deputy Commissioner of the Met, dismissed concerns that the initiative represented a 'politically correct' agenda. Instead he stated:

> it is change for the most basic of business reasons. The future survival of this organisation . . . which needs to recruit two-thirds of its police staff over the next ten years, depends on its ability to attract and retain the most talented employees from all our communities.
> *(Police Review,* 2001b)

Sometime later the operational advantages of recruiting minority ethnic officers were stressed by Peter Herbert, a member of the Metropolitan Police Authority, who argued that minority ethnic officers ought to be deployed with specialist operational units of the Met, 'whether they like it or not'. This would, Herbert argued, bring operational benefits:

> how on earth are we supposed to have any insight into a terrorist group that is not from Northern Ireland without having anyone that, for example, speaks another language . . . In the cause of common sense and good policing it has got to be imposed.
> *(Police Review,* 2002d)

The absence of minority ethnic officers from elite police units has been a matter of concern – Home Office data from 2003, for example, indicates that there were just 1.3 and 3.1 per cent respectively of staff in the National Crime Squad and National Criminal Intelligence Service who were minority ethnic officers. Herbert's argument, however, runs the risk of repeating the compartmentalising of black and Asian officers into roles that relate specifically to their ethnicity. To argue that more minority ethnic officers ought to be recruited for these reasons is problematic: there is nothing to preclude officers from learning other languages regardless of their ethnic background. Furthermore, the suggestion that minority officers do this 'whether they like it or not' seems to ignore the discrimination that minority officers have had to face when they have attempted to develop their careers in elite specialist departments.

More benignly, though, many have argued that there are benefits to be had in operational terms if more minority officers are able to win the trust and confidence of their 'own' communities. A police service that is seen to incorporate sections of society that are otherwise excluded or marginalised will be more likely, the argument goes, to secure the cooperation of members of those communities. Thus victims will more readily report crimes; intelligence and information will be offered; witnesses will be forthcoming; and participants in identity parades more easily recruited. While these arguments seem appealing as common sense, there are reasons to doubt that the operational benefits will flow speedily from the recruitment of a more diverse workforce. Firstly, they overlook the considerable evidence that suggests that minority ethnic recruits experience a process of isolation from the broader community of which they are a part. A common finding of surveys of actual and potential black and Asian recruits to the police service is that they come to be regarded with some suspicion among others of a similar ethnic background. One interviewee, a police officer with experience of training in diversity issues with one of the bigger forces in England and Wales, told the author:

> When I worked for the Met my black colleague received more abuse from members of the black community than any other officer I have known has experienced. He was regarded as a traitor [by the black community] and used to receive no end of verbal abuse and intimidation.

Accusations that minority officers are 'coconuts' (black on the outside, white on the inside) might, in part, be testament to the sorry state of police relations with minority communities. While such accusations are clearly not experienced by all minority ethnic officers, the fact that they have been widely noted suggests that claims that the increased recruitment of black or Asian officers will forge closer links with these communities is certainly not inevitable.

A further difficulty with assumptions that improved community relations will flow from better representation of minority ethnic communities in the police service arises from the foregrounding of the ethnic identity of these officers over other potential identities to which they might subscribe. Many of the arguments that emphasise the pragmatic benefits of a more representative police service assume that the ethnicity of an officer who belongs to a minority community is the most salient aspect of their identity; the age, gender, sexuality, religion, educational background, and so on, are assumed to be only of secondary importance. Sherman (1983) made a similar point in analysing reasons for improvements in the state of police–black relations in the United States, when he argued that black police officers were as likely as their white colleagues to hold negative perceptions about those sections of the black community who received most frequent police attention. That the police officers shared an ethnic background with these victims and suspects was of little significance since their class, level of education, residential profile and other factors were markedly different. Holdaway (1996: 199) expressed similar concerns in the British context and argued that, among other factors, the impact of police occupational culture transcended the ethnic, or any other, identity of individual officers, so that 'there is no evidence that the values and tactics of policing employed by black and Asian officers are radically different from those of white officers'.

Many of the claims made in respect of recruitment betray a naïve approach to the nature of communities, and one that seems very unlikely to be made about the white population. As the concept of diversity becomes more salient in policy-making within policing, it is fundamentally problematic to continue to conceive of minority ethnic communities in one-dimensional terms. It is clearly not the case that the 'Asian community' contained in a Basic Command Unit or police service area is a unified or coherent entity, and claims that increasing the number of Asian officers will provide better relations with that community are at best complacent and at worst extremely problematic for the officers concerned. A parallel can be noted here with debates from the late 1970s and 1980s about the potential power of the 'ethnic vote' when it came to general elections. While exaggerated claims of the potential power of black and Asian voters to 'tip the balance' in key wards and constituencies, and so wield disproportionate political clout, might have served to awaken the interest of complacent mainstream parties, the foundations on which this analysis were based proved extremely shaky. Psephological and opinion poll evidence tended to suggest that the 'black and Asian vote', which had been conceived as a single 'bloc', was much less coherent than it initially seemed, and was fluid and related to class factors. In short, it closely resembled the voting behaviour of the population as a whole (Saggar, 1998; Rowe,

2002b). Similarly, there is no reason to assume that minority ethnic communities inevitably have a coherent set of demands when it comes to policing, that their demands are substantially different from the public more generally, or that their demands are primarily determined by their ethnicity.

In terms of improving relations between the police and minority ethnic communities, it seems unlikely that the recruitment of a relatively small number of minority ethnic officers will make very much difference. This is not to say, though, that securing a 'critical mass' of a significant number of officers at all ranks and all roles within the service would make no difference. As Sherman (1983) noted in the case of the United States, it seems likely that the presence of a relatively substantial number of minority ethnic officers, especially if they come to occupy relatively powerful positions within the organisation, might begin to positively influence culture, policies, and procedures in ways that do bring about meaningful change. Discussion of these issues continues in the following chapter, but it is important to reiterate that critical analysis of the purported pragmatic benefits that might flow from increasing minority ethnic recruitment should not be taken as a rejection of the policy itself; as is argued in the next section, there are important symbolic gains to be had in terms of police legitimacy.

Police legitimacy

In addition to the legal and pragmatic benefits seen to flow from increased recruitment and retention of minority ethnic officers is the symbolic importance of a more representative police service. Although not always explicitly stated, a central component of the discourse of policing by consent is that those responsible for maintaining law and order ought to represent their fellow citizens and be embedded in the communities that they serve. Historians of policing in England and Wales have argued that those responsible for the establishment of the modern professional police service in the early decades of the nineteenth century saw political advantage in stressing that the new constabulary would continue long-standing traditions of policing by consent and would approach the public with servility and a polite demeanour (Emsley, 1996; Reiner, 2000). Other aspects of the discourse used to describe the police service within this liberal democratic framework, such as the notion that the police officer is the 'citizen in uniform', also imply representativeness. While this often remains a relatively abstract conceptual dimension of the police–public relationship, it also has very literal application when it comes to the composition of the personnel employed by the police service and the extent to which that mirrors the demographics of the population in general.

While much is made of the importance of the doctrine of minimal use of force in the British policing tradition, it remains the case that the implicit recourse to coercive power underpins much of the routine activity of the police service. For these reasons it is clear that the police represent, as well as the citizen in uniform, the state in uniform, embodying as the police service does state sovereignty in the form of the legitimate use of force in a given territory, as Weber's definition has it. The police historian Charles Reith summed up the position succinctly: 'the police are the public and the public are the police' (Reith, 1956: 287, cited in Reiner, 1992: 68). For Reith the symbolic engagement of the police and the public was crucial to the success of the British police. As I have argued elsewhere (Rowe, 1998), urban unrest in British history has been explained in terms of a national identity based upon respect for the law, tolerance and order. As many incidents of disorder during the twentieth century became heavily racialised, the position of the police service as a 'thin blue line' between social order and chaos was frequently emphasised. From these conceptual foundations of police–state relations it is but a short step to suggesting that the police service needs to represent symbolically a broader political consensus if it is to secure legitimacy. Achieving this ambition might also deliver some of the pragmatic benefits outlined above, of course.

In more practical terms, it might be argued that a police service explicitly committed to meeting the aspirations of a diverse society must establish its internal credentials in terms of equal opportunities and reflecting the demographic profile of the communities that constitute its clients. Comments, such as those by Lord Harris, chair of the Metropolitan Police Authority, that minority ethnic candidates are dissuaded from applying to the Met because they perceive it to be institutionally racist, carry the corollary that increasing levels of applications indicate a perception that the problems identified by Macpherson are being overcome (*Police Review*, 2001c). Conversely, if the aspirations of minority ethnic potential recruits and established police officers cannot be secured, then questions arise about claims to commitments to providing an anti-racist police service. As Holdaway and Barron (1997: 39) argued in their study of officers who resigned from the service, '. . . the loss of one officer from an ethnic minority is a matter of concern because it may signal deeper organisational problems of race relations within a constabulary . . .'. For these reasons it might be argued that improving the police record in terms of attracting greater numbers of minority and female officers acts as a symbolic testament that the service is facing up to the problems identified by Macpherson's and other reports. It is in a similar manner that Brown (1997: 24) describes attempts to recruit greater numbers of female officers in terms of a 'moral imperative'. When, in 2003, an investigation into alleged corruption of a senior minority ethnic officer in the Metropolitan Police collapsed amid accusations of racism, the Black Police Association were reported to warn black and Asian people not to join the police service (*Guardian*, 2003f). Considered in this light, it can be argued that the establishment of specific recruitment targets for each police service that relate to the ethnic profile of the area places a numerical value on the more abstract notion of policing by consent. Since the 'genius' of the British policing tradition, much contested though it is, is often held to stem from securing legitimacy among the broad mass of the public – and that this foundation has been much undermined in recent decades – it seems that efforts to shore up public support are of more than abstract interest to the contemporary police service.

Chapter 3

Racism and the role of police culture

Unlike many of the other issues discussed in this book, the Macpherson Report does not address police culture as a discrete topic. Nonetheless, much of the analysis contained in the report relates to the values, attitudes and world-view of police officers as they responded to the murder of Stephen Lawrence. Although many of the reforms introduced since publication of the Macpherson Report in 1999 have sought to affect the way in which police officers behave – by changing regulations on the recording of stop and search, for example, requiring officers to detail the ethnicity of those involved – several have also entailed attempts to affect the attitudes and values that officers hold. As is seen below, much of the debate surrounding racism in the police service has conceptualised the problem in cultural terms. This chapter reviews how debates about police subculture developed in academic literature and more recent critiques about the nature and explanatory reach of the concept. It is argued that the notion of police culture is important to analysis of racism within the service in a number of ways.

Police culture has often been addressed in relatively narrow terms to explain the pervasiveness of police stereotypes of minority ethnic and other groups and the impact that this has on relations with the public. However, police culture also needs to be understood in broader and more complex terms if efforts to overcome racism within the service are to succeed. One of the ways in which this has been attempted in the period since publication of the Lawrence Report has been via a programme of training intended to encourage staff to reflect upon their attitudes and values and the impact that these might have on their working practices. This is discussed at length in the following chapter. This chapter concludes with a discussion of the development and role of the Black Police Association, which seeks to challenge aspects of the occupational subculture that have served to marginalise minority ethnic officers.

As Reiner (1994) has noted, police research prior to the 1960s was relatively marginal within broader criminological analysis and tended to be within a positivist tradition. Underlying much of this work was an assumption that the police fulfilled the functional role of applying laws that reflected consensus within a liberal democratic society in a manner that was straightforward and unproblematic. Reiner argues that the wider sociological interest in labelling theory that emerged in the United States in the 1960s led to reappraisal of the role of the police officer as law enforcer and greater recognition that police officers have considerable scope to exercise discretion and partiality in the application of the law. The impact that discretion has on police activity is discussed in the context of stop and search practices in Chapter 5. However, the desire to examine the use and abuse of police discretion led to a series of ethnographic studies of police work in Britain and the United States from the mid-1960s onwards. Many of these have identified racism as a prevailing feature of police subculture. As Waddington (1999a: 287) argued, police culture has been understood to comprise beliefs and values:

> ... widely regarded as having a malign influence upon criminal justice, being responsible for many of the routine injustices that are perpetrated against vulnerable people and also mobilizing lower ranks to resist enlightened change. Thus, the notion of the sub culture of lower ranks is frequently invoked by academic re-searchers and commentators to explain and condemn a broad spectrum of policing practice.

The Macpherson Inquiry demonstrated that cultural features of the police service had a negative impact on various aspects of the response to the fatal attack on Stephen Lawrence. Stereotypical attitudes towards Lawrence and his friend, Duwayne Brooks, hindered the initial investigation of the case and had a negative impact upon police relations with the Lawrence family in the longer term. Evidence presented to the Inquiry by senior police officers and officials often described the problem of institutional racism in the police service as being, in part, a cultural problem. The Lawrence Report referred favourably to views of HM Chief Inspector of Constabulary that cultural properties of the police service had been a major source of a formidable challenge that confronted the service. Similarly, the president of ACPO suggested that institutional racism stemmed from (Macpherson, 1999: 6.50):

> ... racism which is inherent in wider society which shapes our attitudes and behaviour. Those attitudes and behaviour are then

reinforced or reshaped by the culture of the organisation that the person works for. In the police service there is a distinct tendency for officers to stereotype people. That creates problems in a number of areas, but particularly in the way officers deal with black people.

The elasticity of the concept of institutional racism, as discussed at greater length in the final chapter of this book, is illustrated succinctly by the manner in which the ACPO president relates the problem to the culture of the police service. In Lord Scarman's report into the Brixton disorders of 1981, the cultural values of some junior officers are used to argue against the claim that the police service is institutionally racist. Scarman prefers the 'rotten apples' explanation of police racism, which focuses on the behaviour and values of a small minority of overtly racist officers. Scarman (1981: 4.62 and 4.63) clearly locates the problem of police racism in the lower ranks of the service:

The allegation that the police are the oppressive arm of a racist state not only displays a complete ignorance of the constitutional arrange- ments for controlling the police: it is an injustice to the senior officers of the force. Such plausibility as this attack has achieved is due, sadly, to the ill-considered, immature and racially prejudiced actions of some officers in their dealings on the street with young black people.

Thus Scarman reflects the view that a few racist police officers 'infect' the broader organisational milieu and so 'taint' what would otherwise be a non-racist service. From this analysis of the problem it follows that Scarman's recommendations in this area refer to the need to develop psychological tests to screen out potential recruits who are tacit or explicit racists; training in 'race relations' to ensure that the majority of officers are immune from infection; and disciplinary measures to remove malign officers and so protect the vitality of the police service as a whole. Metaphors of disease and infection have been common in analysis of public policy and racism in Britain, as Jenkins and Solomos (1987) have demonstrated. Conceptualising the problem in these terms implies that racism is in some way the dysfunctional property of recalcitrant individuals, rather than, as more recent analysis of institutional racism has tended to suggest, a property embedded in the policies and working practices of organisations.

As the above paragraphs illustrate, the notion of police culture has been cited by senior officers giving evidence to the Macpherson Inquiry as they explained their understanding of institutional racism and by others – and the Scarman Report is just one example – who seek to deny that the police service is institutionally racist. This apparent paradox can only be understood if police culture is conceived as a more complex and multi-dimensional phenomenon than has usually been the case. The following sections will explore police culture in narrow terms as it has been related to problems of stereotyping and racist attitudes and behaviour. While there are grounds to argue that these cultural properties of the police service have often been exaggerated and over-emphasised, there is considerable evidence from ethnographic and other studies that such features continue to be present within the police service. The training programmes discussed in the next chapter have been introduced in an effort to confront inappropriate values and behaviours of police staff. This chapter continues by outlining other aspects of police culture that, while not explicitly racist, hinder various efforts to promote anti-racism and diversity within the service. Along these lines, it is argued that the nature of police culture has proven to be an obstacle to efforts to reform the service by promoting the agenda established in the wake of the Lawrence Report. However, this is related to aspects of police culture that value pragmatism and crime control and reject top-down reform instigated by senior management and politicians or that is caricatured as 'politically correct'.

Stereotyping and 'cop culture'

Many studies of police officers in Britain and elsewhere have described an occupational culture that generates a view of the world that underpins police behaviour. Keith's (1993) study of the policing of urban unrest in London during the 1980s emphasised the importance of a collective police memory that partly determined the development of 'authoritative policing geographies' that provided a mental map guiding police activity. Along with other influences, including those from sources outside of the police service, such collective memory is determined by a police culture characterised by Reiner's (1978) study as 'hard boiled, pessimistic, at best tragic, at worst cynical and bitter, conservative in the broad moral sense . . .'.

The cynicism Reiner refers to is often manifested in racist attitudes, according to other reports of police officers' perceptions. In reviewing ethnographic and other accounts of police behaviour, from Britain and more widely, Waddington, who has been highly critical of the way in which the concept of police subculture has been used in these debates, concludes that 'there is compelling evidence to support the view that the police – especially the lower ranks – are hostile to racial and ethnic minorities' (1999b: 101). One collection of attitudes and perspectives of police officers was compiled by Graef in the late 1980s (Graef, 1989: 125–6, 131, 132). Among the views of 'race' that Graef noted were the following expressed by police officers:

Detective Sergeant: You know why there aren't more black coppers? They're too fucking lazy, that's why. I think they're scared of their people. And I don't think they've got the brain power for it either. I'm sorry but that's how I feel. You can get a whole community, you wouldn't get an O level between them. They're so bloody arrogant, they really are, certainly the people I come across in the West Indian community. I do know a couple who are quite nice guys, but 90 per cent of them – they really are arrogant. And totally 'anti'. Most of them are bloody born here. Yet they all live in their own communities, which is not right. What's the matter with other people? They think there's a war between them and us.

Police Sergeant: Our society's in a mess, and one of the few agencies that understand the problem is the police force, because we have to deal with it all the time ... Why are we being constantly got at because of racism? They can't even get on with themselves. Indian castes can't get on with other Indian castes. We're all racists in our own way. There's a presumption that racism is against blacks, which is rubbish. If you're told that the person you're looking for is a 3-foot midget, then every 3-foot person is going to come under suspicion.

Police Constable: What annoys me is the sheer arrogance of these arseholes who try and teach us Human Awareness Training. Theirs is the only one point of view. In my opinion, that coon with the ghetto blaster is a man who is terribly selfish. He doesn't give a monkey's about anybody else. He could be just as happy more quietly but, having no self-discipline, he doesn't give a shit about anything. Why is their point of view right and my one wrong? 'You're a racist'. It's absolute crap. It's become a moron's chant.

These extracts, selective though they are, illustrate some wider themes that have been identified in studies of police culture. In the first and second, the officers rationalise their derogatory views of minority ethnic communities by referring to their practical experience of police work. In the first, the detective sergeant relates his view that black people lack the intelligence and commitment needed to be a police officer to his experience that the black community is 'anti' police. The implication is that it is from that experience of hostility that the officer's broader perspective of the black community has developed. In the second extract the police sergeant similarly relates her views of the community to the particular insights into the condition of society that police work provides, and that any tendency to over-police minority communities is based upon the operational requirements of crime-fighting. Such arguments hold that it is the over-involvement of certain groups in criminal activity that result in higher rates of contact with the police. In a later chapter arguments that the over-representation of minority ethnic groups in stop and search is due to the nature of the crime reports presented to the police by the public are reviewed, and it is argued that this 'defence' of disproportionate police practice is untenable.

These extracts illustrate several features of 'cop culture' outlined by Reiner (2000), particularly a sense of mission, cynicism and isolation/ solidarity from the wider community. The notion that the police service is 'one of the few agencies that understands the problem' of wider society frequently has been noted in studies of policing. The suggestion that the police service represents the 'thin blue line' between social order and chaos has been expressed in different ways at various times since the establishment of the modern police service in the first decades of the nineteenth century. Storch (1975: 496) describes the manner in which the nineteenth-century police in English industrial cities acted as 'domestic missionaries' intended to 'act as a lever of moral reform on the mysterious terrain of the industrial city's inner core'. Sir Robert Mark, Commissioner of the Metropolitan Police in the mid-1970s, argued that the police service represented a moral buffer against social decay and degeneration (Mark, 1977). Hall *et al.* (1978) described the way in which such perspectives on the role of the police in society became racialised in the early 1970s, during a period in which 'mugging' became associated with black youth and acted as a metaphor for a wider social crisis. Claims that police officers have particular experience of and insight into the ugly reality of contemporary society underpin the sense of mission surrounding police work and the identification of certain groups as 'police property' that can be targeted legitimately.

The cynicism apparent in the quotes from Graef's study has been widely noted as a functionally useful approach to policing. Reiner (2000: 90) suggests that police 'cynicism is the Janus face of [the] commitment' inherent in the sense of mission central to police culture. Closely related to cynicism is the suspicion and stereotyping widely observed as officers seek to preserve social order on the street. That police officers approach the public with suspicion may be an inevitable prerequisite of the crime-fighting mandate, but it clearly poses extreme dangers to the legitimacy of a police service predicated on notions of public consent. The isolation of police officers from black and Asian people in routine contexts, not associated with offending or victimisation, partly reflects the wider tendency of police officers to remain apart from non-police officers even while off-duty. However, a lack of interaction with minority ethnic communities in everyday life makes it more likely that officers will develop stereotypical views predicated on the interactions that they do have, which are based on crime and victimisation. In this way it can be seen that the occupational arrangements of policing, characterised by shift-work and long periods of boredom coupled with occasional experiences of excitement and danger, lead to a strong sense of professional identity and social isolation. These elements of the occupational culture of the police service have implications for relations with a wide range of the public, but given the considerable under-representation of minority ethnic communities in the ranks of the police service, they have particular implications in terms of police prejudice and racism.

Much of the debate about the origins of police occupational culture has focused on the impact of the relatively narrow range of recruitment. There have been recurrent concerns about the quality of police recruits ever since the high turnover of officers in the early days of the Met was attributed in part to their being unfit for duty due to drunkenness (Emsley, 1996: 200). More recently recruitment into the police service has been primarily from the working class, and, as discussed in the previous chapter, women and minorities have been hugely under-represented. Against such a background it is argued that the parochial and insular nature of police culture is a result of the lack of diversity among those recruited to the service. That police culture is partly characterised by racist stereotyping, it is suggested, is a reflection of wider attitudes and prejudices predominant in the sections of society from which police officers are predominantly drawn (Skolnick, 1967; Scripture, 1997).

In contrast with explanations of police culture that emphasise its relation to broader values present in society, there are those arguments which stress that police officers have markedly different attitudes and values from the mainstream. In particular it is suggested that a career in policing is particularly attractive to those with 'authoritarian personalities' who are likely to display chauvinistic attitudes towards those sections of society with whom they come into contact (Adorno et al., 1950). While it has been suggested that the experience of police work itself serves to reinforce isolation from a cross-section of society and perpetuates negative stereotypes about groups not encountered by officers in anything other than a crime-related context, there is some evidence that recruits are predisposed to such attitudes even before they begin patrolling the streets. In 1982 John Fernandes, a lecturer at the Met's training school in Hendon, leaked details of essays written by police cadets that revealed extreme racist attitudes towards minority ethnic communities. The essays were reported to contain comments such as 'do blacks burn better with petrol or oil?' and 'blacks in Britain are a pest'. Much of the media coverage focused on arguments about whether the lecturer was justified in exposing such attitudes or had betrayed the confidence of his students, but the exposé of racism among new recruits was politically charged, given that it occurred shortly after the Scarman Report had recommended that 'racial prejudice' be made a specific offence against the police discipline code.

In the same year, Colman and Gorman (1982) published a study comparing the attitudes of new recruits with a control group on a range of social issues, and concluded that the new recruits tended to be more authoritarian and conservative than the norm. In other words, they argued that police officers did not represent the prevalent attitudes of the social strata from which they were drawn. While initial training had some liberalising effect on their attitudes, this was soon undermined once officers left the training school for the police station. As length of service increased, Colman and Gorman argued, attitudes became increasingly illiberal. Critics of this study suggest it is misleading to imply that police recruits are more authoritarian than the norm, since the control group used in the study, found to be less authoritarian, was not representative of the public at large (Cochrane and Butler, 1980; Butler, 1982). Given this, it seems unlikely that the cultural properties of suspicion and cynicism noted within the police service are a result of the prior attitudes of those interested in a career in policing, and more likely that the working practices and informal rules of policing condition officers to develop these perspectives.

One aspect of police work regarded as contributing to the cultural values outlined here is the relative isolation of police officers from wider society. However, the separation of rank-and-file police officers also applies in terms of the internal organisational arrangements of the service. A prevalent feature in the literature on cop culture identified by Reiner (2000) is the distinction between the lower ranks and more senior officers, or 'street cops' and 'management cops', as Ianni and Ianni (1983, cited in Reiner, 2000: 92) termed them. That police officers in relatively junior ranks regard themselves as distinct from their seniors is particularly important given the extent of discretion that they enjoy in terms of their routine working practices. Much has been written about the extent to which the junior ranks are able to resist initiatives emanating from police leaders and managers that do not coincide with their views of what police work should be about. In particular, analysis of the impact of the 1984 Police and Criminal Evidence Act, which, among other things, sought to restrict the autonomy of officers as they interviewed suspects, has noted the ability of junior ranks to circumvent regulations seen to be impeding their ability to carry out their core mandate of bringing known offenders 'to book' (Dixon, 1997). Efforts implemented by senior police management or by external bodies such as the Home Office or police authorities to improve community relations or to challenge racism are often regarded as unwarranted interference in this core mandate, and are viewed by junior officers as further evidence that their bosses are out of touch with 'real' police work. The officer quoted earlier (from Graef, 1989) who referred to the 'sheer arrogance' of those responsible for human awareness training reflects a tendency to discredit such initiatives on the grounds that they are a sop to political correctness and are detrimental to policing. These attitudes are explored more fully in relation to community and race relations training in the next chapter. Similar cultural problems stemming from the lower ranks' preference for 'traditional coppering' have been identified more generally in terms of developing community policing methods that have been regarded by many officers as undermining the crime-fighting role (Bennett, 1994). Similarly, efforts to introduce problem-oriented policing methods in Britain have also fallen foul of an occupational subculture resistant to tackling neighbourhood problems not previously regarded as part of the police remit (Leigh *et al.*, 1998).

Recognition of cultural tensions within the police service, between lower and senior ranks, points to a wider series of problems that have been identified with debates about police occupational culture. While it is broadly agreed that there is evidence of racism within the police service, and that the culture of the organisation is derived from some combination of factors emanating from the demographic profile of officers, reinforced by the working environment of the police service, it is important to recognise serious limitations on the extent to which cultural explanations can account for racism in the service. Reiner (2000: 106) warns that the explanatory power of the concept is limited by the fact that 'police culture is neither monolithic nor unchanging'. The nature and implications of this caveat for understanding racism in the police service are explored below.

A central criticism of the notion of police culture is that it has been used in a manner that is generalised and, ironically in the context of the topic of this book, stereotypical. While the idea that police officers share an occupational set of values, attitudes and beliefs provides a convenient explanation of many aspects of the service that are regarded as problematic, such approaches to police deviancy are deeply flawed. Images of rogue or 'bent' coppers have become a mainstay of popular cultural representations of police officers and, while racist police officers are rarely presented as tragic heroes in TV series or in the cinema, others who break the rules, especially in pursuit of 'real villains', are familiar staples of the genre. Clarke's (1996: 79) analysis of fictional detective narratives contrasts representations of the 'gentleman detective' with US portrayals of the private investigator, but suggests that a new realism has emerged since the 1960s, which:

> ... might best be described as the 'thin blue line' view of policing as an activity that stands between civilization and anarchy. The police embody and personify order but feel themselves increasingly isolated from the world beyond the station doors. What is represented here is a growing 'siege mentality' on the part of the police and

the density of mutual support and affirmation provided by the occupational culture.

A number of studies of police subculture have suggested that the perspectives of police work that new recruits to the service have gleaned from fictional representations, which tend to focus on the dramatic and glamorous crime-fighting role that actually forms but a minor part of most police work, serve to reinforce the 'canteen culture' outlined in this chapter (Reiner, 1978; Graef, 1989). Whatever the impact of fiction on reality might be, it must be stressed that such portrayals themselves amount to stereotypes, and as such are a very unreliable guide to the values and attitudes of individual police officers.

While the extent to which racist aspects of cop culture are actually subscribed to by police officers is a matter for debate, Waddington (1999a) has offered a powerful critique of the explanatory power of the notion of police subculture that relates to assumptions about its influence on operational behaviour. He argues that prevailing approaches to the study of police culture suggest either that it develops as a means of interpreting the officers' experience in order to make sense of the world, or that it exists as an independent variable that predetermines the behaviour of officers 'on the street'. Waddington expresses the relation in the following terms (1999a: 288):

> Talk and action are related in either of two ways: on the one hand, 'police sub-culture' might be conceived narrowly as attitudinal variables that seek to explain police behaviour. Alternatively, 'police sub-culture' might be conceptualized as a hypothetical construct that lends coherence and continuity to the broad spectrum of police thought and practice.

Waddington (1999a) points to research findings that highlight a disjuncture between the attitudes and behaviour of police officers. Several studies that note the prevalence of racism and stereotyping find that this has little impact in terms of the way in which officers go about their duties. For example, the 1983 Policy Studies Institute study of policing in London explicitly noted that those officers who expressed clear racist sentiments in the privacy of the canteen or the patrol car, delivered an unbiased service to black and Asian people, suggesting a clear distinction between their private attitudes and their professional behaviour (Smith, 1983). Waddington argues that 'if there is little relationship between the privately expressed views of police officers and their actual behaviour on the streets, it appears that the concept of police sub-culture contributes little to the explanation of policing' (1999a: 289). Waddington (1999a) clearly recognises that there are subcultural features of policing that endure across time and in markedly different societies. Traits such as mission and cynicism feature in research reports of police work in Europe and North America and in countries with very different policing systems, such as Japan and India. The important qualification that Waddington makes relates to the explanatory power of the concept of cop culture in respect of the actual delivery of policing.

In terms of the concept of institutional racism that is central to the Lawrence Report, there is a danger that prevalent understanding of police subculture focuses attention too narrowly on the deviant characteristics of junior ranks, and so ignores the structural and organisational features noted by Macpherson. As Waddington (1999a) argues, one reason why the alleged cultural propensities of police officers has been identified as a cause of unacceptable practice is that this serves to deflect attention away from structural problems that might have broader ramifications for the police role. It was noted above that Scarman condemned the subcultural proclivities of a minority of junior officers that were racist and in so doing exonerated senior officers whose motives he regarded as sound. Waddington (1999a: 293) argues that the concept of police culture is useful, not for its explanatory power, but that 'its "convenience" lies in its condemnatory potential: the police are *to blame* for the injustices perpetrated by the criminal justice system' (emphasis in original). As is noted elsewhere in this book, there has been a general tendency to overlook the precise implications of the concept of institutional racism advanced by the Lawrence Report and to reduce the problems identified by it to an individualistic level. Many aspects of the debate about police culture have tended to reinforce such views.

In contrast to such problematic interpretations of police culture has been Chan's (1996, 1997) work, which draws attention to the need to recognise the importance of broader institutional, social and structural dimensions of policing. Chan draws upon the approach of Bourdieu (1990), who sees culture in relational terms, emerging from the interaction between field and habitus. The concept of *field* refers to the structural, organisational and institutional context in which policing is conducted. This might include the internal framework of a particular police service or the style of policing developed by a senior officer. More broadly, it may also refer to wider debates about crime and policing prevalent in society, or the status and position of certain groups and the legal powers and historical dynamics that shape their relation to the police. *Habitus*, in contrast, relates to the means by which individuals make sense of the broader context in which they find themselves. The knowledge and understanding that constitute habitus are complex and exist at different levels within an organisation; for example, there may be tension between the understanding of senior officers who wish to see police relations with minority communities develop along certain lines and the perceptions of those engaged in policing 'on the street'. Police culture, Chan argues, emerges from the relation between field and habitus, but in ways that are neither consistent nor easily predicted. Chan's study of attempts to improve police relations with minority communities in New South Wales suggests that these remained limited when the field of policing was unaffected by reform that addressed police culture solely in narrow terms of habitus. In contrast, earlier efforts to tackle corruption within the New South Wales police were relatively successful as they addressed the attitudes, knowledge and understanding of officers but also the broader 'field' in which the police were located.

From this review of the literature on police culture, a number of key points arise relating to racism within the service. First, many ethnographic accounts have found racist language and attitudes are commonplace among police officers. It is important to recognise that police subculture does not comprise a singular coherent phenomenon to which all officers subscribe – indeed, many studies have identified different cultural values among officers of different ranks and performing different roles. Furthermore, it is not clear whether the cultural properties of police officers play a determining role when it comes to their behaviour as they go about their various duties. In terms of explaining racism within the police service, it seems that the concept of police culture is of limited value. It is difficult to determine to what extent officers subscribe to the racism often noted within the culture or the extent to which it is acted upon. It is also not clear that elements of racism are distinct to the police service. If they are part and parcel of racist attitudes that are prevalent across society, then it may not be useful to isolate these in terms of a distinct occupational subculture but rather to seek to address racism within society more generally. Having offered these various caveats, though, the next section will explore elements of police culture that seem to be associated more strongly with the particular occupational context. While these may not cause racism in the service, it is argued that they serve as important obstacles to efforts to address the problem.

Police culture as an obstacle to reform

Even if it is unclear that the cause of racism within the police service can be traced back to the occupational subculture, there are grounds for believing that this might prove an important obstacle to attempts at reforming the service. As will be argued further in the following chapter on police training, resistance on the part of lower ranks to what they regard as politically driven management initiatives is a hallmark of the culture of the police service. In part this stems from the frequently observed feature of policing that junior ranks enjoy considerable discretion as they carry out their routine activities. In addition to being able to selectively enforce the law, junior officers are able to undermine or negate initiatives emanating from senior management if they see fit. McLaughlin (1996: 75) describes this aspect of police subculture in the following terms:

> It ... has the capacity to resist, subvert, block or co-opt any 'top-down' management initiatives that do not correspond to the 'lived realities' of police work, plays down the 'crime control' function or attempts to restrict officers' autonomy. Senior officers have had to recognize that they are, to a degree, prisoners of the culture and that control over the work situation is pragmatic and 'bottom up' rather than strategic and 'top down'.

In the wake of publication of the Lawrence Report, several senior police officers publicly stated that they accepted that the service was institutionally racist, which drew considerable hostility from some of the junior officers. Among the police officers who wrote to *Police Review* magazine following the Chief Constable of Greater Manchester Police's acceptance of the charge of institutional racism, were a number of officers who claimed to be contemplating legal action for defamation. The impact of the concept of institutional racism for training in community and race relations is discussed in the next chapter and later in this book. What is clear from interviews conducted by the author is that many officers of relatively junior rank have regarded the post-Lawrence agenda as a politically motivated response of senior officers to a high-profile public inquiry that has little bearing on the routine business of the police service. Officers have suggested that the Lawrence case demonstrated that the Metropolitan Police could be inept in handling serious crimes but that it did not mean that the police service more generally was institutionally racist. One officer interviewed by the author stressed that he had 25 years' service and was of the view that the post-Lawrence reforms were 'there for a purpose – and that purpose is to make sure the Chief Constable is protected'. Another officer, of 29 years' service, reported that the diversity training programme he had undertaken had been introduced so that senior management could avoid ramifications of any future controversies: 'they can wash their hands, if anything happens "you've done the course, we can wash our hands of you, you're standing on your own" '.

In addition to resistance to 'top-down' initiatives, the occupational culture can challenge police reform emanating from lower levels of the organisation. In particular it can inhibit efforts by minority ethnic or other officers who might otherwise wish to confront racism. As has been outlined above, a much-noted aspect of police culture, among lower ranks, is the strong internal solidarity produced by the working environment in which long periods of time are spent 'backstage' in personnel carriers, canteens or patrol cars. Coupled with the occasional exposure to danger, this tends to produce a culture in which camaraderie and belonging are important features. A similar emphasis on loyalty and group membership has been noted in studies of professional footballers (Garland and Rowe, 2001), so this is clearly not confined to police officers. In that context, too, it was noted that these cultural dimensions, which are highly functional in other respects, can inhibit those who might otherwise seek to challenge racist banter or other unprofessional or inappropriate attitudes and behaviour. Holdaway has noted the impact that this aspect of police culture can have on attempts to retain minority ethnic officers, as discussed in the previous chapter (1999: 8.ii):

> The occupational culture has specific features that marginalise members of minorities within the workforce. Without change to the occupational culture, recruitment programmes will be opening their front door of constabularies to ethnic minorities whilst presenting them with a context of work that encourages them to consider resigning by exit through the back door.

The alternative to exiting the service was outlined in evidence presented to the Macpherson Inquiry by the National Black Police Association, which noted that 'some of us [black and Asian officers] may think we rise above it on some occasions, but, generally speaking, we tend to conform, to the norms of this occupational culture' (Macpherson, 1999: 6.28). The limits that predominant cultural values place on efforts to improve police community relations by increased recruitment of minority ethnic officers were noted in the previous chapter, as was the perception among members of the public that minority ethnic police recruits might not receive sufficient levels of support from their white colleagues in dangerous circumstances (Stone and Tuffin, 2000). The need to maintain good working relations with colleagues has been cited as a reason not to challenge racism by minority ethnic officers. David Michael, who completed a 30-year career with the Met, during which time he was a prominent activist in the Black Police Association, told the author that being seen to fit into the working environment dissuaded him from directly confronting racism in the early stages of his career:

> You can imagine a nineteen year old cop had joined this massive organisation, at a time when racist language and behaviour was totally unchallenged by any supervising officer, anywhere in the Met ... I would not have done thirty years service [if I had

challenged that], you have to get through your probationary period to be confirmed as a constable. If I had challenged that . . . I would never have been confirmed as a constable.

Michael argued that the dilemma that this position caused him was not one peculiar to black, Asian or other minority officers, but was a general difficulty for all new police officers. The cultural barriers to challenging sexism within the police service, due to a similar need to maintain group loyalty, have been well documented in a number of studies (see, for example, Walklate, 1996) and in particular in the case of Alison Halford who, when Assistant Chief Constable of Merseyside Police, sued the police authority for failing to promote her. In her study of gender and policing, Westmarland (2001) explicitly relates the perpetuation of sexism within the service to predominant cultural values that place considerable emphasis on belonging and loyalty to colleagues. The role of culture in normalising corruption among police officers has also been well documented (see, for example, Bunyard, 2003). In his account of his policing career, Malcolm Young (1991: 81) noted that the cultural values of the police service in the mid-1960s were such that 'in many cases becoming a detective [relied] on a quiet system of patronage; of being invited in by those already inside with power'. Complying with the cultural pressure to conform and generate solidarity with colleagues is a task that junior officers need to fulfil, as noted by another interviewee who reflected on his own reaction to the racism he encountered in the early stages of his career:

As a black officer, it didn't cause me a problem, as a probationer it did. In the sense that you were expected to sort of fall into the system in order to become a substantive officer – to get your probation confirmed. So in that sense, if you didn't sort of fall into the system, fall into expectations, then quite clearly they would say that you didn't make the grade.

That there are aspects of the occupational culture of policing that encourage officers to tolerate attitudes and behaviour from their colleagues that they know to be unprofessional, offensive or, in the context of corruption or malpractice, even illegal is clearly recognised by the service in a number of ways. In particular, service race equality schemes and diversity training programmes, discussed in greater detail in the following chapter, often emphasise the need for officers to confront unacceptable behaviour among colleagues. The extent to which such statements of intent and policy-level initiatives have been able to overcome entrenched cultural propensities of police services is unclear. Since relatively little attention has been paid to addressing the structural components that shape police culture, referred to as the 'field' by Bourdieu and Chan, it seems unlikely that these developments, in themselves, will undermine those aspects that value group solidarity and belonging, which are in other respects functionally useful, but hinder efforts to tackle racism within the police service. One of the more substantive efforts to develop an environment in which racism can be challenged within the service has been the work of the Black Police Association (BPA), and it is to a review of this that the final part of this chapter now turns.

Rank-and-file culture as an obstacle to reform: the case of the Black Police Association

In the early 1990s the Metropolitan Police Service organised an 'away day' seminar for minority ethnic staff, intended to provide officers with an opportunity to network with one another and develop mutual support. According to David Michael, founder member and twice chair of the Met's BPA, this was against a context of concern in the Met about the difficulties of recruiting and retaining minority ethnic officers, and at a time when the occupational culture was such that black officers were reluctant to engage with one another: 'if we walked into a police building and saw another black person we wouldn't acknowledge them' (interview with the author). From this relatively limited ambition developed the Met's Black Police Association, formally established in 1994 with the stated aim 'to improve the working environment of Black Personnel within the Metropolitan Police Service with a view to enhancing the quality of service to the public'. The BPA adopts a 'broad' approach to the term 'black', including anyone of African, African Caribbean or Asian descent, and membership is open to all officers, civilian staff and special constables (Hope, 1995). Staff in other forces across England and Wales began to form their own BPAs and, following several years of discussion and planning, a National Black Police Association was established in November 1998 with the active support of the Home Secretary, a few months prior to publication of the Lawrence Report. Five years later there were approximately 36 force-level BPAs affiliated to the national organisation, which has become a powerful voice within the police service. Although the leadership of the BPA has maintained that it is not a rival organisation to the long established Police Federation, which is effectively the trade union for officers below the rank of superintendent, anecdotal evidence suggests the Federation was sceptical about the BPA and felt that the new organisation would be divisive and that, in any event, it was representative of all officers. Hope's (1995) account of the early development of the BPA reflects the initial suspicion of the Federation concerning the BPA. Although David Michael also referred to similar problems, he noted that he has subsequently enjoyed positive relations with some groups within the Police Federation. In the wake of the establishment of the BPA has come a range of staff associations intended to represent the interests of various minority groups, including among others the Lesbian and Gay Police Association, Muslim Police Association, Jewish Police Association and Christian Police Association.

Holdaway (1996, 1999) has argued that the establishment of BPAs offers a real opportunity for reform of police occupational culture and, relatedly, to increase the recruitment of officers from a minority ethnic background. Crucial to these prospects, Holdaway suggested, is the high-profile support that senior officers have pledged to BPAs. In the case of the Metropolitan Police BPA, to take the most well known example, Holdaway (1996: 194) argued that the commitment offered, in terms of moral support and the provision of resources, by Commissioner Paul Condon would prove crucial to the success of the BPA. Holdaway suggested that the further development of BPA-style organisations more widely across the service would lead to 'some interesting stances to be taken by chief constables and officials of the Police Federation who felt unable to fully support the initial launch of the Metropolitan Association'. Holdaway's prediction may have been valid in the context of policing prior to the establishment of the Macpherson Inquiry, but the experience of the last few years has been that most police services now have established BPAs and these have tended to be positively championed by senior officers keen to demonstrate their anti-racist credentials. Force annual reports and newsletters have featured the establishment and further activity of local BPAs at some length; there seems to have been nothing but unqualified public support for these and similar organisations among senior echelons in the post-Macpherson era.

Holdaway (1996) may have been right to value this support, but subsequent experience suggests that the impact that the endorsement from high-ranking officers has had has been somewhat limited. As discussed earlier in the chapter, a much-noted aspect of police subculture is suspicion about change or reform that is regarded as 'management interference' in routine working practices. Given this, it is perhaps not surprising that Holdaway's optimism has not been fulfilled as senior managers' support has been regarded as counterproductive in some cases. When interviewed, David Michael reflected on the difficulties that the BPA had in winning support from middle and senior management, despite – or even because of? – Condon's public support:

> We had serious obstruction by some people in human resources, some borough commanders, some operational unit commanders

and some people in charge of human resources locally. So basically, many of these people just openly repudiated what the commissioner had said.

While those indisposed to the aims and objectives of the BPA may have been able to frustrate the development of the organisation via institutional means, there have also been suspicions that high-profile activists have been subject to false allegations of misconduct and corruption. A number of leading figures within the NBPA and the Metropolitan Police BPA have been subject to malicious charges, subsequently demonstrated to be unfounded. For example, Sgt Girpul Virdi of the Metropolitan Police, and an executive member of the Met's BPA, was sacked after being convicted by an internal disciplinary panel of sending racist hate mail to himself and minority ethnic colleagues. It was suggested that his motive had been to fabricate a reason for being overlooked for promotion in 2000. An employment tribunal subsequently ruled that he had been discriminated against and that there was no way in which the racist mail could have been sent by Virdi himself. He was awarded compensation, the Met apologised to him and he was reinstated. When interviewed about claims of financial irregularities, misuse of drugs and fabrication of racist mail that have been made against various prominent figures within the BPA, Mike Franklin of HMIC reflected (BBC, 2001):

> The BPA can be forgiven for taking the view that there's a campaign to destroy the Black Police Association . . . I would need to hear the explanations as to why that isn't the case when I'm hearing so many examples of members of the BPA who are under investigation and have been suspended. The BPA need to be very, very careful about witch hunts. Anybody who stands up to be counted lays themselves open for attack and there are risks attached to speaking out.

The vulnerability of organisations such as the BPA belies the official endorsements that it has received from many officers of senior rank and politicians. This is a further demonstration of the capacity of those lower down in the police service to effectively frustrate and undermine anti-racist initiatives that they might regard as outside of the core ambit of routine police work. In this respect, as mentioned earlier in this chapter, police culture, which entails suspicion and mistrust of senior officers who are categorised, alongside politicians and the public more generally, as not understanding the harsh reality of police work, may not directly cause racism within the service, which has more complex roots than that, but it does provide barriers to reform.

Chapter 4

Community and race relations training[1]

As outlined in the introduction, the Macpherson Inquiry repeatedly found that the police officers who responded to the attack on Stephen Lawrence had failed to understand the dynamics of racist violence, or that it provided a context for criminal investigation and family liaison that was markedly different from similar crimes of a non-racist nature. To address this shortcoming the Lawrence Report instigated a wide-ranging review of police training, some of which related to first aid training. In terms of racism and diversity, though, the report made the following recommendations:

Rec'n. 48. That there should be an immediate review and revision of racism awareness training within Police Services to ensure:
(a) that there exists a consistent strategy to deliver appropriate training within all Police Services, based upon the value of our cultural diversity;
(b) that training courses are designed and delivered in order to develop the full understanding that good community relations are essential to good policing and that a racist officer is an incompetent officer.

49. That all police officers, including CID and civilian staff, should be trained in racism awareness and valuing cultural diversity.

50. That police training and practical experience in the field of racism awareness and valuing cultural diversity should

[1] I am grateful to Jon Garland and acknowledge the contribution that he made to an earlier version of this chapter, and to Sam Johnson for his contribution to the research study discussed here.

	regularly be conducted at local level. And that it should be recognised that local minority ethnic communities should be involved in such training and experience.
51.	That consideration be given by Police Services to promoting joint training with members of other organisations or professions otherwise than on police premises.
52.	That the Home Office together with Police Services should publish recognised standards of training aims and objectives in the field of racism awareness and valuing cultural diversity.
53.	That there should be independent and regular monitoring of training within all Police Services to test both implementation and achievement of such training.
54.	That consideration be given to a review of the provision of training in racism awareness and valuing cultural diversity in local Government and other agencies including other sections of the Criminal Justice system.

In the light of the Lawrence Report many police services and the Home Office have trained officers and civilian staff in large numbers, as is outlined below. In this chapter the use of training as a means of influencing the attitudes and behaviour of police officers is reviewed. In contrast to some of the other approaches detailed in this book that have sought to utilise rules and regulations in order to reform the way in which police officers behave, much of the emphasis of training programmes has been to transform the values and attitudes held to underpin behaviour. This represents a challenging and relatively new dimension to police training, which has, historically, centred on the provision of instruction in the legal powers of the police, in practices and procedures employed and on military-style drill (Knights, 1988). Since the 1970s the traditional curriculum has been extended – in piecemeal fashion – to encompass a range of 'human awareness' or 'social scientific' aspects of policing. Much of this new approach has focused on what has been variously described as 'race relations awareness', 'community and race relations' (CRR), or 'policing diversity' issues. This chapter examines the development of these training programmes and outlines findings from an evaluation study conducted between 1998 and 2001, which explored the impact of CRR training. It is argued that the nature of CRR training is relatively unusual in terms of the broad sweep of police training and that this, coupled with the high-profile and controversial debates surrounding racism and policing more generally in British society, means that the training programmes delivered will have only a limited impact. Police managers need to ensure that more is done to embed the principles conveyed in training into the working practices of police organisations.

Before exploring the development of police training in this area, it is important to note that provisions are to a large extent coordinated by individual forces, which may result in considerable differences between the training delivered in one area compared with another. The 43 separate police services of England and Wales do not operate a single framework for CRR training. Even though this evaluation study was of a training programme supported by the Home Office and delivered along a two-day format to several of the 43 services, it was still, in practice, subject to local variation. Indeed, the training providers were encouraged by the Home Office to take the local context into account when devising the course contents. Therefore, it is not possible to discuss police CRR training in England and Wales as though this were a singular programme. Furthermore, a distinction needs to be drawn between training provided to probationer constables and that done 'in service' to staff as they progress through their careers. The development of both forms of training is outlined in the initial section of this chapter, but the evaluation study which informs the detailed discussion of current arrangement was only of 'in service' training.

The primary research findings referred to below arose from a three-year evaluation study, conducted on behalf of the UK Home Office, of the CRR training delivered to the police service by Ionann Management Consultants, a private training and consultancy company. The evaluation focused on the work carried out in two police service areas selected for the research team by the Home Office, one of which was a large metropolitan force and the other a smaller, more rural, one. The training was delivered by associates employed by Ionann in conjunction with full-time police trainers.

Before a discussion of the evaluation findings it is important to place them in context by providing a brief overview of the development of police CRR training, and it is to this overview that this chapter now turns.

A brief history of police CRR training

According to Her Majesty's Inspectorate of Constabulary (HMIC) (1997), the Metropolitan Police introduced elements of 'social and humanitarian' skills into probationer training in the early 1970s and 'race and community relations' became a specific part of the curriculum in 1973. Much of this early training lacked focus and was poorly conceived, as Southgate noted (1982: 1):

There has been a lack of certainty as to precisely what probationer police officers need to learn about dealing with ethnic minorities, and about the best methods of teaching them. In particular, there has been uncertainty as to whether emphasis should be upon giving information, upon trying to mould attitudes, or upon teaching procedures and modes of behaviour which are appropriate for dealing with minorities.

The 'lack of certainty' to which Southgate referred is apparent twenty years later, as this chapter will demonstrate. It was in response to this dissatisfaction with CRR training provisions and in particular as a result of recommendations contained in Lord Scarman's (1981) report into urban unrest, that the Police Training Council (PTC) undertook a review of what was offered. The PTC (1983: 3) referred to a strategic tension relating to the provision of CRR training, which continues to the present time:

> It is often assumed that race relations training should aim to ensure that the attitudes of individuals towards persons of a different race are tolerant or sympathetic. Others feel it is unsound, and can be counterproductive, to seek to modify attitudes and that the focus of training should be on the overt behaviour desired.

The PTC made a series of recommendations that remain the cornerstones of contemporary thinking in this field. Among these were that the aims of CRR training need to be clearly defined; that all officers should receive 'substantial' training on such topics throughout their careers; that training ought to be directly related to the specific circumstances and demands of the police role; that minority ethnic communities be closely involved in the design and delivery of courses; and that the training be monitored and assessed in order that it can keep apace with changing circumstances (PTC, 1983: 10–11).

These recommendations led the Home Office to contract Brunel University to provide CRR training to police services. The programme devised was predicated on a 'reflective practitioner' approach whereby participants were encouraged to reflect on the impact that their attitudes and behaviour had on minority ethnic communities (Oakley, 1989). However, Oakley suggested that there were a number of irresolvable problems that inhibited the programme's success (ibid.). Two of the most important of these were: firstly, since the police service was reluctant to admit that there was an institutional problem of racism, the courses had to be broached in terms of 'community relations', which conceptually shifted the emphasis away from the notion of racism. Secondly, Oakley suggested that an ongoing tension existed between the wish of the training providers to offer in-depth challenging courses and the demands of the police service for shorter, high-turnover programmes that could quickly train large numbers of staff.

However, the subsequent Home Office contractor employed to offer support in this field focused less on the values of participants in favour of an approach that concentrated on behaviour. The method adopted has become known as the 'Turvey model' (after the name of the village in which the company was based) and was run by Equalities Associates. The cornerstone of this approach was the provision of intensive residential training programmes for police trainers, who would then return to their respective police services galvanised and prepared to roll out to their colleagues the training they had received.

The training was based on the premise that the primary goal ought to be to change the behaviour of individuals within the workplace; and that this would eventually lead to a change in attitudes and values. However, it seems that there were practical problems that hindered the 'training the trainers' strategy. Anecdotal evidence suggests that the major difficulty was that those who had been sent on the programme lacked the organisational support required to further promulgate the lessons learnt within the police service. While police services might have been amenable to sending members of their training staff on courses at Turvey, they seem not to have developed a structured approach to enable them to deliver effective CRR training based on their experience once they returned to their posts.

The most recent approach to the provision of in-service training in CRR can be seen in the work of Ionann Management Consultants who, during the period of the evaluation discussed here, were contracted to the Home Office to provide support to the police services of England and Wales in this respect. Before some detailed discussion of recent developments, based on a three-year programme of evaluation, a brief overview of the 'Ionann model' is offered, in order to contrast with the two earlier approaches outlined above.

If a distinction can be drawn between training that seeks to address behaviour and that which focuses on attitudes and values, then the Ionann model was clearly placed in the latter camp, as its common aim was to tackle trainees' attitudes and values toward a range of CRR topics. A key emphasis was placed on the inclusion of lay representatives of minority ethnic communities in the training process. Perhaps one of the key differences between this model and its predecessors is that the programme was predicated on the notion of 'anti-racist policing', and the question of police institutional racism – although extremely contentious – was 'officially' acknowledged and included in the curriculum, even though – as is discussed below – this was not always reflected in classroom delivery.

Following this outline of the history of police CRR training and how Ionann's approach fits in with these developments, the next section will discuss the findings from the three-year evaluation of such training. In order to place these findings within the boundaries of the discussion above, what follows is a necessarily broad outline of the conclusions of the evaluation. Therefore, for example, precise details of the survey's results are not included, but instead the key relevant themes of the overall evaluation are extracted and assessed.

Challenges in contemporary CRR training

When participants in the training were asked to reflect on their experience of the course, a recurring theme uncovered by the evaluation was that they found their two-day course enjoyable, despite their prior misgivings. It was frequently apparent that trainees discussed forthcoming courses with their colleagues and were often anxious about what they may be 'subjected' to. One of those interviewed after the training reflected on the rumours that had circulated beforehand: 'A few said right at the beginning that you go there and you sit there and they call you all a load of racist pigs'; similarly, another respondent reported that 'I think the attitude of some [was] "Well we're going to get brainwashed, and if I say the wrong thing I'm going to get told off"'.

A number of factors might explain these concerns: first, many of those interviewed were civilian members of staff who were concerned because they had not had CRR training in the past, unlike police officers who would at least have had some experience of it as probationers. Additionally, it was often suggested that civilian staff receive less training of any kind than police officers, and so it may have been that they were concerned about being in a relatively unusual environment. However, police officers interviewed also reported that they viewed forthcoming courses with trepidation, so other factors must have been involved. One such might stem from the broader debate of police relations with minority ethnic communities that has followed the publication in 1999 of the Macpherson Report. Since the Chief Constable of Greater Manchester Police and, subsequently, the Commissioner of the Metropolitan Police and other senior officers have publicly stated that the police service is institutionally racist, there has been sustained controversy over the state of racism within the police (see Marlow and Loveday, 2000; Rowe, 2002a). Put simply, the training was being delivered in a context where the content was a source of considerable debate within the service and the public at large. Given this, it is perhaps unsurprising that participants viewed it with suspicion; as one police officer reported the perceptions of his colleagues prior to the training:

I think there was an air of suspicion around some of the training, certainly as a supervisor there were other people who I knew in my section who I'd arranged to go on this training and they had very negative thoughts and attitudes about it and about, silly rumours about the room being bugged and things like that, ridiculous, but that's what they were saying and some people felt that it wasn't a forum where they could speak freely.

Even when participants did not report prior hostility to the training process, it was often regarded as an unnecessary process by interviewees who stressed that they were not motivated by racial prejudice or stereotyped attitudes. Typical was the reaction of one respondent who did not regard the training as necessary:

It was condescending really . . . you're being told how to act [when] your common decency and the way you've been brought up tells you to do that. So I don't see the need for anyone to tell me how to deal with other people . . . if they wanted to do something like that then they could have probably done it in a morning.

A notable feature of Ionann's CRR training was that the programmes were delivered jointly to police officers and civilian staff. This was a relatively unusual approach, and one that may reflect the increased role of civilian staff within the police service in recent years. The evaluation project suggested that there were perceived institutional advantages to training both groups of staff together, as a relatively senior officer stated:

. . . some of our support staff actually recognised that they had a role to play and it's not just about police officers. We were pushing support staff onto [Basic Command Units] to do jobs, administrative posts, for example. So they need to know what it is all about. I just think it's important if you are going to have a corporate approach to the way we deliver, that everybody knows exactly where we're going.

Many of the police officers and civilian staff interviewed also recognised potential benefits to being trained jointly – indeed, none opposed the principle. However, it was often suggested that in practice the training continued to be focused on the needs and experiences of police officers, and that their civilian colleagues were somewhat marginalised. This problem was evident both in terms of the curriculum design, since the illustrations and exercises involved tended to be drawn from the realms of operational policing, and in terms of the management of the classroom environment, in which, it was suggested by respondents, police officers tended to dominate discussions at the expense of their civilian colleagues. One civilian member of staff reflected some of these concerns, observing that:

I felt that for me it was a bit of a waste of time. It was more geared up really for front line policing ... I don't even speak to the public. My job revolves around dealing with police officers. It was very much going through stop-and-search procedures, it was very police orientated, some of us were sitting there thinking 'What are they talking about?', I don't really know anything about that ... at least half the day wasn't really relevant to what we did.

The provision of diversity training to all staff seems likely to exacerbate the tension between the necessity of providing for a well-trained police service and the need of police managers to ensure that the minimum number of staff are available to perform their primary roles (HMIC, 1999a; Langmead-Jones, 1999). The position of civilian staff in this debate seems to have been largely overlooked: while they may be able to offer benefits in terms of efficiency and economy, it seems clear that if they are to be equal partners to their police colleagues, then they too will need considerable training on issues such as CRR. The extension of the 'police family' to include community support officers, as introduced by the 2002 Police Reform Act, raises other concerns about the recruitment, training and monitoring of non-police officer staff. While proponents of these ancillary staff suggest that they will enable the service to provide a stronger presence on the street and so contribute to public reassurance, any such benefits may quickly disappear if they behave inappropriately. Providing more officers, whether sworn constables or otherwise, in communities where police activities have been contentious may exacerbate rather than ease tensions. That training provided in the wake of the Lawrence Report has continued to be primarily organised around the perceived needs of police officers, and has marginalised civilian staff in terms of curriculum design, suggests that meeting the training requirements of community support officers will be a challenge to existing training providers.

Historically, 'lay involvement' in the training process has often involved members of minority ethnic communities participating in training sessions in order to provide their perspective on police CRR. Hall (1988) suggested that there have been four key approaches to this incorporation:

- the black experience approach – in which black individuals are asked to 'tell us where it hurts';

- the intellectual approach – in which (mostly) white professionals from academic institutions discuss the minority ethnic community, without first-hand knowledge of their subject;

- the balancing act – in which responsibility for poor CRR is apportioned equally to the police and to minority ethnic communities; and

- the information focus approach – which stems from the belief that the problems arose because whites failed to understand non-white cultures.

Traditionally, much police CRR training has focused on the last of these approaches, which has led to a concentration on the ethnic and cultural practices, such as arranged marriages or the caste system, that were 'not central to our real problems' (Hall, 1988: 56), thus diverting attention away from institutional patterns of racism and discrimination.

The approach adopted by the training programme under discussion in this chapter fell within the first of the categories outlined above: the black experience. Two techniques were used to bring this experience to the training sessions. In one police service, a video had been made of a variety of individuals from different ethnic groups who discussed their experiences of policing and their perceptions of police racism and relations with the community. In the other police service, one session of the training programme involved various members of local minority ethnic communities speaking about their perceptions of policing. The advantage of the former approach might be that a consistent set of issues could be introduced into all training sessions, since the same videotape was used in each. Additionally, the use of the video meant that a range of perspectives from different ethnic groups, and people of different backgrounds, could be represented in the sessions. The latter approach had the potential advantage of allowing for interaction between the lay representatives and the course participants. A set of problems surrounds this approach, though, since it runs the risk of suggesting that selected participants can 'represent' a wider community. In extreme cases this may lead to situations in which the lay participant becomes the focus of hostility and suspicion from course members – as Hall (1988: 55) described in the following terms:

> The dangers here are that the black men and women who are able to express their experiences are dismissed as radicals, political extremists, exceptions to the norm, having chips on their shoulders, anti-establishment activists; in other words their experience is dismissed under the guise of 'they do not understand the way we do things here'.

While problems were identified in this aspect of training, these types of sessions can have a positive impact beyond the training outcomes. In one of the police service areas included in the evaluation study, a considerable number of individuals – around 70 – from what was a relatively small local minority ethnic population were involved in the community consultation segment of the course, which in itself represented a conduit for consultation and liaison between officers and local communities. It is argued later in relation to police accountability that consultation, liaison and 'dialogue' with the community provide only a limited basis from which relations can be improved, since they do nothing to address structural and institutional problems. While the obstacle to good relations between the police service and minority communities may not simply have been mutual misunderstanding, it remains the case that improving routine mundane communications can provide opportunities to make progress in limited circumstances. Even this is not always possible, as highlighted by an HMIC report (2003: 35), which found that the vast majority of communities 'had no direct contact with the forces' training departments nor were aware that training was taking place'.

Even in those areas where communities were involved in the delivery of training there was little role for minority groups in the design of courses, which generally remained in the hands of police training departments and independent consultants. While the Ionann training evaluated did incorporate a 'benchmarking' process whereby members of minority groups participated in focus groups prior to the design of the training programme, this has been a limited practice and it is generally far from clear that this aspect of the 1983 Police Training Council report has been widely implemented (HMIC, 2003). In addition, the Lawrence Inquiry report (Macpherson, 1999) recommended that minority communities also be involved in the monitoring and assessment of police CRR training: an aspect that has been widely neglected in general terms (HMIC, 1999a). There is no evidence to suggest that any police service actively engages minority ethnic communities in this respect.

A recurring theme in studies of police training on CRR and similar subjects relates to the impact that the training had on those involved in its delivery in the classroom. It is important to outline the strain that delivering CRR training appears to have on those involved, which partly stems from the delivery of a high volume of courses over an extended period, as one police trainer interviewed for this evaluation project noted:

> You know beforehand that this is going to be stressful, emotional . . . I think there's also a degree of, shall I say, Groundhog Day. With 41 courses you are crying out for a change at the end of it. We were only supposed to do one course a week. During the summer of last year we were doing back-to-back courses. I did something like five courses in eleven days. I needed a break from all this. Then when we were getting towards the end of it you could see people start to lighten up. It was physically, as well as mentally, probably the hardest thing I've ever done.

The particular nature of training in the area of community and race relations makes it more challenging to trainers. Several of the trainers interviewed for this evaluation study reported that the suspicion surrounding the training meant that trainers had to seek to overcome resistance and to convince some trainees that it was even appropriate to be providing courses on these topics. One trainer interviewed expressed the specific challenges associated with CRR training in the following terms:

> Because we're talking about people's values, we're talking about what makes them as a person, and we're asking people to look at themselves, reflect on themselves. When teaching normal procedure, if it's the law, it's the law ... But once you talk about doing things that make you as a person, as an individual, things you've grown up with all these years ... it's quite an uncomfortable process for the people. When something's uncomfortable for you, then it's a natural reaction sometimes to be hostile.

There are at least two implications arising from the heightened level of hostility associated with diversity training compared with other fields. First, the impact on those delivering courses, in terms of levels of stress and 'trainer burnout', is a significant human resource problem, not least because such stress might deter trainers from working in what is perceived a 'difficult' area. Another implication is that trainers might tend to adopt a 'line of least resistance' in order to progress through their working day without encountering hostility from those they are training. In the context of delivering a high volume of courses against a tight timetable, this approach might become more common. One police trainer interviewed recognised this potential problem:

> When you've got trainers that are not experienced, they will find their own comfort zones and to get through every day, to know that they've got twelve months ahead of them doing it, they will find easy routes, as simple as that. So if there are any thorny issues, any difficult subjects in there, they will not do it, they will blot them out, some of the objectives were quite difficult. For their own survival, I can't blame them for it.

Given that the content of the courses was supposed to address the 'thorny issue' of police institutional racism, it would be a concern if trainers focused on less controversial aspects of CRR, such as reverting to Hall's (1988) 'information focus approach' in order to avoid conflict with those that they are training. In this manner a key aspect of the training agenda, intended to focus on the nature of policing and racism, might become lost if trainers were unable, and lacked the necessary support, to tackle difficult issues. Thus the substantial pressures on the trainers due to the nature of the topics and the approach the training adopted, presented considerable challenges, and these will be addressed in conceptual terms in the following part of this chapter.

A final issue relating to training programmes outlined here is the extent to which the proper focus should be on issues relating to race and ethnicity, or broadened to include wider dimensions of diversity, such as sexuality, age, gender and disability. One perspective on this question is that issues relating to race and racism have a history and context of their own, which cannot be applied to other interest groups. Others have argued that the attention afforded to these issues by the Lawrence Report was the fruit of years of political struggle and campaigning that should not be jeopardised by allowing other parties to hitch their cause to the bandwagon. In opposition have been those who have argued that the various dimensions of social exclusion share features in common and that the right of minority ethnic communities to have issues relating to racism addressed cannot be justifiably denied to other minorities. A recent report by HMIC (2003: 63) discussed this debate in some detail, but rather fudged any definitive conclusion by recommending that 'wider diversity matters are incorporated into all aspects of police training, while ensuring that the high profile and importance of race relations is maintained'. The complex conceptualisation of diversity and community is analysed further in later chapters of this book, in relation to hate crime and to the policing of diversity.

Approaches to police CRR training: the challenge of the 'affective domain'

As has been noted, the fundamental strategy of CRR training has varied over time and between different programmes. Three main approaches to CRR training have been identified: cognitive, behavioural and affective, and it is argued that it is the latter that is most apparent in contemporary police CRR training, although it is relatively unusual compared with broader police training. In terms of approaches to reforming the police in the post-Lawrence era, the input of training has often focused on changing the attitudes and values of police service staff. Similarly, efforts have been made to change the culture of the service. Conceptually these adopt a different strategy to measures that rely on regulatory or disciplinary frameworks, such as monitoring stop-and-search practices, which seek to effect change by addressing the way in which officers behave, as is outlined in Chapter 5. It is argued that a tension exists between training that seeks to address the values and beliefs of participants and the concept of institutional racism, which focuses on policies and procedures.

Luthra and Oakley (1991) suggested that there was a difficulty with racism awareness training in that it does not, in itself, leave individuals in a commanding position to build upon the process of examining their own values and beliefs. The content of the training programme is not matched by changes to the policing context also necessary to affect institutional performance, a point returned to in the concluding section of this chapter. Two equally negative positions tend to be adopted, as Luthra and Oakley (1991: 25) argued:

> The known effects of this type of training ... are that where participants are not left alienated or resistant, they may be either disabled by guilt or loss of confidence, or alternatively become positively committed crusaders for the cause. All of these personal responses may present difficulties at the organisational level in utilising the outcomes of such training for the purposes of effecting change.

While the training evaluated did not adopt a confrontational approach, it was apparent that participants sometimes resented the training and felt concerned by the perceived implication that they were racist. Although the post-course interviews tended to reveal that participants had enjoyed and valued the training, it was clear that they were often unable to transfer this to their routine working practices. Very rarely were those interviewed able to identify ways in which they behaved differently in the workplace as a result of the training they had received. It seems that this is a problem that needs to be addressed at the organisational level and is not a fault of the training course as such. In addition, the interviews with course participants demonstrated that line managers had not followed the training with debriefing sessions that might identify ways in which the content could be incorporated into working practices. In one of the police services examined, superintendents responsible for running Basic Command Units reported that they had done nothing to follow up the training with other performance reviews or similar techniques. The content of the training was not incorporated into personal development plans, which might have ensured that it represented one dimension in the process of developing reflective practitioners.

There may also be a tension between training that focuses on the personal values and beliefs of individuals and the concept of institutional racism, which, by definition, focuses attention away from the individual toward policy, procedure and structure. If the nature of racism in contemporary policing is an institutional problem, then it is at that level that it needs to be addressed. Questions of institutional power in the perpetuation of racism remain unanswered by an approach that concentrates on the personal norms and mores of staff. This limitation reflects earlier criticisms of racism awareness training and local authority approaches to tackling racism in the 1980s (Sivanandan, 1985; Gilroy, 1990).

None of the above concerns about adopting an affective approach to police CRR training suggests that such a strategy ought to be abandoned. Encouraging officers and civilian staff to become 'reflective practitioners' able to recognise the impact that they personally, and the police service in general, have on the broader community is an important step in improving the 'trust and confidence' of minority ethnic communities in the police, the primary aim established by the Lawrence Report. However, it is not sufficient in itself and it is clear that the organisational and cultural context in which such training is delivered needs to be addressed in order that the dangers implicit in this approach do not fatally undermine the training work currently undertaken. It is to these issues that the concluding section of this chapter now turns.

Reform through training: reconsidering the nature of police culture

Brogden et al. (1988) distinguished two broad strategies of police reform: those that focus on 'rule tightening' and those predicated on cultural reform. The former model assumes that organisational behaviour can be developed via modification of internal and external governance of police services. With regard to improving police relations with minority ethnic communities, there have been a number of initiatives that reflect this approach: for example, the requirement for police services to practise ethnic monitoring in respect of internal personnel management (Fitzgerald and Sibbit, 1997) or to recruit a more ethnically diverse workforce (Home Office, 1999a). Similarly, in the wake of the Scarman Report (Scarman, 1981), changes were made to the police discipline code, so that racially prejudiced behaviour was classified as a particular offence.

Alternatively, the training analysed in this chapter reflects the other strategy Brogden et al. (1988) described: that which seeks organisational change via reconfiguring police culture. However, the approach to culture that implicitly informs the training courses outlined here remains somewhat simplistic. On the one hand, racism is seen as a cultural artefact of renegade officers whose values and beliefs are preventing organisations from improving community and race relations. More positively, police officers and civilian staff are regarded as culturally isolated and in need of development to enable them to respond effectively to the changing demands of policing in a diverse society. If better informed about the various needs of the diverse communities, the argument goes, staff will act appropriately and deliver an effective service. In either case, the problem that needs to be addressed is within individual officers and civilians present in the training sessions. In this way 'cultural problems' such as prejudice and stereotyping are seen in isolation from the broader organisational and institutional framework in which they have developed. It is ironic that training that has been developed in part as a response to the Macpherson Report's definition of institutional racism appears to have marginalised this aspect of the problem of community and race relations in favour of an approach predicated on affecting the norms and perceptions of individual employees.

The work of Chan (1996, 1997), referred to in the previous chapter, illustrates how efforts to change police culture need to understand the complexities and broader context in which that culture is developed; and to recognise that it has structural and organisational dimensions as well as comprising the informal values and 'working personality' of police officers and civilian staff. Chan (1996) reviews prevailing approaches to police culture, such as those outlined by Skolnick (1966) and Reiner (1978), and suggests that they tend to regard it as monolithic, unchanging and universal. Furthermore, Chan (1996: 112) contends that police research often implies a solely passive role for officers in their relation to culture, and so ignores 'the interpretive and active role of officers in structuring their understanding of the organization and its environment'. Thirdly, and crucially in terms of the arguments explored in this chapter, much research assumes that police culture is apart from social, political, legal and organisational context of policing. Overall, Chan suggests that police culture often is seen as an all-powerful, homogenous and deterministic concept. Analysis of police community and race relations training that draws upon some of the complexities of police culture as characterised by Chan provides a number of new directions that might begin to explain why and in what circumstances the training had a positive impact and in what ways it seems to have been less successful.

In terms of Bourdieu's distinction between habitus and field (as discussed in Chapter 3), it appears that police training has had more impact in respect of the former than the latter. There are several reasons for this. First, the results of the interviews discussed above showed that many course participants felt that the sessions had encouraged them to think more carefully about their interactions with colleagues or members of the public. There was clear evidence that it had at least begun to develop 'reflective practitioners' cognisant of the constructive role that they had in terms of shaping the perceptions of others. To this extent some elements of habitus within police culture were addressed as participants actively considered their knowledge and assumptions about their working environment.

However, there was much less evidence that the training offered addressed issues relating to the field of policing. This was apparent in two distinct ways: firstly, it was evident that little had been done to effectively integrate the content of the training sessions into the everyday working practices of the organisations examined: there was little or no opportunity for the content of the training to be developed in the longer term. Such concerns do not amount to a criticism of the training sessions or providers, who were unable to address the broader context concerned. However, it does suggest an institutional failure to develop an effective training strategy capable of reshaping and redirecting the organisation. This lack of strategic direction has been identified in police training more generally (HMIC, 1999a) and in respect of police CRR training it might also be explained by the short-term political expediency of getting relatively large numbers of individuals trained as quickly as practicable, even if that were done with little strategic vision.

The second way in which the role of the 'field of policing' tended to be neglected in the content of the training was evident in the failure to recognise that some of the aspects of police racism tackled may retain some functional use in the eyes of some police officers. Issues such as stereotyping and prejudice were dealt with at some length in the training programme and these relate directly to the field of policing and police culture. One aspect of police culture often noted in the research literature is the central role of suspicion and stereotyping as a means of ordering and understanding the terrain on which the police operate. Such processes were identified in Keith's study of policing in London, which described the way in which police knowledge informed an 'authoritative policing geography' that had impacted upon the way in which operational practice was organised (Keith, 1993: 19–20).

While relying on stereotypes is ultimately a poor and unreliable basis for judgement, it might remain functionally useful in terms of the habitus and the field of policing. Training programmes and other interventions intended to reform the police service must take into account the cultural reasons why processes such as stereotyping persist and have proved impervious to change. Miles (1989: 80) argued that a key feature of much racism is that it is 'practically adequate' in that, while ontologically flawed, it often provides a framework around which complex realities can be interpreted, simplified and (mis)understood.

The training programmes reviewed in this study have overcome many of the concerns relating to earlier interventions of this sort and have begun to develop an approach that encourages police officers and civilian staff to be reflective and self-conscious about the roles that they fulfil. It is evident that the curriculum and mode of delivery encouraged officers to think critically about continuing problems in police community and race relations. That many of these developments do not seem to have been embedded in the subsequent working practices of those who had been trained in this way does not reflect badly on those who delivered the programmes. It does suggest, however, that concerns about police training more generally (HMIC, 1999a) also pertain in this field, even though the curriculum and pedagogical approach that underpinned this particular programme was sound and innovative for the most part. That the training strategy, which ought to be broader than the training programme, did not address the complexity of police culture and that the wider 'field' of policing remained largely intact, suggest that the training will have only a limited impact and that the future trajectory of police community and 'race relations' will have been relatively unaffected.

Similarly, a national review of diversity training (HMIC, 2003) suggested that the positive measures implemented, in some places, in the learning environment were hampered by a lack of institutional strategic direction to embed them into the working routines of the service. The main areas of concern identified by HMIC (2003: 31–35) were the failure to develop a 'coherent, integrated, structured and long-term approach', the absence of a systematic needs analysis to identify areas where it was considered the service should improve CRR training, a lack of leadership, and insufficient evaluation of the training that was delivered. Additionally, HMIC (2003) argued that training was not properly related to staff appraisal systems and line management, that diversity issues were not incorporated into general training programmes, and the selection, assessment, management, support and training of trainers were insufficient. Given that the HMIC report made repeated reference to the failure of the police service to heed the findings of previous reports into these matters, it seems that at a strategic and leadership level action is needed if training is to prove more effective.

Chapter 5

Stop and search

Claims that the police misuse their powers of stop and search and disproportionately target minority ethnic communities have been a consistent feature of wider debates about the problematic nature of police 'race relations' for several decades in Britain. As with many of the other issues covered in this book, such concerns can be traced back much further than the post-Second World War era. Indeed, analysis of police relations with minority communities is complicated by the fact that associations between criminal behaviour and ethnic or 'racial' origin appear to pre-date the establishment of professional policing institutions along modern lines. Prior to the foundation of the Metropolitan Police service in 1829, English society had become familiar with the notion that some forms of crime were somehow linked with particular groups. Media claims that various types of offending were associated with certain ethnic groups were a feature of eighteenth-century England. For example, during this time an apparent rise in 'footpad crime' was blamed on migrant Irish workers who were also held to cause problems for the authorities as they 'brought with them the foreign habit of resistance to street arrest' (Pearson, 1983: 236).

Similar concerns continued in the period after the establishment of the 'new police'. Certainly, in the second half of the nineteenth century it seems that the police reflected prevailing fears about the 'dangerous classes' in Victorian London and other cities in such a way that led them to act against sections of the Irish and Jewish community in a manner that today would likely lead to suggestions of 'racial profiling' (Emsley, 1987: 86–7). What is more, the rise in urban lawlessness widely identified during this period was often explained in terms that were strongly biologically and genetically deterministic. The claimed propensity of certain ethnic groups and social classes to frequently commit crime was not explained in relation to their demographic profiles, social and economic circumstances or the urban milieu in which new migrants have often found themselves – all factors which, as will be examined later in this chapter, have featured in more recent discussions of street crime and stop and search. Instead the biological tenets of scientific racism seemed to explain the threat such groups posed to both the 'respectable poor' and society more generally. It was the supposed degradation of the racial character of the English people that many regarded as the fundamental cause of disorder and conflict in the burgeoning industrial cities. Miles' (1993) account of the emergence of 'race thinking' during this period outlines the manner in which notions of biological racial difference, widely used as an ideological framework in the exterior of the Empire, were also applied domestically in order to explain, and thereby rationalise, the parlous position of the lower orders. Emsley (1987: 60) illustrates this parallel application of racialised explanations of criminal behaviour in his account of the representation of crime in the popular press of the mid-nineteenth century:

> During the 1850s to 1870s a succession of explorers picked up their notebooks, as often as not found trusty guides among the stout-hearted, blue uniformed, helmeted guardians of law and order, and penetrated the dark and teeming recesses of poor working-class districts. They then wrote up their exploits for the vicarious delights of the reading public as journeys into criminal districts where the inhabitants were best compared with Red Indians or varieties of black 'savages'.

While more recent debates about minority ethnic communities and stop and search have not always reproduced the crude racist stereotypes of earlier eras, many of the themes briefly referred to above continue to be reflected. Criminality has been a major feature in US and UK discussions of the underclass, and some of the most vociferous participants in such debates have argued strongly that there is a genetic component to membership of the underclass and subsequently to offending behaviour. Jencks (1992: 98), for example, argues that 'the conclusion that blacks are five to ten times more likely than whites to commit most violent crimes is inescapable. This means that the genes determining skin colour are as closely correlated with criminal violence in the United States as genes determining gender' (cited in Morris, 1994: 90). While such arguments are deeply flawed – unable as they are to account for the social construction of crime and mistaking correlation for causality – they do provide a straightforward explanation of the likelihood that some minority ethnic communities will come into greater contact with the police. If the genetically reductionist accounts were correct, then all that follows in this chapter would be more or less irrelevant and claims that there is an over-representation of black people in stop and searches would be refuted by the fact that such statistical evidence simply reflects the greater likelihood of these groups committing offences. That the chapter continues below indicates that these arguments are not convincing, although it is not possible for a thorough discussion of genetic determinism to be included here. These controversies indicate that, although a broad consensus that some minority groups are over-represented in terms of stop and search has developed in the period since the publication of the Lawrence Report (Macpherson, 1999), there is much less agreement about the causes of this disproportionality. Before reviewing these key issues and controversies, and the implications that they have had for police practice, the contemporary history of this issue in Britain will be outlined.

Suspicious minds: stop and search before the 1984 Police and Criminal Evidence Act

In an early contribution to the development of the 'left realist' approach to crime and policing, Lea and Young (1984) argued that the increasing numbers of people stopped by the police in London during the 1970s were indicative of a more fundamental trend towards paramilitary policing. Suggestions such as these provide further illustration of the manner in which many of the debates about the relation of the police to minority ethnic communities have had broader implications that raise fundamental questions about the role of the police in a liberal democratic society. Lea and Young (1984: 176) claimed that the use by the Metropolitan Police of the Special Patrol Group, a mobile reserve unit, was:

> . . . compatible with the development of some of the characteristics of military policing. The growth in the number of people stopped and searched indicates a situation in which the police are not so much stopping people on the basis of some particular suspicion, based on information that the individual concerned is likely to have committed a crime, but as part of a generalized screening of the population of an area for information, and as a generalized deterrent. The police officers concerned in such activities acted on the basis of a stereotype, that the population of the area – young blacks – were 'very likely' to have committed crimes.

Until the end of the 1970s the Metropolitan Police, but not other police forces, had legal power to stop and search individuals under the terms of the 1824 Vagrancy Act. That this legislation had been passed to deal with the public delinquency and drunkenness regarded as a major threat to public order in the first decades of the nineteenth century further demonstrates the historical endurance of contemporary concerns. The Act enabled officers to stop and search a person if they suspected that the individual was about to commit an offence. Similarly, the 1839 Metropolitan Police Act gave powers to stop and search if it was 'reasonably suspected' that an individual was in possession of stolen property. Under the terms of these pieces of legislation the necessary criterion to stop and search an individual was the highly subjective grounds that a police officer was suspicious of their behaviour: no external objective factors, such as a potential victim or even type of offence, need be referred to. That the officer was suspicious was, in and of itself, sufficient legal basis for action. It is the importance of officer suspicion to this policing practice that has given rise to the phrase 'sus laws', often used in discussion of stop and search.

During a period in which the police service in Britain contained strong subcultural patterns of racism and machismo – as detailed elsewhere in this book – it is perhaps unsurprising that the extensive scope that such legislation provided for officers to exercise their discretion resulted in minority ethnic communities being targets for stop and search. Even in circumstances where individual or groups of officers did not deliberately direct their attention towards particular sections of society, there is every reason to suppose that broader moral panics and the perpetuation in the media relating to 'race' and crime provided a context in which black and Asian people were more likely to be stopped than others. As earlier periods saw concern about 'footpad' robberies and 'garrotting' (Pearson, 1983) and the notion of 'taxing' has had some currency more recently, during the 1970s sensational media coverage of 'mugging' assumed the status of a racialised moral panic. Hall et al. (1978) describe how the phenomenon developed in the early 1970s and served as a metaphor for a wide range of perceived social, economic and cultural concerns about law and order, urban decline and declining national fortune. Central to this process was the establishment in popular discourse of the image of the black 'mugger', preying on white victims. As Hall et al. (1978) and others (for example, Gilroy, 1987) have made clear, there was no reliable basis on which it could have been argued that black youths were disproportionately involved in such crimes or that this type of offending tended to be directed at white victims. What was apparent, however, was that the development of racialised stereotypes of this sort fitted neatly into media news agendas and, Sim (1982: 58) argues, the police 'utilised and emphasised one crucial factor – their belief that black people were disproportionately involved in street robbery' as they sought to undermine elements of the 1981 Scarman Report into the disorders in Brixton. Keith (1991: 190) suggests that the developments of such stereotypes during this period had broader connotations, as the black community in British cities became 'the incarnation of a threatening *other* that could always serve as both a frightening cautionary tale of urban decline and convenient scapegoat for the ills of society'.

Another feature of the controversy surrounding the use of stop and search during the 1970s was that the legal basis and practice among different police services varied considerably in the absence of any robust national legal or policy framework. Coupled with the lack of reliable recording practices, this meant that quantitative data by which stop and search could be ethnically monitored was unavailable. While it was clear that the stop and searches often did not result in arrest, suggesting that at most only minor offences, or no offences, were detected, there was little coherent information on which a final judgement could be made. Lea and Young (1984: 176–7) reported that 42 per cent of those arrested in 1976 under the 1824 Vagrancy Act were black, compared with 12 per cent of those arrested under other provisions. Such data only revealed limited information about the situation in London, and revealed nothing about arguably the most important group: those stopped and searched who turned out to be innocent. In the absence of statistical information, campaigning groups referred to the growing weight of anecdotal evidence. A comprehensive example is that contained in an Institute of Race Relations report (1979: 12), which details numerous cases of concern and refers to circumstances in south London in which:

> ... black parents were constantly worried whenever their children went out. They were liable to be stopped on the way to school or work, at bus stops and in the underground, not return home when expected and only hours later would parents discover that they were being held in the local police station.

While some of these concerns were assuaged by the repeal of the Vagrancy Acts on the advice of the 1979 Royal Commission on Criminal Procedure, it became apparent in the aftermath of Lord Scarman's Inquiry into the 1981 disorders in Brixton that some of the fundamental problems of the disproportionate representation of minority ethnic communities in stop and searches continued. Scarman (1981: 56–8) described the manner in which the police in Lambeth devised 'Operation Swamp '81' in order to arrest street robbers and burglars. During the six days that the Operation was in place, some 943 stops were carried out, leading to 118 arrests and the subsequent charging of 75 people with a variety of offences. Although local police claimed that the number of street robberies and burglaries committed during the period fell by 50 per cent, there was little evidence in the report that these claims could be robustly defended – for example, the notion that some of these offences had simply been displaced, now a staple of crime-prevention evaluation, was not addressed. Coupled with the activities of the Special Patrol Group, which had been drafted into the area on several occasions between 1978 and 1980, the impact of such policing operations on relations with the black community was outlined by Scarman (1981: 51–2) in the following terms:

> They provoked the hostility of young black people, who felt they were being hunted irrespectively of their innocence or guilt. And their hostility infected older members of the community, who, hearing stories of many innocent young people who had been stopped and searched, began themselves to lose confidence in, and respect for, the police.

The PACE framework

Scarman's (1981: 113) robust analysis of the legal framework for stop and search during this period was that 'the state of the law is . . . a mess'. The patchwork of powers affecting police forces across the country, which often tended to afford officers considerable discretion in terms of who was stopped and searched, and for what reason, was eventually consolidated by the 1984 Police and Criminal Evidence Act (PACE). In addition to regulating the conduct of stop and search, PACE, described as 'the greatest single reform of police powers' (Jason-Lloyd, 2000), legislated on the police complaints system, powers of seizure, entry and arrest, and the gathering and presentation of evidence. In terms of stop and search, Section 1 of PACE states that a constable may stop, search and detain an individual if there is reasonable suspicion that they are carrying stolen or prohibited articles. Such powers extend to vehicles, and must be conducted in a public place. As far as the precise legal terms of the statute are concerned, it appears that the threshold for stopping and searching continued to be whether the officer had 'reasonable suspicion'. However, PACE contains provisions for codes of practice to be issued that provide more detailed advice on the implementation of the Act, and these explicitly state that such suspicion must have some objective basis. A recent code of practice, issued in 1999, outlines what constitutes reasonable suspicion in the following terms (Sampson, 2001: 346):

> Reasonable suspicion may exist, for example, where information has been received such as a description of an article being carried or of a suspected offender; a person is seen acting covertly or warily, or attempting to hide something; or a person is carrying a certain type

of article at an unusual time or in a place where a number of burglaries or thefts are known to have taken place recently.

The code goes on to advise that the personal characteristics of an individual, such as their 'colour, age, hairstyle or manner of dress', do not constitute 'reasonable grounds'. Neither are these provided 'on the basis of stereotypical images of certain persons or groups as more likely to be committing these offences' (Sampson, 2001: 346). However, the code continues by referring to circumstances in which reliable information or intelligence that gang members carry knives or drugs means that there can be reasonable grounds to stop an individual who is wearing a '... distinctive item of clothing or other means of identification' that signals they belong to the gang. Popular concern about apparent escalation in gang-related crime and the use of knives and guns in street crime, which have recurred in recent years, have been heavily racialised and have formed an important context against which the powers of the police have been debated, a point returned to later in this chapter. Despite the warnings contained in the code, there is evidence that officers find it difficult in practice to interpret which aspects of a person's outward appearance constitute an acceptable basis for a stop and which do not (Miller *et al.*, 2000). While skin colour is expressly ruled out by the code, 'other means of identification', which remain unspecified, can be used to justify a stop: against a context in which minority ethnic youth are criminalised in ways that are complex and enduring, it seems probable that the subtle distinction that the code tries to negotiate, in practice will not often be recognised by police officers.

In addition to codifying the nature of 'reasonable suspicion', PACE has also provided for improved recording of stop and searches. Wherever practicable, an officer must provide the person stopped with a record of the incident, including details of the object of the stop and search, the grounds for making it, the outcome of the stop, and the identity of the officer concerned. Among the personal details collected are the age of the person stopped, their name and ethnic origin. The purpose of such recording practice is threefold. First, by advising the public that they are entitled to a written record of their encounter, it is intended that officers will be inhibited from using their powers arbitrarily. Second, in terms of securing public trust and confidence in the police it is held to be important that the practice of stop and search be accountable and transparent. Providing the person stopped with details of the incident and instructions on how they might complain, should they so wish, is held to be an important means of promoting openness. Third, recording and monitoring of stop and search patterns provides senior police officers with the wherewithal to identify more junior staff who might be over- or under-using these powers. The discretion afforded to police officers when 'on the beat' is considerable and has been widely discussed in police studies for several decades (Goldstein, 1960, 1964; Skolnick, 1975). Equally, improvements in information technology and data monitoring systems have long been held to improve the visibility of an officer's behaviour. The PACE Code makes it clear that (Sampson, 2001: 352):

> Supervising officers, in monitoring the exercise of officers' stop and search powers, should consider in particular whether there is any evidence that officers are exercising their discretion on the basis of stereotyped images of certain persons or groups contrary to the provisions of this code. It is important that any such evidence should be addressed.

Although officers provided members of the public stopped with records from the mid-1980s onwards, it was not until 1993 that Her Majesty's Inspector of Constabulary required forces to monitor these for ethnic differences on a constabulary-wide basis. Initially the data gathered only distinguished between 'ethnic minorities' and 'white' communities, and in 1994–95, the first year for which information was presented, it was apparent that overall ethnic minorities were more than four times more likely to be stopped and searched than whites, at 44 per 1,000 of the population compared with a rate of 10 per 1,000 for whites. The precise figures are shown in Table 5.1 for selected police forces.

Table 5.1 clearly indicates considerable differences in the extent to which forces use stop and search, regardless of the ethnicity of those involved, as Greater Manchester, Leicestershire and the Metropolitan

Table 5.1 Stop and searches per 1,000 population 1994/95, selected forces

Force	Ethnic minorities	Whites	Ratio ethnic minority:white
Bedfordshire	8	4	2.7:1
Greater Manchester	25	17	1.5:1
Hertfordshire	13	5	2.6:1
Lancashire	9	7	1.3:1
Leicestershire	21	20	1.1:1
Metropolitan Police	84	33	2.5:1
Nottinghamshire	5	2	2.5:1
Thames Valley	8	3	2.7:1
West Midlands	7	2	3.5:1
West Yorkshire	4	2	2:1

Source: derived from FitzGerald and Sibbitt (1997: 41)

Police forces had higher rates than others. In each force the proportion of ethnic minorities stopped and searched was greater than whites, although the difference was only marginal in respect of Leicestershire Constabulary (1.1: 1). Whatever the patterns between forces, the overall position seemed clear and these figures were seen to provide 'the first "official" proof that concerns about the disproportionate stopping of black people have been justified' (FitzGerald and Sibbitt, 1997: 40).

Since these figures were published the ethnic monitoring of stop and search has continued and it is now possible to review trends over a period of years. Table 5.2 indicates that the number of stop and searches recorded fell, year by year, from a total for England and Wales of 1,011,533 in 1997–98 to 686,114 in 2000–01. Several commentators suggested that this decline in the use of stop and search powers by the police was a consequence of the Lawrence Inquiry report (Macpherson, 1999), which demonstrated that police officers were suffering from low morale and were reluctant to stop people from fear of being accused of racism. For example, the then leader of the Conservative Party, William Hague, explicitly linked the decline in stop and search figures with the publication of the report, arguing in December 2000 that 'the Macpherson Report is . . . being used to brand every police officer as racist . . . the result is that there has been a post-Macpherson crisis that has led to a collapse in police morale and recruitment, and a rise in street crime' (Hague, 2000). More recently, a representative of the Metropolitan Police Federation suggested that the declining numbers reflected the fact that 'officers are wary of stopping people because they are open to complaint' (*Police Review*, 2002a).

The Lawrence Inquiry report was not centrally concerned with the question of police stop-and-search powers and their application to minority ethnic communities. The report notes that debate of this issue is complex, and must include analysis of demographic matters, social exclusion and recording practices. Nonetheless, the report argues that 'there remains . . . a clear core conclusion of racist stereotyping' (Macpherson, 1999: 6.45b). Much of the subsequent research into stop and search, most of which is outlined below, was instigated by the Home Office in response to the Lawrence Inquiry report's recommendations on these matters, which were (Macpherson, 1999: 333–4):

Rec'n 60. That the powers of the police under current legislation are required for the prevention and detection of crime and should remain unchanged.

61. That the Home Secretary, in consultation with Police Services, should ensure that a record is made by police officers of all 'stops' and 'stops and searches' made under any legislative provision (not just PACE). Non-statutory or

Table 5.2 Stop and searches of persons under Section of 1 PACE 1984 and other legislation, by ethnicity, 1997–2002, per 1,000 of population and total number

	1997–98		1998–99		1999–2000		2000–01		2001–02	
	England & Wales[1]	MPS[2]	England & Wales	MPS	England & Wales	MPS	England & Wales	MPS	England & Wales	MPS
White	19	37	20	33	16	19	13	17	13	18
Black	139	180	118	148	81	95	86	101	106	132
Asian	45	75	42	64	26	37	27	38	35	54
Other	20	25	21	21	15	13	14	12	16	16
Total (per 1,000 population)	22	51	22	45	18	27	15	25	16	29
Total (N)	1,011,533	337,339	1,037,271	296,072	818,203	178,280	686,114	167,074	713,683	197,333

Source: Home Office
[1] Includes MPS
[2] MPS = Metropolitan Police Service, including City of London police.

87

	so called 'voluntary' stops must also be recorded. The record to include the reason for the stop, the outcome, and the self-defined ethnic identity of the person stopped. A copy of the record shall be given to the person stopped.
62.	That these records should be monitored and analysed by Police Services and Police Authorities, and reviewed by HMIC on inspections. The information and analysis should be published.
63.	That Police Authorities be given the duty to undertake publicity campaigns to ensure that the public is aware of 'stop and search' provisions and the right to receive a record in all circumstances.

While the debate that has followed publication of the Macpherson Report is considered at greater length elsewhere in this book, it is worth noting some difficulties with the interpretations of the impact that it has had in respect of stop and search. Two points in particular might be noted. First, the decline in the use of stop and search that Hague referred to in December 2000 reflected a trend that pre-dated the Lawrence Inquiry report, and so could not be simply attributed to it. Of itself this does not mean that the Macpherson Report had no impact in these terms, but clearly other factors were also at play, including, perhaps, attempts to use stop-and-search powers in a more targeted manner in response to particular criminal incidents or as part of focused operations rather than as a routine activity of policing. One illustration of this is that, from 1997 onwards, the Metropolitan Police Service ceased using stop and search as a performance indicator, thus reducing any incentive for officers to use these powers unnecessarily (FitzGerald, 1999: v).

A second difficulty with arguments that suggest that stop-and-search practices have been adversely affected by the impact of the Macpherson Report is that, as discussed below, the pattern in terms of the disproportionate impact of stop and search on black and Asian people appears fairly consistent in Table 5.2. It is not the case, these figures suggest, that the disproportionate representation of minority ethnic communities in stop-and-search data decreased subsequent to Macpherson's report.

The trend of declining numbers of stop and search reversed in 2001–02, however, when the total number increased from the previous year by 4.0 per cent to 713,683. When considered in terms of stop and searches per 1,000 of the population, a similar pattern emerges, with the proportion declining from 22 in 1,000 in 1997–98 to 15 per 1,000 in 2001–02 before rising again to 16 per 1,000 in 2001–02.

It is also apparent that the Metropolitan Police Service accounted for a substantial proportion of stop and searches in England and Wales as a whole. This is the case in terms of the actual number of stop and searches, with the MPS accounting for 33.3 per cent of the total in 1997–98 and 27.6 per cent in 2001–02, and when considered per 1,000 of the population, with 51 and 29 people stopped and searched in 1997–98 and 2001–02 respectively. Results of more detailed research into stop and search in London are discussed further below.

Table 5.2 also indicates that the pattern outlined in Table 5.1, which referred only to ethnic minorities in generic terms, has continued to apply in the subsequent period, although it is also apparent that black people are disproportionately represented to a much greater extent than any other ethnic group. In 1997–98 black people were represented at 139 per 1,000 in England and Wales and 180 per 1,000 in the Metropolitan Police Service area. In the former case this amounts to a rate seven times greater than for whites. While the rate for both groups had fallen by 2001–02, the extent of the disproportionality actually increased, since blacks had a rate more than eight times greater than whites in England and Wales that year. Asian people were also more likely to be stopped and searched than whites across the period shown in Table 5.2 (45 per 1,000 in 1997–98 and 35 per 1,000 in 2001–02). As mentioned above, the persistence of the over-representation of minority ethnic groups from the pre- to the post-Macpherson period undermines claims that the Lawrence Report has had a dramatic impact on police officers' behaviour in respect of stop and search.

Post-Macpherson developments

While the overall picture clearly seems to support long-standing claims that black and Asian people are stopped and searched more often than the overall population, more detailed research carried out since the Macpherson Report suggests a somewhat different conclusion, although not necessarily one that exonerates the police service in this regard. A study conducted for the Home Office (MVA and Miller, 2000) analysed stop-and-search patterns in five areas on the basis, not of the proportion of ethnic groups resident, as presented in Tables 5.1 and 5.2, but instead in terms of the *available* population. This approach is based on research that suggests that the profile of people who are present in public places at times and in areas where stops and searches are more likely to be conducted is not the same as the profile of those resident. Specifically this research indicates that young men and minority ethnic communities are more heavily represented in the available than the resident population, which may explain their disproportionality in stop-and-search data. When compared with the benchmark of the available population, stop-and-search data 'did not suggest any general pattern of bias against people from minority ethnic groups' (MVA and Miller, 2000: vi). The ethnic differences identified by this study of available populations found that white people were over-represented, Asian people under-represented and black people had a mixed experience in terms of stop and search.

Superficially at least, this analysis appears to discount one of the most frequent explanations of black and Asian people's experiences of stop and search, which suggests that police officers, whether deliberately or unwittingly, unduly target their powers against minority ethnic groups. Since these powers appear to be used in proportion to the pattern of the population actually present in public places and so available to stop and search, it might appear that officers practise what Young (1994) referred to as 'democratic suspicion' in terms of the ethnicity of those targeted. This interpretation of the behaviour of individual officers is reinforced by the additional finding of MVA and Miller's study (2000: 86), which was that:

> There is a fair degree of consistency between the patterns of crime and patterns of both stops and searches. In other words, the patterns of stops and searches appeared, to a large extent, to be justified by the patterns of crime . . .

The conclusion to be drawn is that the over-representation of minority groups in overall terms seems largely to be because they are more likely to reside in areas where stop and search is targeted as these are relatively high-crime neighbourhoods. Even within these areas there may be various reasons why minority ethnic people are more likely to be present on the street and so 'available' to the police. FitzGerald (1999) argues that higher unemployment and school exclusion rates, and a greater tendency to socialise in public places, explain this pattern. This offers scant comfort to the police service, however, since broader patterns of discrimination and disadvantage, albeit not directly arising from policing, need to be addressed if the increased availability of minority groups to the police is to be tackled.

If the over-representation in terms of the wider population data is explicable in socio-geographical terms suggesting that individual officers are not engaging in 'racial profiling' when it comes to stop and search, this does not mean that the police service institutionally has no cause for concern. If the deployment of the officers who conduct stop and search is linked with recorded crime figures, and this happens to take them into districts with relatively high minority ethnic communities, concerns remain. The 'authoritative policing geographies' that Keith suggests (1993: 20) form police operational decision-making, may themselves reflect stereotypical labelling processes that establish a self-perpetuating cycle whereby higher rates of recorded crime both justify, and result from, the deployment of greater numbers of officers to the areas concerned. That there continues to be a general perception of black people as offenders was highlighted by FitzGerald and Sibbitt's (1997: 57) analysis of police activity on the streets, when they noted that 'the day-to-day business of responding to crime reports appeared to be reinforced by collective memories of the riots ... reinforced by officers' experiences and perceptions of black hostility towards the police'.

A further reason why the apparent proportionality of stop and search in terms of the ethnicity of those available to the police does not provide comfort relates to the importance of public perception and the related imperative to improve trust and confidence in the police among minority ethnic communities. The extent to which individuals feel confident that the police use their stop-and-search powers responsibly relates not only to the overall trends in the way in which they are used, but also to the experiences that individuals have of such encounters with the police. Waddington (1999b: 52) argues that the broader context of police relations with minority ethnic groups plays a crucial role in this respect:

> ... the significance of being stopped by the police is not considered in isolation, but against wider experiences of being stopped repeatedly and knowing that one's friends and acquaintances are also frequently stopped. Those experiences are refracted through a culture that attributes meaning and significance and contains oppositional components ... If this is so for one party to such encounters – black people, especially young black men – it is equally true for the other party – the police. Their experience is no less partial and no less subject to interpretation.

While research evidence suggests that all ethnic groups support the general stop-and-search powers available to the police, it is also apparent that minority ethnic groups are more likely to be dissatisfied in terms of personal experiences of particular incidents. Survey research undertaken for the Home Office (Stone and Pettigrew, 2000: 52) found that:

> There was a very strong perception that the way in which stops and searches are currently handled causes more distrust, antagonism, and resentment than any of the positive effects they can have. Despite this, respondents from all ethnic groups felt that if there were fundamental changes in the ways they are used, who they are targeted at, attitudes of the police, and reasons given, then there was a role for stops and searches.

Other studies have demonstrated that minority ethnic groups are less satisfied than whites with the treatment that they receive from officers during the stop-and-search encounter. Analysis of the 2000 British Crime

Survey found that minority ethnic people were less satisfied with the attitude and behaviour of officers in terms of the perceived fairness of the action, and the attitude and behaviour of the officers involved (Clancy *et al.*, 2001: 68–70). The notion that the interactions between police officers and minority ethnic individuals were qualitatively different from those involving the white population has been a persistent aspect of the debate surrounding the misuse of stop and search. Partly these concerns have reflected the greater likelihood that minority ethnic individuals who are stopped are more likely to then be searched, and that an arrest is more likely to be the final result of the encounter. Benyon's (1986: 58) review of the literature from the early 1980s noted a common feature was that 'police officers complained that young black people would not respond as co-operatively and respectfully as young whites, while young West Indians resented the formality of police officers'. Reiner (1992) argues that the broader context and history of poor relations between the police and sections of the minority ethnic community had a negative impact on what would otherwise be routine interactions. In such circumstances, Reiner (1992: 170) suggests that black youths were often arrested for 'contempt of cop' as:

... a vicious cycle develops whereby police officers and their 'property' approach encounters warily with pre-existing hostility and suspiciousness, and interact in ways which only exacerbate the tension.

More recent research has suggested that the tendency for those stopped to be arrested as a result of the fraught nature of the interface, rather than due to any prior offence being committed, continues. While it was noted above that the Metropolitan Police no longer use stop-and-search data as a performance indicator, Mooney and Young's (2000: 83) study of policing in North London concludes that it continues to be replete with informal power dynamics:

The arrests which arise from such confrontations we called ... 'meta-crimes' – crimes created by the confrontation rather than crimes in themselves. It is difficult not to view these situations as an attempt to bolster arrest statistics or, as one police officer interviewed put it succinctly, the suspects had 'failed the attitude test'.

It was in order to bring greater transparency and accountability to the conduct of stop and search that officers were required by PACE to issue records to those stopped. As outlined above, the Macpherson Report recommended that this practice be widened to incorporate a wider range of police encounters with the public, including those that are voluntary.

Stone and Pettigrew's (2000: viii) survey of public opinion found that 'the most important focus for change requested by members of all ethnic groups, was for officers to give credible explanations for each stop or search'. A programme of public consultation conducted by the Association of Police Authorities (APA, 2001) found a consensus that a wide range of stops should be recorded. While increasing scrutiny of an officer's behaviour along these lines appears to provide an opportunity to curtail the misuse of powers, it may be that extending recording practices in these ways will have a negative impact by formalising routine encounters. A senior officer suggested that the requirement to record all such encounters would result in one million incidents being recorded each year in London alone (Mulraney, 2002). Such an escalation in the number of interactions that would be recorded would introduce greater bureaucracy and possibly a deleterious impact in terms of legitimacy. It may be counterproductive to formalise and codify in this way what would otherwise be routine interchanges between the police and members of the public, since the requirement to complete records might deter officers from engaging with members of the public. Alternatively, it may be unhelpful if officers issue records to those individuals who they anticipate might prove troublesome but not to those regarded as unlikely to have complaints. Concerns have been expressed that requiring police officers to ask members of the public for personal information during an otherwise informal exchange might raise concerns about data protection and the invasion of privacy. Towards the end of 2002 a pilot study established to test these concerns was introduced in seven police force areas (Home Office, 2002a) and it remains unclear how this issue will develop.

Discretion, street crime and measuring police performance

At the heart of debates about police use of stop and search is the issue of discretion. As mentioned briefly above, a long-standing feature of attempts to manage the routine activity of police officers when out on the beat is the difficulty faced by those responsible for police governance arising from the low visibility of much police work. Elsewhere in this book the roles that training, disciplinary procedures, complaints and accountability systems variously play in regulating the actions taken by officers as they interact with the public are discussed. Much of the effort expended to control officers' behaviour in relation to stop and search has employed the development of regulations and monitoring procedures.

The discretion available to officers in terms of their powers to stop and search is considerable for a number of reasons. Even though PACE tightened the requirement for police officers to have reasonable suspicion before using stop and search and the codes of practice stipulate in some detail how this ought to be applied, it remains the case that such guidelines require interpretation in a myriad of circumstances. In such situations informal practices and norms influence the application of formal regulations and the working knowledge of policing provides a basis for officers' action. The nature and impact of police subculture has been discussed elsewhere in this book, but machismo and racism have been much noted in studies into this issue and the concern has been that these filter officers' discretion so that black people and other minorities come to be regarded as police 'property'. Since most police officers are white males, the extent to which they have contact with minority communities in a non-policing environment has been found to be limited and so the process of stereotyping becomes reinforced to the extent that black people, and other groups, are only encountered in crime-related contexts. Against this background, there is only a short mental leap to be made before officers use stereotypes to order and make sense of the complex shifting environment in which they work (Rowe, 1995).

Interestingly, though, FitzGerald's (1999) study of stop and search in London found that officers tended to deny that they implemented their powers on the basis of their own discretion. Instead, it was argued, such decision-making was removed from the individual officer who responded instead to crime reports provided to them or to information supplied by the public, described by FitzGerald as 'low-discretion' stop and searches. However, FitzGerald's analysis of data relating to stop and searches suggested that officers' perceptions were not borne out since approximately three-quarters of these encounters were implemented at the discretion of the police officer. Another explanation FitzGerald was given by officers was that they tended to use their powers to target 'prominent nominals', i.e. individuals who were 'known offenders'. Again, though, FitzGerald's (1999: 41) analysis sheds doubt on this explanation of officers' use of stop and search:

In interviews, police officers constantly asserted that their patterns of search simply mirrored patterns of offending, as witnessed by victims of crime; and their insistence that they focused their attention on 'known' offenders was clearly a further reflection of this. These perceptions cannot be fully reconciled with the objective facts ... around half the people they search but do not arrest have no criminal record.

The manner in which officers rationalise and reflect on their behaviour may be interpreted as attempts at self-justification of the sort offered to external researchers even though it may bear little comparison to reality. Earlier discussion of officers' reaction to diversity training found a common denial of the need for such 'politically correct' activity on the basis that individuals perceived themselves to be fair, open-minded and tolerant. While the anecdotal and research evidence might point to a catalogue of experiences to the contrary that cannot easily be reconciled with this self-perspective, it is difficult to conceive of efforts to challenge or reform the activity of police officers, or any other group, unless this perception is taken seriously. Robert Miles (1989) has argued that racism often provides a 'practically adequate' way of understanding and rationalising complex social realities; that it is ultimately flawed is, on some levels, beside the point.

Section 60: a return to 'sus'?

Almost all of the above discussion and the research that has been conducted into the use and abuse of stop and search have related to those powers available to the police under the 1984 PACE. As has been outlined, PACE attempted to regulate more closely the manner in which stop and search was carried out, and other efforts have also been made to ensure that the 'reasonable grounds' requirement provides a real check on potential abuse. Concerns have arisen, however, that other legal powers available to the police are being increasingly used which do not require that officers have strong grounds for stopping individuals. Most important has been the increasing use that many police forces have made of powers under Section 60 of the 1994 Criminal Justice and Public Order Act. This legislation allows for officers of the rank of inspector and above to authorise individuals to be stopped and searched in particular locations for a period of up to 24 hours, should they reasonably anticipate incidents of serious violence or suspect that individuals may be carrying offensive weapons. Of particular importance for police relations with minority ethnic communities is that such searches do not require an officer to have 'reasonable suspicion' of an individual's behaviour or intention: their presence in an area covered by a Section 60 certificate is all that is required for them to be stopped.

While these powers are often used in public order situations, to allow, for example, for widespread search powers to be used at political demonstrations or football matches, there is some evidence that they are also starting to be used in routine policing. Certainly the number of 'Section 60' searches has increased in recent years, from 7,054 in 1998–9, to 7,153 in 1999–2000, to 11,203 in 2000–1 and to 18,639 in 2001–2. Clearly such searches are relatively rare compared with those carried out under PACE (which amounted to some 713,683 in 2001–2) and the increase in their use might be partly explained by the fact that Section 60 orders can now be given by inspectors, rather than the higher-ranking

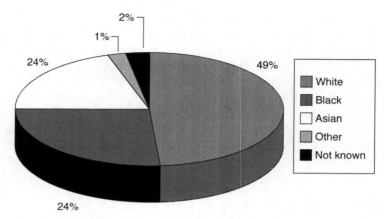

Figure 5.1 Section 60 stop and searches by ethnicity, England and Wales, 1998–2002
Source: Home Office

superintendents whose authorisation was required when the legislation was first introduced. While used less often than PACE legislation, it is clear that, in overall terms, the proportion of Section 60 searches involving black and Asian people is greater than their presence in the population (see Figure 5.1).

While there is a dearth of research into the use of Section 60 stop and searches relative to that investigating PACE-based activity, there are anecdotal grounds for concern. In February 2003, for example, the case of a senior executive from a media company was highlighted after he was dragged from his car by officers apparently suspicious of a black man driving an expensive vehicle. The executive concerned argued that little appeared to have changed in the post-Macpherson era since 'the police find it difficult to understand the resentment they cause when they judge people on such meaningless markers as the colour of their skin or the cost of the car they drive' (Eboda, 2003).

Other reasons why Section 60 stop and searches, which do not require 'reasonable suspicion', are cause for concern relate to recurring debates in Britain in the period since publication of the Lawrence Report about various aspects of street crime. Media coverage and political and police reaction to problems of 'taxing', the most recent euphemism for the centuries-old phenomenon of street robbery, mobile phone theft, drug-dealing and gang and gun-related crime have all been heavily racialised in recent times. The fatal shooting of two young women at a New Year party in January 2003 in Birmingham gave rise to considerable media coverage of gang crime and the use of guns. Some of this coverage spoke directly of such problems in terms of perceived dysfunctionality within the black community, which has led, it was argued, to a situation where young black males are marginalised and disaffected to such a degree that crime and gang membership provide an attractive route to wealth and status.

The jailing of Ashley D from rap group *So Solid Crew* for firearm possession in 2002 re-opened debates about the influence of pop stars on young audiences. Following the shootings in Birmingham, senior police officers were reportedly concerned about the negative impact of elements of popular culture that glamorise weapons (Hinsliff *et al.*, 2003) and fuel a 'trend towards so-called "respect shootings" where black youths have resorted to firearms to settle minor scores' (Gadher *et al.*, 2003). While such views, emanating from within the black community, have been subject to much debate and criticism, the Metropolitan Police have been engaged in Operation Trident, explicitly designed to tackle gun and drug crime among London's black community. Interestingly, a major element of the operation has centred on maintaining transparency and accounta- bility with the black community itself, so that police actions are not regarded as confrontational. Such operations can, and must be, conduc- ted along such lines in order to maintain the trust and confidence of the public, as prioritised by the Lawrence Inquiry report.

While popular debate around these topics has not explicitly stated that these are problems particularly associated with some minority ethnic communities, such claims are often only thinly veiled. As commentators previously referred to in relation to the mugging moral panics of the 1970s noted, once a particular media definition of a problem has become established, it is no longer necessary for all the details to be reiterated and key phrases act as synonyms for the, in this case, racial or ethnic identity of those purportedly involved. Hall *et al.* (1978: 329) argue that the use of place names often served a similar purpose: 'the specification of certain *venues*, however, reactivates earlier and subsequent associ- ations'. The relatively subtle way in which racialised images are woven around media coverage of the problems of street crime provide an important context against which stop and search is conducted. Although it remains difficult to measure the impact that these debates have had on police officers in the period since the Lawrence Report was published, it seems unlikely that they are immune from images of gang culture and crime that are heavily racialised.

Political responses to these issues, such as the commitment made by the Prime Minister, Tony Blair, in 2002 to reduce street crime and a plethora of initiatives from Home Secretary, David Blunkett, also seem likely to encourage officers to use stop and search more widely; even if official police policy remains that such powers be carefully targeted. Associations of criminal behaviour with ethnicity may be reinforced by developments such as those in January 2003, whereby visa restrictions were placed on individuals from Jamaica travelling to Britain, because of fears relating to an apparent rise in gun-related crime and drug smuggling.

In addition to the political pressures directly relating to street crime are those applied more generally in terms of the monitoring of police performance. Although the police service may no longer use stop-and-search data as a crude measure of the activity of officers, maintaining symbolic and actual control of the streets continues to be a central component of policing, both in legal and cultural terms. Cashmore (2001: 652) outlines how such attempts to manage performance more closely might have a detrimental impact in terms of relations with the public:

> Behaviour such as this is motivated by the attempt to maintain a respectable performance profile. The action may not be triggered by a racist motive, but, of course, the result is just the same as if it was. Professional pressure to keep up 'numbers' manifests itself in several ways, the most obvious – and, for most officers, easiest – one being to perform more searches, to issue more cautions or to detain more motorists. On this account, racism among white police officers is not the result of deep-rooted prejudices, bigotry or authoritarian personalities; less still of fixed ideological positions. More likely, racism is at least partly the product of practical necessities. It emerges from the attempt to ascertain how to do one's job effectively.

Considered against the distinction made by Chan (1997) in her study of police culture and reform in Australia between the field and habitus of policing, it appears that the recent British experience in terms of stop and search provides further evidence that both dimensions need to be fully recognised. Much of the attempts to scrutinise and control the ways in which officers apply their considerable powers to stop and search members of the public have involved particular management and information systems to monitor officer behaviour. Additionally, as described elsewhere in this book, training has been carried out intended to address cultural issues and stereotyping. The extent to which such measures have proved effective is, inevitably, open to interpretation and the reasons for successes and failures a matter for debate. What is clear, though, and what will be discussed at greater length in the final chapter of this book, is that such internal reforms cannot be considered in isolation from broader developments. While the research evidence suggests some limited signs that stop and search is being used proportionately by individual police officers, it seems clear that broader developments, including continuing racism within society more generally, mean that legitimate concerns about the use and abuse of stop and search persist.

Chapter 6

Racist incidents, policing and 'hate crimes'

As the broad range of topics reviewed in the Macpherson Report indicates, many aspects of policing are involved in responding to hate crime. First aid training, victim liaison and many of the routine tasks of criminal investigation apply to racist incidents as to any other crime. This chapter takes a relatively narrow focus as it explores the recent history of concern about the failure of policing racist violence and the developments that have sought to rectify the situation. Many of the reforms outlined below, most notably those stemming from the 1998 Crime and Disorder Act, pre-date the Lawrence Report, but were implemented against the context of the debate surrounding racist violence, of which the murder of Stephen Lawrence formed a large part. An important aspect of this debate, which developed in the United States, has related to the notion of 'hate crime', which is also explored below.

The question of whether racist incidents be classified and treated as 'hate crimes' will be addressed along two dimensions. Firstly, the notion will be explored that certain offences ought to be more thoroughly investigated and, where convictions result, subjected to more stringent punishment on the basis of the motivation of the offender, rather than – as with most types of crime – on the basis of the magnitude of the incident itself. Secondly, the debate is considered in terms of the practical impact that the application of the label 'hate crime' might have on the response of the police, local authorities and the criminal justice system more generally to racist incidents. It is argued here that, whatever position is taken on the value judgement about whether certain categories of offence be treated more harshly than others, the notion of 'hate crime' is unlikely to be helpful in terms of focusing the attention of police officers on racist incidents.

Much of the academic and 'campaigning' literature on 'racial violence', or 'racist violence' as it now tends, quite properly, to be called, agrees that the problem was first established on the political agenda in the early 1980s. Two key reports were published in the late 1970s (Bethnal Green and Stepney Trades Council, 1978; Institute of Race Relations, 1979), which drew attention to the extent and nature of racist violence and harassment experienced by minority ethnic communities in British society. Shortly afterwards, official recognition of both the problem and the paucity of the policing response to it came in the 1982 Home Affairs Committee report *Racial Attacks*, which was instrumental in the development of multi-agency approaches to the problem (House of Commons Home Affairs Committee, 1982).

More than two decades later, when reviewing this literature, it is apparent that many of the recommendations made and problems identified seem to have been addressed, at least at the level of policy even if not always implementation. Many of these studies, for example Forbes (1988) and Gordon (1986), drew attention to the need for local authority housing departments to take more effective action against the perpetrators of racist incidents. Others, such as Blagg *et al.* (1988) and Saulsbury and Bowling (1991), called for greater coordination via a multi-agency response to racist incidents. These and other reports also suggested that a common complaint of victims of racist incidents was that police officers often refused to acknowledge that the incidents of violence and harassment were motivated by racism (see Hesse *et al.*, 1992, for example).

Since this period it can be argued that progress has been made to address each of these three areas of concern. In terms of housing departments it is now common for local authorities and housing associations to explicitly prohibit racist and other forms of harassment, and to adopt policies whereby the perpetrators of such incidents will be subject to sanctions up to and including eviction. The 1996 Housing Act strengthened the power of local authority housing departments to act against a range of 'antisocial' behaviour. Other policy and legislative initiatives have meant that demands for concerted 'multi-agency' responses to racist incidents have also been largely met – most notably in the 1998 Crime and Disorder Act which, for the first time, gave local authorities statutory responsibilities in the field of community safety and crime prevention. Numerous reports from the 1980s and 1990s demanded that police, housing departments, education authorities, the voluntary and business sector develop a coordinated approach to the problem of racist violence and harassment, and it might be argued that not only has this been widely adopted in the context of these particular offences, but that it has become the hallmark of much policing and criminal justice policy in general. Again, it might be argued that the denial of the racist motivation, seen as a fundamental problem by many commentators in the 1980s and 1990s, has been addressed, at least in policy terms. Most significant has been the widespread acceptance among criminal justice and local government agencies of the definition of a racist incident recommended in the Lawrence Report, which is that: 'A racist incident is any incident which is perceived to be racist by the victim or any other person' (Macpherson, 1999: 328).

The most significant development in terms of addressing the problem of racist violence and harassment in recent years, at least in legal and policing terms, has been the measures outlined in the 1998 Crime and Disorder Act (CDA), which created a separate class of offences that were 'racially aggravated'. Arguments in favour of establishing a distinct legal offence of racially motivated crime had been resisted by previous governments, usually on the grounds that a requirement to establish the motivation of an offender would create a legal hurdle that would often be difficult to overcome. This would mean, it was held, that it would be more difficult to prove racially motivated offences than other types of crime – rendering such legal provisions at best no more than symbolic and at worst counterproductive, since false expectations would be raised. The CDA 1998 overcame this problem by enshrining in law the principle that 'racial aggravation', where it could be proved, provided grounds to impose a more serious penalty than for an offender who had been convicted of a similar offence, but where 'racial aggravation' was not present. To this end the CDA provides for a stiffer tariff for offences where it can be established that the offender was motivated by racism. For example, an offender convicted of common assault is liable to a maximum penalty of six months in prison or a level five fine. If, however, it can be established that the offence was 'racially aggravated', then the maximum penalty increases to two years' imprisonment and/or an unlimited fine.

The Act defines 'racial aggravation' fairly broadly, stating in Section 28 that such an offence is:

- one motivated by racial hostility; or if

- racial hostility was demonstrated towards the victim either at the time of committing the offence, or immediately before or after.

The notion of motivation is itself open to fairly wide interpretation under Section 28 and the inclusion of the demonstration of 'racial hostility' means that such charges might be brought where the offender uses racist language or displays racist symbols (for example on their clothing) during an offence. In these terms, then, a prosecution need not rely solely on establishing the motivation of an attack, which may be a subjective exercise in many cases, since the presence of more objective factors – what was said or demonstrated prior to, during or after an incident – are sufficient to establish 'racial aggravation' (Home Office, 1998b).

Unlike the situation in the United States, Britain does not have generic legislation against 'hate crime' and in this context the provisions against racially aggravated offences outlined above represent the closest equivalent for comparison. Since the introduction of the CDA, a body of evidence has emerged against which demands for more generic hate crime legislation can be judged. In what follows, two broad areas of debate are identified. First, the conceptual ambiguities surrounding the notion of hate crime will be considered in the light of the British experience of responding to racist violence and harassment. Second, the challenges of implementing these provisions as they have emerged since the CDA came into effect will be reviewed. In conclusion it is argued here that the introduction of more general 'hate crime' laws might serve some useful symbolic purpose, but that there is a serious risk that such legislation would not be properly enforced and that sustained effort would be needed if the criminal justice system were to translate the letter of such laws into practice.

The conceptual ambiguities of hate crime

One of the most fundamental criticisms of the notion of hate crimes relates to the attention concentrated on the motivation of the offender. As has already been mentioned in respect of the CDA in Britain, the legislation was framed in such a way that the notion of motivation could be approached in fairly broad terms, thus avoiding legal wrangling over the precise psychological mindset of an alleged offender. Morsch (1991) argues that motivation is subtly distinct from other concepts, such as 'intent', relating to *mens rea* on which the criminal law more usually focuses. One reason why motivation proves difficult for the law to come to terms with, Morsch (1991: 667) suggests, is because 'the exact contours of motive ... will be within each individual's knowledge alone as personality and psyche are inherently subjective'. The CDA was framed in terms of motivation for practical reasons, though, and opponents of the general terrain of hate crime legislation sometimes make a more fundamental objection, which is that such laws focus on the motivation of offenders and thus are at odds with the generality of criminal law, which concentrates on the actions of offenders, and is largely unconcerned with what motivated them.

Phillips (2002) objects to laws proposed in the UK in the wake of the 11 September 2001 terrorist attacks in the United States prohibiting incitement to religious hatred, on the grounds that they are unlikely to combat effectively problems of racism or religious intolerance. In addition she argued against such measures because they represent an unacceptable extension of the criminal law into the realms of individual beliefs. Many objections to hate crime legislation in the United States have centred on whether such prohibitions run counter to the constitutional rights to free speech enshrined in the first amendment (Jacobs and Potter, 1998). While such legal arguments do not translate easily to the United Kingdom, in which there is no written constitution against which other legislation might be found wanting – although the Human Rights Act 2000 complicates this – it does seem that the provisions against racially aggravated offences contained in the CDA are relatively unusual because they explicitly provide for more serious sanctions against offences committed on some grounds rather than others. This is not entirely a recent development, though. The 1991 Criminal Justice Act allowed for stronger penalties in cases where racial motivation could be established (Iganski, 1999: 391). In addition, in 1992, the Code for Crown Prosecutors was amended such that the presence of a racial motivation was an aggravating factor that added to the public interest grounds on which prosecution should be pursued (Hare, 1997: 437). Furthermore, in 1995 the Lord Chief Justice advised that offences in which it could be established that an offender had been motivated by racism be treated more seriously when it came to sentencing (Iganski, 1999: 391).

Although it might be simplistic to argue that the hate crime laws represent a distinct and worrying development whereby the law becomes embroiled in the policing of individual thought and motivation, there are other reasons for questioning the conceptual basis of legislation such as the CDA prohibition of 'racially aggravated' offences. Jenness (2002) argues that an unintended consequence of interest group pressure to establish certain offences as hate crimes is that the process of translating concern to protect particular interests into legal statute involves moving from the particular – for example, safeguarding the rights of black and Asian communities in Britain – into more generic legal terminology. Jenness (2002: 24–5) has argued that pressure to protect identified groups who tend to experience disproportionate levels of crime have, in the United States, run up against a fundamental tenet of the legal system, which is that all groups be treated equally: what she describes as the 'norm of sameness':

> In the case of hate crime, the norm of sameness ensures that terms like 'race', 'religion' and 'gender', instead of 'Blacks', 'Jews' and 'women', anchor various formulations of hate crime law and attendant discourse. Hate crime laws are written in a way that elides the historical basis and meaning of such crimes by translating specific categories of persons (such as Blacks, Jews, gays and

103

lesbians, Mexicans, etc.) into all encompassing and seemingly neutral categories (such as race, religion, sexual orientation and national origin). In doing so, the laws do not offer these groups any remedies or protections that are not simultaneously available to all other races, religions, genders, sexual orientations, nationalities and so on. Minorities are treated the same as their counterparts.

Perversely, then, one outcome of hate crime legislation might be that the particular ideologies, prejudices and social dynamics that cause problems for certain groups in society – in the context of this discussion, racism and racial prejudice – are marginalised by legal formulations that must hold that any 'racial' or ethnic group can become victimised by hate crime. This is reflected in the findings of the 1999 British Crime Survey of victims of crime, which found that 65 per cent of those who claimed to have been the victim of a racially motivated incident were white (Clancy *et al.*, 2001: 28).

Further evidence that the 'norm of sameness' might obfuscate the particular experiences of minority ethnic communities can be drawn from analysis of the impact of racially motivated offences on victims from different ethnic backgrounds. Although there is a lack of substantial evidence on the impact that racist crime has on victims and the wider community, what there is suggests that it is more severe than for non-racist crimes. Clearly, most commentators also agree that incidents motivated by racism are more invidious than those caused by 'ordinary' criminal motivation and this is usually cited as a reason for punishing hate crimes more seriously. Iganski (2001) suggests that the impact of hate crimes is felt at a variety of levels: by the direct victim, by the wider community to which the victim belongs, and by society as a whole. While discussion of the impact of hate crime often seems to take it for granted that the negative impact of such offences is greater than for non-hate alternatives, there is some evidence that this is the case, at least when it comes to the reaction of those victims directly involved. Clancy *et al.* (2001) analyse the findings of the 1999 British Crime Survey (BCS), the largest victimisation study in the country, which asks victims to gauge the seriousness of their experience on a scale between 0 (most minor) and 20 (most serious). The results are summarised in Table 6.1.

While the average scores shown in the table indicate that victims regard racially motivated crime more seriously, the other data in the table suggest that further research is needed into what may be a more complex situation. White victims appear to regard racially motivated incidents less seriously than their minority ethnic counterparts – which may reflect the BCS finding that the nature of the incidents reported as racially motivated varies between white and minority ethnic communi-

Table 6.1 Victim perceptions of the seriousness of racially motivated and non-racially motivated crime

	White victim	Black victim	Asian victim	Average
Racially motivated incidents	8.6	10.9	9.3	9.1
Non-racially motivated incidents	5.1	7.7	7.9	5.2

Source: Clancy *et al.* (2001: 39)

ties – and minority ethnic respondents seem to regard non-racially motivated offending as more serious than do white victims. One implication of this may be that the broader social context of racism and disadvantage has an impact on how serious victims regard crimes to be. It might be that white victims of racially motivated offences do not regard them as so grave because they do not form part of a wider experience of racism. Conversely, black or Asian victims might feel that their experience of non-racially motivated crime is more serious since it occurs against a background of racism and social exclusion. Without more detailed research into the experience of the victims of these crimes, it is difficult to draw more definite conclusions about the impact of racially motivated crimes on their victims, particularly when it comes to the effect that such crimes have on the wider community.

A different set of concerns surrounds another reason often given in support of hate crime legislation, namely that acts specified under hate crime law are qualitatively more abhorrent than other types of criminal behaviour, since they undermine the multi-cultural fabric of diverse society. Iganski's (2001) research in the United States found that a common justification for hate crime legislation was that hate crime had a broad negative impact on society that did not apply with other types of crime. Tatchell (2002) outlines his – ultimately fruitless – attempts to persuade the British Home Office that other types of offence be included in the CDA in such a way that mirrored the establishment of 'racially aggravated' offences. Tatchell argued that religion; sexual orientation; political opinion; disability; sex; medical condition; national or social origin; gender identity; and physical appearance could also provide criteria by which offences could be aggravated and thus liable to stronger sentences. The difficulty with this position is that the notion of 'hate crime' becomes increasingly conceptually ambiguous as it expands, but at the same time there is no clear reason why it should remain limited only to certain types of offence. It might be readily agreed that racist offences be understood as 'hate crimes' in particular circumstances, and that many offences against women also be labelled in this manner.

Heterosexist assaults on gays and lesbians or crime targeted at the disabled might also be included in some cases. The difficulty is that almost any incident might come to be understood as a hate crime, and so a category so broadly drawn loses its power to highlight the peculiarly reprehensible nature of certain types of crime. The difficulty of conceptualising diversity was mentioned in an earlier discussion of police training initiatives that followed the Lawrence Report, and is considered at greater length in Chapter 8.

Jenness (2002) argued that the growth of hate crime legislation in the United States has reflected the development of various interest groups: as new coalitions have formed, their demands have begun to be reflected in hate crime legislation. In this way, the original forms of hate crime to be recognised in that country related to the civil rights movements of the 1960s that targeted crime, prejudice and discrimination against minority ethnic communities. Since that time, other pressure groups and campaigns, relating, for example, to women's rights and those of gay and lesbian communities, have emerged and gradually these too have come under the umbrella of hate crime. While this gradualist or evolutionary approach may reflect broader processes of community political activism, it seems to run counter to the very spirit of hate crime legislation if minority interest groups must rely on securing their place on a greasy political pole in order to gain the level of legal protection that such laws have to offer, especially since the advance of one group's cause may be at the expense of another claim. That minority or interest groups need to court public opinion in order to secure protection from hate crime legislation is also problematic, since those groups most in need of such support might be so marginalised that they are unable to garner the political momentum they need in order to advance their claims.

An important reason for introducing hate crime legislation against racist violence and harassment, it has been argued, is because of the broader symbolic legal capital to be gained from prohibiting behaviour widely held by society to be especially reprehensible. Iganski (1999: 388) suggested that many argued in favour of Section 28 of the CDA on the grounds that:

> ... the legislation will provide an educative function by sending a message that racist bigotry and acts of violence, harassment and damage motivated by such bigotry are socially unacceptable. The potential educative role of legislation cannot be undervalued in light of the social context in which racist incidents occur. Recent research ... suggests that the attitudes of perpetrators of racist incidents are shared by the wider communities to which they belong, and the absence of community condemnation of incidents reinforces the perpetrator's behaviour.

As Iganski (1999) notes, there are a number of grounds to regard this as problematic. For one thing, the CDA did not invent condemnation of racist violence and harassment: such behaviour has been widely reviled by public and private agencies for a considerable period. As was mentioned earlier, provisions for stronger sentences can be traced back in legislation at least as far as 1991. If the symbol of prohibiting such behaviour was ineffective following that legislation, it is not apparent why it would be any different in the wake of the 1998 CDA. The notion that the law is capable of sending signals about what society regards as acceptable or unacceptable is simplistic. ACPO welcomed the symbolic capital of the CDA, arguing that:

> The legislative changes will do much to reinforce the seriousness with which the vast majority of members of our society view crime and conduct motivated by racial hatred. It will send out important messages to perpetrators and victims alike, that racist violence and harassment will not be tolerated and that positive action will be taken where this is exhibited.
>
> (Iganski, 1999: 389)

Another limitation of the position exemplified here by ACPO, as Tatchell's (2002) argument makes clear, is that those groups not explicitly included in hate crime legislation may feel that their exclusion symbolises that their victimisation is not treated seriously. Also, it may be that the short-term benefits of such a symbolic message are soon outweighed by a longer-term failure to actually take the positive action suggested. It will be argued below that the experience in England and Wales in the period since the CDA came into force has been that the prosecution of racially aggravated offences has been relatively rare, and that the recording of cases has varied enormously between police forces. Given this, it seems likely that the positive impact that the passing of such legislation might have on minority ethnic communities may be negated by a subsequent failure to implement effectively the legal powers made available by law. This point is further developed in the following section.

Applying hate crime law in practice

Thus far the discussion has centred on concerns relating to the conceptual and jurisprudential foundations of hate crime. While this was applied in some aspects to the precise context of the response to racist violence and harassment in the UK, many of the points raised relate to hate crime generically. In the remainder of this chapter some of the more practical difficulties of applying the discourse of hate crime to racist incidents will be explored. Three particular aspects of recent research and policy development in this field are focused on to illustrate some of the problems that have been faced in terms of translating the letter of the CDA provisions into actual policing 'on the ground'. The first issue to be discussed relates to the work conducted by Bowling (1998), which suggested that many of the racist incidents experienced in Britain are offences that have traditionally been regarded as relatively insignificant by the police service. Although there have been recent attempts, not least those occasioned by the CDA itself, to stress the links between 'low-level' crime and disorder and 'serious' crime, it seems likely that the fact that most racist incidents fall in the former category means that the concept of 'hate crime' is peculiarly unsuited to addressing them.

Related to this is the second factor arising from research into racist violence and harassment, which suggests that this type of victimisation is more likely to be experienced as an ongoing process rather than a discrete incident. It is argued below that this poses something of a challenge to policing which has traditionally been incident-driven. As with the previous point, it is recognised that broader changes to the style of policing introduced by the CDA and models such as problem-oriented policing have sought to change this focus on isolated incidents.

The third finding from recent research that has a bearing on the extent to which the hate crime legislation contained in the CDA has proved effective is the lack of objective evidence needed for police to classify an incident as 'racially motivated'. Police officers are used to dealing with evidence, collecting statements, recording details of 'what happened'; they are not used to considering what motivated an offender. Such problems might help to explain the available statistical evidence that indicates that there are considerable differences in the number of racially aggravated offences recorded by police forces.

Before considering these issues at greater length it is important to provide some statistical evidence of the nature and extent of crimes recorded as racially aggravated in terms of the CDA. The data presented below provide an imperfect overview of the racially aggravated incidents in England and Wales in 1999–2000. Since the data refer only to the recorded crime statistics, it is important to stress that the usual important caveats apply about these data being an imperfect representation of reality. It is not possible to review all of the limitations surrounding officially recorded statistics in this brief discussion, and a fuller account of these is available elsewhere (Maguire, 1994; Burrows *et al.*, 2000). One reason to be particularly concerned that the data recorded by the police do not represent an accurate picture of the extent of racist violence and harassment experienced by the public comes from British

Crime Survey data, which indicate that only approximately one-third of such incidents are reported to the police – although this proportion has increased since the late 1990s (Clancy *et al.*, 2001: 40). Nonetheless, the recorded data do provide some useful indicators, not least because they allow for some comparison of information from the 43 different police services of England and Wales.

Table 6.2 shows the number of racially aggravated incidents recorded in 42 of the police forces in England and Wales during 1999–2000, excluding the City of London police. The table indicates that the proportion of total recorded crime that is racially aggravated is less than half of one per cent across England and Wales as a whole (0.410 per cent), including a very large proportion of the total that is recorded in the Metropolitan Police area. It seems likely that this reflects the tendency of victims of racist incidents not to report offences to the police, as was mentioned above. Additionally, of course, it might be that the extent of racially aggravated crime, as a proportion of all crimes, varies from area to area, and so the recorded figures might partly reflect that. For these reasons the information provided in the table does not provide a reliable indication of the extent of racist violence and harassment. What can be gleaned, however, is that the relative performance of the police forces listed varies considerably in terms of the proportion of all crime that is recorded as being racially aggravated. Lincolnshire had the lowest figure in terms of the proportion of total recorded crime that was racially aggravated (0.026 per cent) and the Metropolitan Police recorded the highest figure, indeed the only case in which more than 1 per cent was racially aggravated, at 1.316 per cent. This may, of course, reflect real differences in levels of racist crime, although there is emerging evidence of such incidents being under-recorded in rural areas (Chakraborti and Garland, 2003b). Additionally, it reflects the role of the police service as gatekeepers in terms of crime-recording practices and a wealth of research evidence suggests that they have often denied the racist motivation of incidents. It seems likely that one explanation of the differences outlined in the table relates to the differences in recording practices across police force areas.

That police practices vary in respect of this type of offence is further illustrated by consideration of the number of incidents identified in case files passed to the Crown Prosecution Service (CPS). Under terms of a nationwide agreement, the police indicate on the files submitted to the CPS if a case is identified as a 'racist incident', since, as was outlined earlier, this provides additional public-interest grounds for pursuing a prosecution. All case files received by the CPS are reviewed and can be identified as racist incidents at this stage by the CPS itself. Table 6.3 provides a breakdown of which organisation identified racist incidents in each police service area.

Table 6.2 Racially aggravated offences, 1999–2000, by police service area

	Recorded offences	Percentage of total recorded offences racially aggravated
Avon and Somerset	240	0.163
Bedfordshire	42	0.078
Cambridgeshire	222	0.323
Cheshire	98	0.152
Cleveland	29	0.044
Cumbria	27	0.072
Derbyshire	263	0.307
Devon and Cornwall	120	0.109
Dorset	83	0.159
Durham	30	0.061
Essex	87	0.085
Gloucestershire	147	0.288
Greater Manchester	693	0.184
Hampshire	273	0.202
Hertfordshire	148	0.281
Humberside	70	0.058
Kent	339	0.271
Lancashire	232	0.213
Leicestershire	169	0.179
Lincolnshire	12	0.026
Merseyside	234	0.158
Metropolitan Police	13,850	1.316
Norfolk	76	0.128
North Yorkshire	6	0.011
Northamptonshire	126	0.206
Northumbria	199	0.140
Nottinghamshire	312	0.228
South Yorkshire	48	0.036
Staffordshire	110	0.111
Suffolk	83	0.191
Surrey	105	0.227
Sussex	112	0.082
Thames Valley	420	0.219
Warwickshire	36	0.093
West Mercia	146	0.172
West Midlands	388	0.106
West Yorkshire	126	0.048
Wiltshire	36	0.094
Dyfed Powys	43	0.181
Gwent	81	0.135
North Wales	14	0.031
South Wales	226	0.178
England and Wales	*21,750*	*0.410*

Source: Home Office (2000a)

Table 6.3 Identification of racist incidents by police service and CPS, 1999–2000, per cent

	Police	CPS
Avon and Somerset	87	13
Bedfordshire	56	44
Cambridgeshire	86	14
Cheshire	90	10
Cleveland	100	0
Cumbria	50	50
Derbyshire	78	22
Devon and Cornwall	69	31
Dorset	89	11
Durham	58	42
Essex	91	9
Gloucestershire	85	15
Greater Manchester	74	26
Hampshire	74	26
Hertfordshire	92	8
Humberside	92	8
Kent	68	32
Lancashire	82	18
Leicestershire	88	12
Lincolnshire	38	62
Merseyside	85	15
Metropolitan Police & City of London Police	79	21
Norfolk	84	16
North Yorkshire	71	29
Northamptonshire	76	24
Northumbria	90	10
Nottinghamshire	82	18
South Yorkshire	70	30
Staffordshire	60	40
Suffolk	92	8
Surrey	100	0
Sussex	66	34
Thames Valley	88	12
Warwickshire	65	35
West Mercia	78	22
West Midlands	68	32
West Yorkshire	86	14
Wiltshire	95	5
Dyfed Powys	73	27
Gwent	76	24
North Wales	57	43
South Wales	56	44
England and Wales	*78*	*22*

Source: Crown Prosecution Service, 2001

The table shows that, for England and Wales as a whole, the police were responsible for classifying 78 per cent of cases that were identified as racist incidents. Conversely, in 22 per cent of cases the CPS found grounds to identify an incident as racist where the police had not done so. By examining this data, some indication can be gleaned of the differential performance of police services when it comes to identifying cases that are racist. In two areas (Cleveland and Surrey) the police service identified all of the racist incidents during 1999–2000 – in other words, there were no cases in which the CPS found racist incidents that had not already been identified by the police. On the other hand, the CPS were responsible for identifying evidence of racism in most cases recorded in Lincolnshire, where the police only noted that there were grounds for defining an incident as racist in 38 per cent of instances, and in South Wales the proportion identified by the police, 56 per cent, was only marginally higher than that identified by the CPS (44 per cent).

The above discussion has shown that both the recording of racially aggravated offences and the identification of such offences in case files provided to the CPS vary considerably between police services. There might be a number of reasons for this. First, it could be that the actual level of racist incidents and racially aggravated offences varies significantly from area to area, and that this explains the differences in the data. Table 6.2 shows the number of racially aggravated incidents recorded in the various police service areas, indicating that 13,850 of the 21,750 (63.7 per cent) occurred in the Metropolitan Police Service area. Comparable data relating to racially motivated incidents derived from the British Crime Survey showed that some 35 per cent of incidents in 1999 occurred in London. This suggests that the higher reporting and recording rates in the MPS area cannot be explained solely by a greater prevalence of racially aggravated or motivated incidents in that area, and that other factors also need to be considered. Among these might be the high-profile response that the MPS has taken in respect of 'hate crimes', such as the establishment of the Racial and Violent Crime Taskforce, which oversaw a raft of measures to encourage the public to report incidents.

That different police services may have done more or less than others to encourage the reporting and recording of racially aggravated offences and racially motivated offences partly reflects the tradition of local autonomy for each of the 43 police services and the fact that each can determine its own priorities. There might be a host of reasons why the response to racist crime has been more pronounced and thoroughgoing in one police service area than in another. This level of autonomy applies to many aspects of policing and is not solely related to the response to racist or other forms of hate crime. However, when it comes to the propensity for individual officers to understand racist incidents and

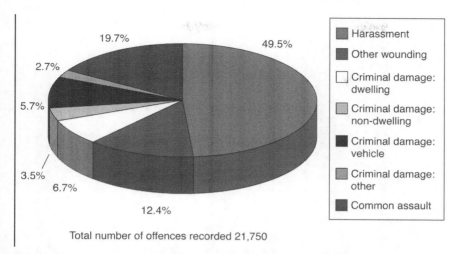

Total number of offences recorded 21,750

Figure 6.1 Breakdown of racially aggravated offences recorded by the police in England and Wales, 1999–2000
Source: Home Office (2000a)

respond to them effectively, it does appear that the nature of racially motivated offending is unlike many other forms of criminal activity and that this might explain why such incidents have often been under-recorded by officers. The second main theme that has emerged from much recent research in this area strongly suggests that the patterns and type of offending associated with racially motivated crime are relatively unusual. Before considering the implications of this for the broader debate about hate crime, an overview of these findings is provided.

Figure 6.1 indicates the types of racially aggravated offences recorded by police services in 1999–2000. As can be seen, the largest single category is harassment, at 49.5 per cent, followed by common assault at 19.7 per cent, and 'other wounding' at 12.4 per cent. The various types of criminal damage indicated in the figure collectively amount to 18.6 per cent of the total.

Figure 6.2 indicates that the relative detection rates for racially aggravated offences tend to be lower than for the comparable crimes that are not racially aggravated. Racially aggravated harassment, for example, was detected in 39 per cent of cases, whereas the base offence was detected in 78 per cent of instances. Only in respect of criminal damage to vehicles or criminal damage to non-dwellings were racially aggravated cases more likely to be detected than in 'ordinary' circumstances.

Of course, the likelihood of an offence being detected depends on a number of factors, and it might be that the different characteristics of racially motivated compared with non-racially motivated crimes, in part,

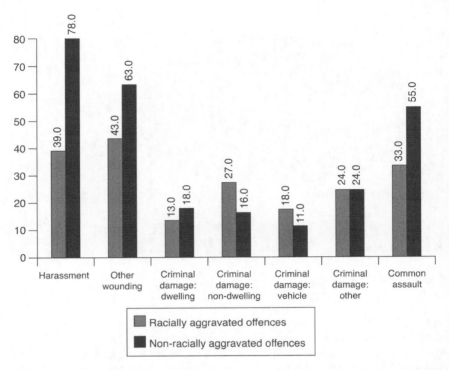

Figure 6.2 Detection rates of racially aggravated and non-racially aggravated offences, 1999–2000
Source: Home Office (2000a)

explain the lower detection rates for the former as outlined in Figure 6.2. One explanation might be that the encouragement of a *prima facie* approach to police recording of racially aggravated offences means that these are more likely to be recorded than general crimes in cases where there is not enough evidence for charges to be brought. The inclusion of weaker cases in evidential terms at the recording stage might explain why the detection rate is lower (Burney and Rose, 2002: 53). Other factors might also account for these differences in detection rates. Analysis of data from the BCS suggests that racially motivated crimes were more likely to be perpetrated by more than one offender whereas non-racially motivated incidents were most likely to be carried out by a lone offender. Additionally, the perpetrators of racially motivated incidents were much less likely to be well known to the victim than is the case with non-racially motivated cases. It might be that such qualitative differences between racially motivated and other offences make it more difficult to succeed in detecting offences. Another important factor in accounting for differences in detection rates is the response and perceptions of police officers. There are at least three reasons for arguing that police officers might be less effective in responding to crimes motivated by racism.

First, the available research evidence suggests that the nature of many racist incidents does not coincide with what police officers tend to regard as serious crime. As has been noted, the single largest category of racially aggravated offences recorded was 'harassment' and several studies have suggested that the routine racist harassment and intimidation experienced by many victims is not the type of behaviour that has traditionally been afforded a high priority by the police (Chakraborti and Garland, 2003a: 10–11). Perhaps the most comprehensive of these studies was Bowling's examination of racial violence and harassment in East London. He described the following (Bowling, 1998: 182):

> The incidents were frequently described [by practitioners] as being 'low level' but 'persistent' and included such incidents as criminal damage, graffiti, spreading rubbish, abusive behaviour, egg throwing, stone throwing, threatening behaviour, and 'knock-down-ginger', often forming patterns of harassing behaviour. More serious incidents such as physical assaults and arson were believed to occur, though less frequently than mundane but persistent behaviour.

One reason why this type of 'low-level' racial harassment may not lead to detections, Bowling argued, is that officers will often be likely to seek relatively informal resolution of disputes and thus follow an 'order maintenance' strategy rather than one of law enforcement. Officers will seek to prevent further incidents occurring and to ensure that harassment or intimidation is ceased, but they may prefer to use informal techniques to resolve these problems and so return the situation to normality, rather than deal with it by strictly enforcing the letter of the law. As Bowling (1998: 280) notes, however, this type of response – where 'normal' circumstances are restored without resort to legal sanction against perpetrators:

> ... may simply serve to maintain the on-going process of ... victimization. If the threat of violence and occasional use of actual violence is used to intimidate, exclude, or terrorize, the balance of power between victim and perpetrator remains.

A second reason, as has already been alluded to, is that much of the routine of racist violence and harassment is experienced by victims as a continuing process, rather than a single incident. While any single episode within the series might be regarded by officers as of relatively low priority, the extended nature of the victimisation embeds the experience into the routine lifestyle of the victim in such a way that makes it graver. This may be exacerbated by the more general impact of racism and disadvantage that the victim of violence or harassment might experience. That it is part of the routine of the victim's daily experience makes the process more, not less, serious; but this may not be understood by a police officer more used to dealing with discrete incidents. As with a number of the other issues reviewed here, this point does not relate exclusively to racist violence and harassment: indeed, much of the thrust of the 1998 Crime and Disorder Act was to focus attention on tackling antisocial behaviour which, while not constituting serious criminal offences, undermine the quality of life of communities affected. Additionally, a key dimension of the problem-oriented policing model is for officers to seek to resolve relatively minor issues before they escalate into more serious criminality (Goldstein, 1979; Leigh *et al.*, 1996). Related to the particular point about the police failing to recognise the nature or the impact of racist incidents is the broader problem identified with problem-oriented policing, which is that officers continue to be focused on criminal incidents (Small, 2001).

The third reason, and related to both of the previous points, is the continuing concern that police officers do not always properly appreciate the correct definition of a racist incident. The period since the publication of the Lawrence Inquiry report (Macpherson, 1999: 328) has seen police services adopt the definition of a racist incident, which was mentioned in the introduction to this chapter, namely that 'a racist incident is any incident which is perceived to be racist by the victim or any other person'. In terms of models of crime recording, the adoption of this definition represents a shift from an evidential approach wherein officers seek proof to corroborate that an incident has occurred to a *prima facie* approach whereby the account of the victim is accepted without question unless there are compelling reasons not to. This shift was intended to overcome widespread concerns that officers acted as gatekeepers, who often denied that incidents were motivated by racism even in circumstances where victims and witnesses were convinced otherwise. Gordon (1990) and Hesse *et al.* (1992) suggest that a serious weakness in the policing of racist violence and harassment in London during the 1980s was that the police tended to deny or marginalise the racist motivation in many cases.

While the post-Macpherson approach has sought to circumvent this problem by removing the need for police officers to make such decisions, concerns remain about the implementation of this *prima facie* definition. In particular, there is evidence to suggest that police officers are misinterpreting the definition in such a way that any incident involving parties of different ethnic backgrounds is being recorded as racist (Burney and Rose, 2002: 41). In addition, analysis of BCS data suggests that the most common reason white victims defined racist incidents as such was because of the ethnic origin of the perpetrator (Clancy *et al.*, 2001: 32). These examples suggest there is a danger that the nature of racist violence and harassment is again being marginalised. In circumstances where any encounter between individuals of different ethnic origin is understood to be racist, the specificity of 'genuine' racist victimisation becomes lost, just as it used to do when police officers were able to deny such motivation in the 'pre-Macpherson' period.

Analysis of the nature of racially aggravated offences recorded by the police indicates considerable variation in the response of the 43 services in England and Wales. Since it is widely accepted that these figures do not provide a reliable indication of the extent of racist violence and harassment, it seems unlikely that this variation in recorded figures reflects real differences in the amount of crime in the respective police service areas. Different recording systems and the level of priority given to these types of crime will also have an impact on the number of offences recorded in each area. The research evidence suggests that these institutional ambiguities are reflected at the level of individual police officers and the nature of their response to racist violence and harassment. Three reasons have been identified that explain why officers are not well placed to respond effectively to this type of crime. First, there continues to be a problem that officers may not recognise the seriousness of racist incidents. Second, officers traditionally respond to specific incidents, which may mean that the extended experience of racist victimisation is not recognised. Third, although there has been a shift in emphasis when it comes to classifying racist incidents, intended to remove the officer as a gatekeeper in the process, there continues to be some misunderstanding of what constitutes a racist incident.

Concluding comments: reconsidering hate

The creation of racially aggravated offences by the Crime and Disorder Act 1998 represents the closest comparison in Britain to the type of hate crime legislation widely introduced in the United States. The evidence reviewed suggests that there are strong grounds to argue against the development of such generic legal prohibitions in Britain. These fall into two broad categories. First, the general arguments surrounding the conceptual basis of hate crime legislation were analysed with particular reference to how these might apply to racially aggravated offences. It was argued that the legislation does not criminalise certain types of thought or speech held to be socially unacceptable. Instead it is actions or behaviour of the offender that are subject to legal sanction, not the subjective state of their mind. A stronger objection to the extension of hate crime legislation stems from what Jenness (2002) refers to as the 'norm of sameness' whereby the development of generic legislation means that the protection intended for particular communities comes to be applied to all sections, including those who have not usually been targeted. The research evidence supports this abstract concern, suggesting as it does that 65 per cent of victims of racially motivated incidents identified by the 1999 British Crime Survey were white (Clancy *et al.*, 2001: 28).

That hate crimes have a greater impact than other types of offending has been advanced as a justification to punish them more harshly. Often this argument is treated as axiomatic and while it may be that there is some evidence that minority ethnic victims of racially motivated incidents do regard them as more serious, as demonstrated in Table 6.1, it also appears that non-racially motivated incidents are also seen as more grave by these groups, which suggests that further research is required into the complexities of this aspect of the impact of hate crimes. Beyond the particular effects of such crimes on the immediate victims it is also argued that those motivated by hate have a particularly detrimental impact on broader society, and so a clear legal prohibition serves as symbolic denunciation. Again it seems that there are logical inconsistencies on this matter, since, at least in the British context, the kinds of behaviour included within the provisions of the CDA had been widely denounced by public authorities for many years. Additionally, the position of those not included by the CDA (such as, for example, the gay, lesbian, bisexual and transgender community) may become even more marginalised if their status is not specifically included in the hate crime provisions.

In addition to these conceptual problems, the second broad area of concern that suggests the hate crime debate might be of limited use in dealing with racist violence relates to the actual application of such measures. The review of the CDA provisions as actually experienced in England and Wales in recent years suggests that other more practical problems might stem from the development of more generic hate crime legislation. Two aspects of the nature of much racist violence and harassment mean that the notion of hate crime is unlikely to improve the policing response. First, as established earlier, many of the incidents currently categorised as racially motivated consist of what would otherwise be regarded as relatively minor incidents of antisocial behaviour and neighbourhood disputes. While it is clear that the presence of racist motivation makes them qualitatively different, it is of concern that police officers may often not appreciate the added dimension that this brings. Given this, it seems likely that 'hate' is not the most appropriate concept to encapsulate the broad range of racist incidents that currently occur and that it may prove detrimental to efforts to tackle the problems.

Burney and Rose argue that ' "hate crime" seems the wrong label for many minor incidents involving ethnic references, and where ethnicity has clearly not been the trigger for the hostility' (2002: 114).

Relatedly, the research evidence suggests that many racist incidents comprise of extended processes of victimisation, rather than isolated events, as may be the case with many other crimes. Maynard and Read (1997) suggest that the concept of 'motivation' might be problematic in the context of racist incidents: ongoing neighbourhood disputes do not fit easily with prevailing approaches that tend to understand motivation in the context of individual incidents. Extending the ambit of hate crime legislation would require officers to make difficult judgements about motivation, and it seems clear that this has proved an obstacle to the effective recording of racist incidents in the past. The danger might be that officers either marginalised the notion of hate crime, which would make any legal provisions redundant, or that it would be applied in such a broad manner that the particular focus it is intended to bring becomes blurred.

Whatever position one takes in respect of the philosophical or political content of the discourse surrounding hate crime – and there is debate to be had and strengths and weaknesses can be identified – it is argued here that there are serious limitations when it comes to operationalising the notion in the context of the contemporary policing of racist incidents in the UK. Simply put, the nature and pattern of racist incidents are not the same as with other types of crime. It has been argued in this chapter that this is one important reason why the police service has found it difficult to respond effectively to the problem: racist incidents often do not directly correspond to the types of criminal incident that the police are routinely expected to deal with. While the Lawrence Report and much of what has flowed from it rightly has sought to redefine police policy on racist violence, it is not clear that this is effectively implemented because of the routine context of policing. Following the example of the United States by developing the notion of 'hate crime' in response to these problems may offer some broad political advantages in terms of demonstrating society's abhorrence to such incidents. If this makes it more difficult for the police to understand and respond effectively to these crimes, though, there is a real risk that these political gains will not be translated into positive action on the ground, and so further advancing the concept of hate crime is likely to create more problems than it resolves.

Chapter 7

Accountability and complaints

A central component of the principle of policing by consent, which has underpinned official discourse on policing in Britain since the establishment of the Met in 1832, is that the police are accountable to the public that they serve. This chapter will explore the various ways in which the principle of accountability has been translated into practice in recent decades. Accountability is discussed in terms of the formal legal mechanisms that govern the police, and – more broadly – as it has developed in informal ways as consultation with local communities has become increasingly important in recent years. Although it is stressed that consultation is qualitatively different from accountability, as relations of power and control are fundamentally changed, it is shown that the two can be closely related. It is argued that debates surrounding accountability, which do not inherently relate to police relations with minority ethnic communities, actually have been greatly influenced by many of the issues that are explored in other chapters in this book. Arguments about the way in which complaints against the police are investigated and managed will be examined. Tension between statutory forms of control, such as those exercised by local police authorities, and the fiscal accountability of the police to central government are explored towards the end of the chapter. In the concluding section it is argued that there has been a process of bifurcation whereby policing has become increasingly devolved to local levels, simultaneously the central Home Office seems to be exercising greater than ever control.

The Lawrence Report does not address the issue of police accountability directly at length, although it makes two recommendations on this issue:

Rec'n 6. ... the formation of the Metropolitan Police Authority ...
7. That the Home Secretary and Police Authorities should seek to ensure that the membership of police authorities

reflects so far as is possible the cultural and ethnic mix of the communities which those authorities serve.

In the wake of the Lawrence Report the Greater London Authority Act established the Metropolitan Police Authority and so transferred the role of holding the Metropolitan Police to account from the Home Secretary to a body comprising 23 members (12 from the Assembly, 4 magistrates selected by the Greater London Magistrates Courts Authority, and 7 independents). This legislation ended the anomalous position whereby, unlike other forces, the Metropolitan Police was not held accountable via a police authority. The Home Secretary responsible for establishing the immediate post-Lawrence agenda, Jack Straw, had, as a junior backbencher in 1979 and 1980, attempted to introduce Bills into the House of Commons to strengthen the position of police authorities and to establish such a body for London (McLaughlin, 1991: 114). Many of those who argued for police reform during the immediate aftermath of the urban unrest in British cities in the early 1980s identified the lack of oversight of the Metropolitan Police as a major weakness in a system claiming democratic credentials (Jefferson and Grimshaw, 1984). At around the same time, as is mentioned below in more detail, the Greater London Council had attempted to fill the perceived gap in the constitutional arrangements governing policing in the capital by establishing a non-statutory police committee that, among other things, funded police monitoring groups to provide local scrutiny of the police (McLaughlin, 1991: 115).

Police authorities have been closely involved in a range of initiatives developed in the post-Lawrence Report period and, following the 2000 Race Relations (Amendment) Act, became, along with chief constables, vicariously liable for discrimination on the part of police officers and co-responsible for the promotion of equality. The ability of police authorities, whatever the ethnic composition of their members, to provide effective scrutiny of operational policing has been called into question for some time, and recent police reform has accrued greater power to central government at the expense of local police authorities, which may further undermine their position. This issue will also be considered at greater length later in this chapter.

Other formal mechanisms designed to ensure police accountability are the arrangements for dealing with complaints against the police, and the 2002 Police Reform Act established an Independent Police Complaints Commission, which replaced the Police Complaints Authority (PCA) in 2004. Concern about the legitimacy of the PCA system was clearly identified in the Macpherson Report and this is considered at greater length in a later section of this chapter.

Alongside formal arrangements intended to enhance police accountability to the public have been a number of initiatives introduced post-

Lawrence intended to make policing more transparent and publicly accessible. Included among these, for example, have been proposals that Metropolitan Police Officers wear name badges in addition to their police numbers in order that the public identify with them more easily. These developments are also returned to later in the chapter.

The principle of police accountability

While those responsible for establishing the professional police in Britain during the nineteenth century were concerned to overcome public suspicion and hostility by stressing the servile position that the new constables would adopt towards law-abiding citizens, there were also more formal measures to ensure accountability to the local public. Municipal police forces, but not those operating at a county level, were established under local by-laws and so were under the control of Watch Committees, which were prestigious and powerful arms of local government. In law the Watch Committees fulfilled the same role at a borough level as chief constables in county forces, and so the organisation, employment and regulation of police activity was under the jurisdiction of local aldermen. Steedman's (1984) account of policing during this era suggests a close, even cosy, relation between Watch Committees and the police. While the committees were powerful and exercised much control, they were semi-autonomous from the mainstream of local government, met in secret, and their activities were rarely reported in the press. Nonetheless, Steedman (1984: 43) demonstrates that Watch Committees did act as an interface between police and public:

> In many places ... it was watch committee members who were considered the peace-keepers, rather than the police. In Cambridge in the 1850s it was the custom of ratepayers to speak privately to a committee member, stopping him in the street, or calling on him at home, about the state of the pavements, the prevalence of street begging, or the improprieties of constables on the beat. By the 1860s a system of formal attendance at watch committee meetings to make complaints had developed. The watch committee constituted itself a committee of inquiry when complaints about police practice were made, and listened to police evidence. When damage was done to private property in the course of police duty, complaints might be recompensed out of the police fund.

Although the catalogue of functions performed by Watch Committees in the Victorian era appear similar to dimensions of accountability that continue into the twenty-first century, it would be simplistic to assume that this represented a progressive modern model. Not only were the proceedings of the committees shrouded in secrecy, they were also, by virtue of their master–servant relation with the police, able to direct constables into activities only marginally related to law and order (Emsley, 1983; Steedman, 1984). Emsley (1987: 182) argues that these arrangements amounted to 'the continuation of "pre-police" traditions and by no means the triumph of any new model'. What is more, it must be remembered that these mechanisms were devised in an era in which the working class and most women were denied the vote, so the democratic credentials of the Watch Committee system were slender by later standards. In respect of county forces, the established mechanism of accountability also survived the creation of the professional police, as magistrates retained their role of overseeing the activity of the new constabularies. The model of community policing whereby the popula-tion were directly involved in policing activity, which was a cornerstone of the pre-modern era, was thus incorporated into the modern period when full-time paid police officers relieved the public of direct respon-sibility for tackling crime and upholding order.

Whatever the extent to which the principles of policing by consent were incorporated in the Watch Committee system, it is clear that the practice of accountability was subject to considerable local variation. Brogden's (1982, cited in Reiner, 2000: 32) analysis of policing in Liverpool suggests that the chief constable established considerable autonomy from the local Watch Committee within just a few years of the constabulary's inception. By the middle of the nineteenth century, as the franchise began to be extended to the working class, Reiner (2000: 44) argues, Watch Committees were beginning to lose control over increas-ingly autonomous chief constables. Although the Watch Committee system continued into the middle of the twentieth century, Reiner (2000: 44) suggests that there is no foundation for the often-made claim that the people controlled the police and that by the end of the nineteenth century the police were becoming increasingly autonomous and unaccountable.

By the mid-1950s concerns were emerging about police corruption and malpractice. One high-profile case of the period concerned allegations that officers had used excessive force while arresting a youth at Thurso (Williams, 2003). Specific issues of police accountability were raised following the refusal of the Chief Constable of Nottinghamshire, Captain Arthur Popkiss, to disclose information about the progress of an inquiry into corruption among local councillors to the Watch Committee. Popkiss argued that the request of the Watch Committee for information on the investigation compromised his operational independence, while the committee argued that they had the right to hold the chief constable to account. The stand-off between the parties foreshadowed similar argu-ments between police authorities and senior officers during the 1980s, which are mentioned below, and led to Popkiss being suspended from office by the committee, although the Home Office subsequently insisted that he be reinstated. While these incidents had nothing directly to do with police relations with minority groups, it was during the same period that racist violence in Nottingham and Notting Hill in London was exposing, for the first time in the post-Second World War era, claims that the police were failing to provide adequate protection for the black community. The 1958–59 disorders developed as white youths attacked recent migrants from the Caribbean in the St Anne's district of Nottingham and later in Notting Hill. Local black people subsequently reported that the failure of the police to protect them meant they were forced to use violence in their own defence (Rowe, 1998).

It was against this background that a Royal Commission on the Police reported in 1962 and the 1964 Police Act carried out many of its recommendations, including the abolition of Watch Committees and the establishment of police authorities. The 1964 Act established the tripartite system that continues to be the framework for police accountability, defining as it does the balance of powers and responsibilities of the chief constable, the Home Office and the local police authority. Initially police authorities comprised two-thirds local councillors and one-third magistrates, thus ensuring that democratically elected representatives were in the majority. Police authorities have statutory responsibilities to provide local funding, to appoint chief constables and assistant chief constables, and to maintain an effective and efficient police service. The extent to which these considerable powers actually provided for effective local control over police services has long been questioned by those who have argued that police authorities were the junior partners of the tripartite system. Stephens (1988) argued that by the 1980s it was apparent that police authorities were often unable to call chief officers to account, since the principle of operational independence could be cited as grounds for refusing to disclose information, in much the same way that Popkiss did in the 1950s. Furthermore, financial control was limited since forces could appeal to the Home Office for central funds if local resources were not forthcoming.

In the aftermath of urban unrest in 1985, during which the Commissioner of the Metropolitan Police had deployed rubber bullets (although none was actually fired), it became clear that the Home Office would authorise police use of non-lethal weapons regardless of the views of local police authorities (Stephens, 1988: 85). Particularly significant has been the inability of police authorities to provide an effective 'voice' for local communities, however limited their role might be. While minority ethnic communities seem to have been under-represented on police authorities, there is a more general problem whereby a relatively small committee simply cannot represent complex diverse communities. Compounding this limitation has been the growing corporate nature of senior ranks as the Association of Chief Police Officers (ACPO) has become an increasingly powerful body both in terms of providing a central voice on policing matters and also in the development of policy and practice in key areas, including those relating to diversity and community relations. Whatever the strengths and weaknesses of ACPO policies in any particular area might be, they are clearly developed outside of the scope of democratic oversight (Loader and Mulcahy, 2001).

Dissatisfaction with the role of police authorities was evident in the early 1980s in a number of metropolitan areas where Labour administrations established monitoring committees to provide non-statutory scrutiny of police activity. In London, where the Home Secretary performed the police authority role, demands to address the democratic deficit on police accountability were made by the Greater London Council, which funded various groups concerned to oversee the police. While such groups were not focused solely on issues relating to police relations with minority ethnic communities, these formed an important part of their activity, as McLaughlin (1991: 115) noted:

Such monitoring groups had their origins in the campaigns around policing issues that had been waged by black communities since the 1960s. These campaigns concerned racist practices, corruption, deaths in police custody and general policing strategies on the streets.

The urban unrest that occurred in many British towns and cities in 1981 and 1985 involved very many white people, although the media and much political response suggested that these were primarily conflicts between black youths and the state (Solomos, 1991; Rowe, 1998). In his report into the Brixton disorders of April 1981, Lord Scarman (1981: 5.64–5.66) argued that the informal mechanisms by which the police in London consulted with the community were useful but needed strengthening if public trust was to be secured. However, Scarman specifically rejected claims for a police authority for London or that the powers of existing authorities elsewhere in the country be increased. Along these lines, Section 106 of the Police and Criminal Evidence Act 1984 required that constabularies establish Police Consultative Committees (PCCs) as forums for discussion between police and public. While commentators have recognised that these committees can provide the opportunity for dialogue and to bring forward matters of concern, they are not robust mechanisms of accountability since they have no powers to demand information, few resources, and no ability to effect redress against the police (Savage, 1984; Stephens, 1988). Keith (1988) has criticised the effectiveness of the consultative committees to deliver significant results since they are based on the spurious notion that problems in police relations with minority ethnic communities could be overcome by improved communication without addressing structural and institutional factors.

Along similar lines, McLaughlin (1991: 116) argued that the Section 106 provisions took no account of the 'interests of those for whom the police were the problem'. Keith's study of PCCs in the mid-1980s led him to record circumstances in which the opportunity for dialogue that they created may have prevented disorder on the streets. Nonetheless, Keith (1988: 69) argued that the PCCs are fundamentally flawed, not least because senior police officers engaged in dialogue may have only very limited powers to bring about change in policing practice. While improved means of consultation might offer some benefits, they do not ensure accountability: as Keith (1988: 76) expressed it: 'accountability is about power relations, consultation is about dialogue'.

Hughes (1994) highlighted the 'theoretical foreclosure' of radical critiques of community consultation, whereby any innovation that fails to address the structural conditions of society is denigrated without the need for empirical examination. Despite these concerns, however, Hughes recognises that most of the research on PCCs has borne out the reservations of Lea and Young's (1984) argument for accountable and democratic policing. In particular, Lea and Young were concerned that PCCs would not properly represent diverse sections of the population and would fail to incorporate the young unemployed (1984, cited in Hughes, 1994: 257). Research on the profile of PCC members and their relations with the police have also suggested that only a narrow demographic profile is included, namely those who are white, male, middle-aged and middle class, and that members tend to become increasingly 'pro-police' as their involvement develops (Morgan, 1992). Hughes (1994: 263) describes the composition of the PCC he studied:

> ... key players in PCCs are generally representatives from or-ganised constituencies (e.g. political parties, special interest groups) together with local government and voluntary agency members. Their representativeness of the local population is dubious but one should not assume that such members of the local political elite are necessarily pro-police in the narrow sense often implied in other studies. Policing is supported but not all police activities.

The main achievement of the PCC that Hughes (1994: 264) studied was that it facilitated local networking that might not otherwise occur among agencies and community groups. However, the extent to which this engaged the wider population was minimal and it seems improbable that those groups most likely to come into conflict with the police, whether they be young people, the homeless, the unemployed or those from minority ethnic backgrounds, have been incorporated by the PCC arrangements.

Requirements for the police to consult the community were further developed by the 1994 Police and Magistrates Court Act, which made police authorities responsible for producing local policing plans. Since chief constables write these plans, the need for local consultation has become an increasingly routine aspect of policy development (Jones and Newburn, 2001). Additionally, the 1998 Crime and Disorder Act has also led to changes in the relationship between police services, local authorities and the community. The 1998 Act gave local authorities statutory responsibilities in terms of crime prevention and community safety and requires the police to work in conjunction with other agencies in 'community safety partnerships'. A key dimension of the role of community safety partnerships is that they audit the local population in order to establish their priorities and concerns and so contribute towards developing the agenda for future work. Edwards and Benyon (2000: 45) suggested that the development of partnerships might incorporate the police, who had previously been isolated from local government, into networks of governance, but that this does not necessarily lead to a net increase in accountability:

> One of the principal arguments for partnerships ... is that they facilitate more responsive policy-making, geared towards the needs of local conditions. However, the shift of decision-making responsibilities from elected councillors to multi-agency partnerships has attracted criticism for undermining accountability. Conversely, advocates of the partnership approach argue that it empowers local populations through the opportunities for direct participation in decision-making.

As with PCCs, however, there are concerns that minority ethnic and other communities are not engaging in practice with the networks that now surround community safety. It has been noted in other contexts that the rhetoric concerning networks and partnerships may hide closed systems that exclude those not thought to belong (Thompson *et al.*, 1993). A review of the early development of community safety partnerships found that the extent to which they engaged minority ethnic communities was improving, but that this remained a difficult area, with 31 per cent of partnerships reporting little success (Audit Commission, 2002: 27). In their study of partnerships in Leicester and Nottingham, Edwards and Benyon noted that members of the public resident in high-crime areas may have been disinclined to engage in the work being undertaken for fear of retaliation, and that there might be other deterrents for minority ethnic communities, as one of their respondents noted:

With the African-Caribbean and Asian members of the community there's an isolation that hasn't been broken down yet ... I feel there's a fear of coming out, certainly after dark, which has prevented their involvement. There's a fear of making oneself known, which comes to just a basic fear of personal safety and security ... You must remember that the National Front had their headquarters on this estate, so you've got an almost endemic racism at times in certain areas of the estate.

(Cited in Edwards and Benyon, 2000: 47–48)

In their review of arrangements to consult with the community, Jones and Newburn (2001) recognise various means by which the police identify and engage with different groups, ranging from formal requirements stipulated by HMIC or the Crime and Disorder Act, to community audits and problem-led initiatives, to informal personal networking. A feature of these practices that stands in contrast to the PCC arrangements developed in the early 1980s is that they often require the police to be proactive in the consultation process, rather than relying on interested parties to emerge and engage in arrangements established by the police in isolation. While it might be of benefit to place the onus for consultation onto the police, it remains unclear that the complexity of communities is addressed. As a number of recent studies have suggested (HMIC, 1999b, 2003; Jones and Newburn, 2001), there remains a tendency for the police to conceive of communities in one-dimensional terms, defined by one salient characteristic (most commonly ethnicity, religion or sexuality). That communities may be internally diverse, fractured, or even in conflict remains unrecognised in much of recent police strategy in this area, a point examined at greater length in the following chapter.

While the requirement for the police to play a proactive role in consultation offers advantages over the arrangements developed in the 1980s, other features that raised concern during that earlier period continue. The introduction of mechanisms of consultation does not amount to local communities holding the police to account. The formal mechanisms by which police are accountable to local populations in an era of multi-agency partnerships remain blurred, partly because the relation between community safety partnerships, local councillors and police authorities remains somewhat ambiguous and fraught (Audit Commission, 2002: 19). However, Jones and Newburn (2001: 25) argue that members of the public who participated in consultation processes did feel able to hold the police to account for particular operational activities and refer to instances where minor complaints and grievances could be aired and successfully resolved. Of course, such informal and *ad hoc* opportunities to hold the police accountable are not available to those sections of the community not engaged in the consultation process. As is discussed at greater length in the concluding section of this chapter, these problems are compounded by the increasing power of central government relative to local factors. Given all of this, it seems that Lea and Young's (1984: 260, cited in Hughes, 1994: 257) complaint that 'it should be the case that the community consults the police as part of the process of formulating its needs, not that the police consult the community in formulating its strategy' applies equally in the post-Macpherson period as it did in the years following the Scarman Report.

Complaints against the police

The manner in which complaints against the police are investigated, and any subsequent disciplinary measures applied, has been a matter of general public concern for many years. The Scarman Report (1981: 7.18) noted that there was pressure to introduce an independent system of investigating complaints against the police, although the report maintained that there were practical obstacles to doing so. In the light of Scarman's recommendations, a series of reforms were introduced in order to increase effectiveness and efficiency by allowing for relatively minor complaints to be resolved informally. In the wake of the Scarman Report, the Police and Criminal Evidence Act (PACE) established the Police Complaints Authority (PCA) in place of the Police Complaints Board. The distinguishing feature of the PCA is that it introduced an independent element in the supervision of complaints by civilian staff who oversee the planning, implementation and results of investigations of complaints. Complaints were still made to individual police forces, who were required to send to the PCA those that might result in disciplinary or criminal proceedings against an officer. In addition, cases in which a member of the public had died had to be referred to the authority and police services could voluntarily refer other matters to the PCA. The investigations were conducted by police officers, although in more serious cases they were drawn from a force other than that to which the officer complained about belonged.

In 2001–02 the PCA dealt with 7,556 complaints, a decrease of 14.9 per cent on the previous year's total of 8,880. This amounted to 125.83 complaints for every 1,000 officers in England and Wales, including those working for the 'non-Home Office forces' such as the Royal Parks Police, the Ministry of Defence Police, the National Crime Squad and the National Criminal Intelligence Service. In 13.87 per cent of cases, allegations were substantiated. While this proportion appears low, it does not take into account the number of cases that are informally resolved and so might bring satisfaction to the complainant. Nonetheless, serious concern was expressed, from diverse quarters, about the efficacy and independence of the PCA system. A report by the House of Commons Home Affairs Select Committee (1997) reflected that the PCA was found wanting by pressure groups such as Inquest and GALOP, which campaign on deaths in custody and the policing of homophobia respectively, by solicitors representing those bringing complaints and by senior police officers who suggested that the system was unable to remove corrupt or mendacious officers. In the second part of the Macpherson Report (1999: 45.22), which dealt with some of the more general matters surrounding police minority relations, dissatisfaction with the formal complaints system was noted:

> It will be no surprise that almost universally we were told that there is little confidence amongst minority ethnic communities in the present system ... there is no doubt but that this lack of confidence affects adversely the atmosphere in which racist incidents and crime have to be addressed.

One explanation of the declining number of cases reported to the PCA has been that a lack of confidence has led people to pursue remedial action through civil courts, rather than the formal system. The House of Commons Home Affairs Select Committee (1997: 32) noted that the amount of compensation that the Metropolitan Police paid out as a result of such actions increased steadily in the 1990s: from £490,000 in 1991 to £2.6 million in 1996. Similarly, Greater Manchester Police paid out £305,019 in compensation in 1993–94, a figure that reached £2,009,565 by 1996–97 (Home Affairs Select Committee, 1998). The Select Committee noted that ACPO suggested that the rise in such actions reflected a desire for financial compensation rather than a lack of confidence in the PCA system, and the apparent growth of 'compensation culture' and 'ambulance-chasing' lawyers has been an issue of more general concern during recent years. However, McLaughlin and Johansen (2002) argued that civil proceedings provide a more equitable environment from the complainant's perspective, since the official complaints system has incorporated substantial safeguards for officers, such as the provision of legal representation, that are not available to complainants. Against this background, McLaughlin and Johansen (2002: 639) argued, civil proceedings held in public, at which the complainant also has legal representation and the burden of proof is lower, have become increasingly attractive:

> To the consternation of the police, the Home Office, and the PCA, in a stream of high profile private actions involving allegations of wrongful arrest, planting and fabricating evidence, malicious pros-

ecution, false imprisonment and assault and intimidation, juries censored the misconduct of officers by awarding exemplary damages against police forces.

It was against this background that Part 2 of the 2002 Police Reform Act established the Independent Police Complaints Commission (IPCC) to replace the PCA in April 2004. The new arrangements provide a broader basis for complaints against the police, as those other than the person directly affected by alleged misconduct can now register cases. Witnesses to incidents and others that the Act describes as 'adversely affected' by incidents are able to register complaints, which may be done via independent organisations. The powers of the IPCC in relation to the police are stronger, at least in statutory terms, than those assigned to the PCA since the IPCC has a team of independent investigators at its disposal, to use instead of police officers where it feels this is necessary, and chief constables are legally obliged to provide relevant documentation to the IPCC. The Police Reform Act also widened the scope in terms of those who are covered by the complaints system. Senior officers, special constables, civilian staff and community safety wardens – a role created by the Act – are covered in the remit of the IPCC.

The extent to which the IPCC proves to be effective will need to be assessed in two senses. First, it will depend upon the degree to which those who make complaints are satisfied that their case has been subject to an impartial investigation and that any subsequent disciplinary procedures have been appropriate. The strengthening of the powers of the IPCC and the emphasis on establishing a system that secures public confidence suggest that the relative weakness of the PCA era will be overcome, at least to some extent. However, as discussed earlier in this book in relation to police stop-and-search powers, attempts to implement legal and regulatory frameworks on policing service have often proved unsuccessful. As Dixon's (1997) review of the impact of law on policing suggested, many studies have revealed that cultural and structural factors provide considerable opportunity for the police to impede legal regulation. Chan (1997) argued that police culture could frustrate efforts at reform in certain circumstances, although she also showed that there were contexts in which regulation of police behaviour did prove effective. In particular, she suggested that this latter outcome had occurred in New South Wales in efforts to tackle police corruption because the frameworks of regulation resonated with more general political, social and structural conditions. While the development of the IPCC in England and Wales has not been primarily to address concerns about endemic corruption, it is perhaps worth noting that concerns about the previous PCA system had been made by senior police officers who were frustrated that they were unable to conduct rigorous disciplinary proceedings against those accused of misconduct or corruption. Even if the complaints system introduced in 2004 proves effective in dealing with such problems, it is far from clear that it will address the issues relating to institutional racism that have shaped relations with minority ethnic communities.

The second perspective against which the IPCC will be assessed relates to the extent to which it is able to address complaints about institutional aspects of policing. McLaughlin and Johansen (2002) expressed concern that the post-2004 arrangements for dealing with complaints against the police continue to be narrowly focused and so will do little to address the structural conditions that bring marginalised groups into repeated conflict with the police. Even though the IPCC arrangements broaden the definition of what constitutes a complaint, so that witnesses and others vicariously involved can instigate proceedings, the focus remains on the micro-level actions of individual officers as they come into contact with the public. Scrutiny of broader issues of concern relating to the priorities identified in local policing plans, for example, is not included in the work of the IPCC. Similarly, the emphasis on remedying incidents of misconduct does little to address concerns about circumstances, such as those often surrounding racist incidents, in which the police service is perceived to be inactive. The IPCC remit might provide stronger redress in cases where staff are responsible for sins of commission but not in respect of those of omission. One solution to this limitation that McLaughlin and Johansen (2002: 650) propose is that the IPCC be enabled to instigate local inquiries into issues of broader concern than individual misdemeanours; they argue that:

> There is every reason to believe that citizen complaints about low-level incivilities and disrespect are symptomatic of conflictual relationships between the police and certain communities ... A combination of institutionalized police misconduct allied to repressive 'in your face' modes of policing can cause serious damage to the fabric of communities already weakened by high levels of crime, disorder, socio-economic stress and political alienation. Repairing relationships between police officers and communities in certain parts of the UK is not a question of restoring respect for human rights and civil liberties, but of establishing that in the first place.

That the establishment of the IPCC provides a greater degree of independence to the system of investigating complaints does not mean that those with grievances will be reassured, since other aspects of the legal system have also been seen as problematic. In addition to identifying widespread dissatisfaction with the PCA-era complaints system, the Macpherson Inquiry noted that controversial deaths in custody involving minority ethnic individuals had been a major cause of concern. In the period since the murder of Stephen Lawrence a number of high-profile instances of people dying in custody have involved black people. Among these have been Joy Gardner, who died in 1993 as a result of the restraining belts and a gag applied by police during an attempt to forcibly deport her. Three officers involved in her death were subsequently acquitted of manslaughter. In 1995 Brian Douglas died after being taken into custody in Clapham, south London. During his arrest officers struck Douglas with long-armed batons and he was not taken to hospital for many hours despite persistently vomiting while held in a police station cell. The inquest into his death returned a verdict of 'misadventure' and a PCA-directed inquiry led to no disciplinary action and the Crown Prosecution Service (CPS) brought no charges. In 1996 Ibrahim Sey, a Gambian asylum-seeker, died in Ilford Police Station. At an inquest into his death it was revealed that Sey had been forcibly restrained by a dozen officers and sprayed with CS gas, following which he was held face-down for 15 minutes until he stopped breathing. While the inquest ruled that Sey was unlawfully killed, the CPS brought no charges against any of the officers involved. These three selected cases – details of which have been gleaned from contemporaneous media reports – represent only a proportion of black and Asian people who have died in police custody: between 1990 and 1996 there were 380 deaths in custody (Leigh *et al.*, 1998). Of these, the majority (87 per cent) of those who died were white, which still suggests that non-whites were over-represented in comparison with their proportion in the general population. However, it is unclear whether this is an over-representation in terms of the ethnic composition of people held in custody (Leigh *et al.*, 1998).

Whatever the appalling circumstances of particular cases where people have died in custody or where blame and responsibility should properly be apportioned, it seems unlikely that recent reforms to the complaints system will remedy problems identified. As the cases referred to above illustrate, the role of the CPS, the courts and the inquest system have all been found wanting by those families and friends of individuals who have died in custody. The campaigning group Inquest, which represents the interests of those affected by deaths in custody, has argued in a number of cases that police officers have been able to rely on stereotypes about black people's supposed physical strength and potential for violence as grounds for defending themselves in court. Against this context it seems that fairly narrow, even if important, reforms to the complaints system in isolation will address public concerns about deaths in custody.

Police–community relations: centralisation vs. devolved policing

One of the more controversial aspects of the 2002 Police Reform Act related to proposals to increase the power of the Home Secretary over chief constables and local police authorities. The government's original proposals, which would have given the Home Secretary power to suspend chief officers on the grounds of public confidence, were considerably reduced in the face of opposition in the House of Lords and elsewhere. Nonetheless, it remained the case that the power of central government to direct the 43 police forces of England and Wales was increased by the Act. Local police services are required to work towards a national policing plan devised by the Home Office and the Home Secretary can intervene, via HMIC, in circumstances where forces are 'failing'. None of these reforms heralds a qualitatively new set of relationships and, as mentioned earlier in the chapter, concern about the degree of influence that central government has over local police authorities has existed for a century or more.

Changes in the regulatory mechanisms binding police to central government run in parallel to less remarked-upon processes of fiscal accountability whereby pressure to demonstrate 'efficiency and effectiveness' creates a disciplinary framework more fundamental than local arrangements for consultation. McLaughlin and Murji (1997) have shown how Conservative governments throughout the 1980s introduced 'new managerialism' as a means of introducing 'private-sector discipline' into the public sector. Although the nomenclature of 'efficiency', 'effectiveness', 'league tables' and 'best value' might have been applied to the police service somewhat later than to other public-sector organisations, by the early 1990s the disciplinary framework of fiscal control was firmly established. Given the controversies surrounding the 2002 Police Reform Act, it is worth noting that the strengthening of the power of the Home Secretary encompassed in the 1994 Police and Magistrates Courts Act was widely regarded at the time as the *de facto* imposition of a national police force. Among many other things, the 1994 Act reduced the number of local councillors on police authorities and introduced members appointed by the Home Secretary. McLaughlin (1996: 98–99) characterised the arguments expressed at that time in the following terms, which seem to prefigure the tone of opponents of the 2002 legislation:

> The battery of powers and levers allocated to the Home Secretary would enable her or him to determine local police practices which would constitute a direct infringement on the operational independence of chief officers. The new police committees would be directly

accountable to central government . . . The foregrounding of crude, over-simplistic, quantitative plans and targets, which highlighted crime control as being the core police task, would be counterproductive and have an adverse effect on the overall quality of policing and police–community relationships. Forces would concentrate on those activities that could be easily identified and quantified and deliver immediate results. Officers would be forced to cut corners, bend the rules and twist the statistics to deliver their targets, resulting in a high level of wrongful convictions. Chief Officers on fixed-term contracts and financial incentives would be forced to collude with central government to protect their jobs. Overall, the 'calculative and contractual' mode of accountability would corrupt the unique ethos of British policing by transforming the police from a local public service into a state-run 'crime control' business.

Given the apparent centralising tendencies of successive governments, it might be argued that the bedrock of accountability on which the British policing tradition has been based has been torn from the grasp of local communities by an ever more powerful central authority. The ability of local communities to influence the policing services available to them has been crucially undermined. Such arguments are partial, however, since there has also been a countervailing tendency in recent years towards devolved policing.

In conjunction with the development of partnership approaches to community safety, crime and disorder that emerged in the late 1990s has been a reorganisation of police structures such that responsibility for almost all service delivery has been devolved to the Basic Command Unit (BCU) level. The national policing plan requires police services and BCUs to develop local plans at this devolved level. Budgets and resources are allocated and policy is developed at the sub-force level by these local policing units that are considered to be closer to the community. As has been described earlier in this chapter, much of the tone of discussion relating to the delivery of policing in recent years has related to local partnerships. While the processes of consultation that these have engaged in does not amount to making police services accountable to local communities, the devolvement of policing does appear to offer opportunities to engage the police more closely with the public. The bifurcation of policing towards central organisation and local devolution provides for some tension and apparent contradictions, but it may offer some space for the re-engagement of the police with the public.

Much of the above discussion relates to police relations with the public in very general terms. While it has been shown that concerns about accountability and complaints have been particularly salient for minority ethnic communities, they are of broader relevance. However, one limitation of the devolution of policing to the BCU level, which appears to bring the police closer to the community, is particularly relevant to minority groups. The geographical organisation of devolved policing units might be of limited benefit to communities that are not organised in and do not conceive of themselves in spatial terms. Those who form only a minority of the community served by one of the 43 constabularies might find themselves in an even smaller minority once the role of that constabulary is devolved into smaller units. Research on the position of minority ethnic communities in rural areas, in which they often constitute very small proportions of the overall population, often emphasises the qualitatively different experiences that they face compared with ethnic groups in areas where they constitute a larger percentage of the population (Chakraborti and Garland, 2003a). While the principle of devolving policing in order to improve consultation with local communities might appear to offer inevitable benefits, these may not flow to those excluded or marginalised within the geographical community that they find themselves. For many minority ethnic people the local community might be the source of the problem, rather than the source of the solution. The complex nature of communities and the implications of this for notions of policing diversity are explored at greater length in the following chapter.

Chapter 8

Policing diversity

As will be outlined in detail later in this chapter, a recurring theme that has been used to describe the development of policing in the period since the Lawrence Report has been 'policing diversity'. While it will be shown that this phrase is used in conceptually ambiguous ways and often appears to be used by police services for its symbolic connotations, it generally features in two distinct ways in the professional and academic literature of recent years. First, the term has been used by those analysing the increasingly important role seen to be played by private and semi-private organisations in the delivery of services usually associated with the public police service. Along these lines, for example, Johnston (2000) uses the phrase 'policing diversity' to describe the increasingly pluralistic provision of policing that incorporates a range of organisations belonging to what the government's recent agenda for reform has labelled the 'extended police family'. The term is used in this sense to refer to the diversity of policing. In contrast, the other way in which the phrase appears, and perhaps the more common usage in the professional context, relates instead to the policing of diversity in terms of the complex composition of contemporary society. In this latter sense, 'policing diversity' denotes the increasingly difficult task apparently facing the police service as it seeks to meet the various demands of a multi-faceted society. While this chapter focuses primarily on the latter meaning of the term, by analysing some of the practical implications and highlighting the conceptual weaknesses of the approach, it also considers the likely ramifications that the increasing role for non-traditional policing agencies might have for the post-Lawrence agenda.

Although the term 'policing diversity' has only come to be used in policy documents and the like in the recent past, and is widely regarded as presenting a new and growing challenge to police–community relations, it is clear that the British police have had problematic encounters with various groups since the inception of the professional police in the mid-nineteenth century. Historians have demonstrated that various sections of the public have been understood as problematic for the police during particular periods (Emsley, 1996; Reiner, 2000). In the early decades of the modern policing era, the 'dangerous classes' located in urban slums were widely regarded as a threat to the police, and to 'respectable society' more generally (Morris, 1994). In the century or so between the foundation of the modern police and the beginning of large-scale migration to Britain from the Commonwealth, Irish people, Jews from Eastern Europe, Arab and African seamen, among others, were in various ways understood as difficult groups for the police (Rowe, 1998). That concern about police relations with minority communities is often regarded as a relatively recent phenomenon is perhaps because contemporary problems are understood against the background of the perceived 'golden era' of British policing that followed the Second World War (Reiner, 2000). If a longer-term perspective is taken, then a rather different picture of police–community relations emerges.

While the fact of policing a diverse and complex society is not a recent challenge to the police service, the recognition that sections of society have legitimate aspirations and distinctive policing needs has been a relatively recent development. The Lawrence Report may have provided additional impetus and created a political climate in which some interest groups have been able to advance their agenda, but this has been against a more fundamental shift in emphasis that has seen the service orientation of the police come to the fore and the restructuring of the public sector. The changing relations between the police service and the public cannot be adequately explained without consideration of reforms in areas such as public housing, health and education, which have also been couched in the language of the marketplace whereby 'citizens' have been replaced with 'customers', whose various needs will be met by a plurality of service providers. Loader and Mulcahy (2003: 10) describe how 'under neo-liberal tutelage, citizens were encouraged to think of themselves as consumers of (once) publicly delivered goods – pensions, education, health care, even policing and security'.

The police service in Britain was subject to the rigour of quasi-market discipline later than other public-sector institutions because it was a relatively powerful lobby group that would prove a difficult challenge politically. Even if the successive Conservative governments of the 1980s, engaged in reform across many other areas, had wished to 'take on' the police, they would have found it difficult. The centrality of the 'law and order' agenda to the Thatcher governments meant that the police were well placed to win the argument that increased resources were the priority in the fight against crime, rather than institutional reform. The close association between the police and the 'project' of Thatcherism is evident from the language used by those who have described its eventual deterioration as a 'fall from grace' (Waddington, 1999b) or compared the attempts at reform in the 1990s with the 'perfidy of the paramour' (Reiner, 1995). It was in response to increasing political and financial scrutiny from central government that senior police officers sought to 'reconfigure the working culture of the police so as to improve the "quality" of the service it offers' (Loader and Mulcahy, 2003: 240). In addition to adopting some of the financial rigours of the private sector, policing co-opted the language of service delivery and customer satisfaction. An early example of this was the launch in 1988 of the Met's 'plus programme', and ACPO's Statement of Common Purpose and Values, both of which sought to emphasise a role for the police beyond the narrow remit of crime-fighting (Reiner, 2000: 75). In the face of a political climate that was becoming chillier, it seems that the police service sought the comfort of reiterating a commitment to community policing. In this way benefit may have arisen from the general warmth that Bauman (2001: 1) suggests is associated with the term 'community':

> Words have meanings: some words, however, also have a 'feel'. The word 'community' is one of them. It feels good: whatever the word 'community' may mean, it is good 'to have a community', 'to be in a community'. If someone wandered off the right track, we would often explain his unwholesome conduct by saying that 'he has fallen into bad *company*'. If someone is miserable, suffers a lot and is consistently denied a dignified life, we promptly accuse *society* – the way it is organized, the way it works. Company or society can be bad; but not the community. Community, we feel, is always a good thing.

Although these attempts to transform the police *force* into a police *service* were not directly related to the policing of minority ethnic communities, they did perhaps represent the point at which Scarman's (1981) reiteration of the doctrine of policing by consent was embraced by senior officers. Scarman's restatement of the importance of policing by consent and community policing did not occur in a vacuum. Other influential commentators, perhaps most notably the former Chief Constable, John Alderson, were also arguing that from the 1960s onwards British policing had become too isolated from the public, and that officers had come to regard themselves as a group separate from society at large (Alderson, 1979). Loader and Mulcahy (2003: 26–9) have argued that an unintended consequence of twin processes of centralisation and technological change was that the opportunities for officers to routinely interact with the communities that they policed were reduced. One high-profile report into police–community relations, published by Her Majesty's Inspectorate of Constabulary (HMIC, 1997: 7), notes that during the 1970s and 1980s:

> Police force amalgamations created larger and sometimes impersonal service providers where policing strategies were decided upon, implemented and changed with a minimum of internal and external consultation. The traditional foot beat system had in many instances been replaced by unit–beat systems supported by 'panda' cars providing less continuity in personal contact between the police and the public. In many areas, particularly those within inner cities, reactive 'fire brigade' style policing had become more and more prevalent.

In addition to concerns that the style of policing as delivered to the public was serving to isolate officers from routine contact with members of the public, debates were also taking place about formal systems of accountability, as was outlined in Chapter 7. The relative powerlessness of local police authorities *vis-à-vis* chief constables and the Home Secretary, within the tripartite framework laid down by the 1964 Police Act, was causing some to argue that a democratic deficit existed in governance of the police (Jefferson and Grimshaw, 1984; Scraton, 1985, 1987). While relations with minority ethnic communities were only one aspect of these broader debates about policing, a series of incidents involving alleged police mistreatment of black people provided many examples that fuelled arguments about the proper role of the police. It has been in the light of these concerns, as well as the specific agenda instigated by the Macpherson Inquiry, that the policing diversity approach outlined here has been developed, and the following section explores this development at greater length.

The impact of the Lawrence Inquiry

In addition to the myriad recommendations that Macpherson made about specific aspects of policing, the report has provided additional impetus to the development of policing diversity policies. It might be that the term 'policing diversity' has at times been employed by police services for its symbolic value as a demonstration of commitment to policing a plural society. The re-casting of policing policy in the language of diversity might be a necessary step for the service to gain public trust and confidence, as prioritised by the Lawrence Report, but there remains considerable conceptual confusion that will limit its effect on service delivery. Before highlighting some of the ambiguities and weaknesses of 'policing diversity', the main features of the model will be contrasted with earlier approaches to police 'race relations'.

Prior to the publication of the Lawrence Report, it might be argued, the predominant policing approach was one predicated upon a 'race relations' or equal opportunities model: broadly based around the provision of a similar level and style of policing to all members of society. The key focus of attention was to ensure that minority ethnic communities received an equitable service, as delivered to all members of society. This perspective characterises the role of the police as essentially neutral, in which the appropriate concern of officers is to enforce the law in a professional, even-handed and effective manner. Often the goal was to ensure that officers refrained from behaving in certain ways considered to be illegal or morally and ethically undesirable.

Post-Lawrence, conceptualisation of the police position in respect of minority ethnic groups has become one in which anti-racism is a central theme. This requires the police service to adopt a proactive and interventionist stance to tackle prejudice, and recognise that minority groups, and not just those that are based on ethnicity, have legitimate needs not shared by the majority. As shown below, the role of the police extends beyond a law-enforcement or crime-fighting responsibility to embrace a broader social agenda. In summary, the previous position was one in which the police occupied a largely neutral, inert role whereby social racism was a given problem to which the police responded, and members of the public, whether victims, witnesses or suspects, were to be treated equitably and in a uniform manner. Perhaps the most significant dimension of reconceptualising the police role has been an emphasis on policing as an explicitly anti-racist activity: one in which a proactive interventionary role is taken to challenge the problem of racism. A guide to combating hate crime, published by the Association of Chief Police Officers (2000: 3) describes the implication of anti-racism in the following terms [emphasis in original]:

> To confront prejudice outside the police service and to eliminate it within it, at work, every member of staff is expected to subscribe to a code of *active* conduct, which requires far more than strict compliance with the law.

The key features of the 'race relations' and 'policing diversity' models are outlined in Table 8.1. It is important to recognise that the two models are simplified representations, and should be regarded as heuristic devices rather than indications of a wholesale shift in direction 'on the ground'. The approaches differ in terms of the relations of the police to society, the way in which racism within the service is conceptualised, the

Table 8.1 Models of police–community relations

	'Race relations' model	'Policing diversity' model
External problem is located in . . .	. . . communities that are problematic, or present difficult or unusual challenges to the police.	. . . social, political and economic structures that discriminate against minority ethnic groups; and socio-ideological beliefs and stereotypes prevalent about them.
Internal problem is located in . . .	. . . a minority of explicitly racist staff – who should be disciplined or sacked once identified.	. . . in addition, the unwitting prejudices and attitudes of all staff need to be confronted; training and the monitoring of performance indicators used to bring about change.
Role of police in relation to racism . . .	. . . passive; neutral arbiters of the law.	. . . pro-active, interventionist.
Role of police leader . . .	. . . ensuring that staff do not behave in a manner deemed unacceptable; preventing certain subcultural patterns developing within the organisation.	. . . in addition, encouraging or requiring staff to develop attitudes and behaviour that confront racism, and other unacceptable behaviour; encouraging a culture in which stereotypical attitudes and behaviour within police organisations can be effectively challenged.

role of the police in tackling racism, and the specific roles of police leaders.

One factor that should be evident in Table 8.1 is that the policing diversity model requires greater commitment and activity of police leaders. In several of the cells of the table, the phrase 'in addition' is included, suggesting a wider role for police leaders in more recent approaches to police–community relations. The role of leadership is particularly significant since many of the components of the policing diversity model require fundamental transformation of the working environment such that, for example, 'unacceptable behaviour' can be

- Macpherson, Sir William (1999) *The Stephen Lawrence Inquiry*

- Her Majesty's Inspectorate of Constabulary (1997, 1999, 2000) *Winning the Race – Policing Plural Communities*, II and III

- Home Office (1999a) *Dismantling Barriers to Reflect the Community We Serve*

- Home Office (1999b) *Stephen Lawrence Inquiry: Home Secretary's Action Plan*

- Home Office (2000d) *Auditing Organisational Culture Within the Police Service, HOC 14/2000*

- ACPO (undated) *Policing Diversity Strategy*

- ACPO (2000) *Guide to Identifying and Combating Hate Crime*

- Metropolitan Police (undated) *Protect and Respect: Diversity Strategy*

- Metropolitan Police (2000) *Policing London – Winning Consent: A Review of Murder Investigation and Community and Race Relations Issues in the Metropolitan Police Service*

- Her Majesty's Inspectorate of Constabulary (2003) *Diversity Matters*

Figure 8.1   Policing diversity: recent official publications

challenged. Recognition that the active pursuit of good community and race relations is central to contemporary police leadership is evident in the remarks of the president of the UK Police Superintendents' Association, who noted that, 'if you are not delivering on this [policing diversity] you should not be a BCU [basic command unit] commander' (*Police Review*, 2001a: 6).

Since the mid-1990s a host of policy statements, strategy documents and reports have been issued by almost all of the major organisations concerned with policing in England and Wales. Partly, the range of these documents reflects the number of agencies variously involved in police governance; but it also illustrates the growing importance of policing diversity to the future of the service. The list in Figure 8.1 represents an incomplete catalogue of the principal official publications relating to this subject that have appeared in recent years; full details are contained in the bibliography.

While each of the publications listed in Figure 8.1 has a distinct focus, and there are issues on which they diverge from one another, considerable areas of overlap can be identified between them. In particular, they tend to be premised on the notion that good relations with all aspects of the community is central to effective policing. For example, the report by Her Majesty's Inspectorate of Constabulary (1997: 19) argued that:

... the real test of a force's community and race relations strategy is not whether it exists in written form but whether it falls out of its policies and practices as well as its organisational strategies at every level. Not only should considerations of community and race relations have a major influence on all aspects of force activity and organisation, but force effectiveness in turn should be measured in terms of its impact on community and race relations.

This suggestion that relations with the community ought to be one of the criteria against which effectiveness is measured has been incorporated into the framework of central government scrutiny established by the Police Reform Act 2002. The National Policing Plan for 2003–06 outlines the various dimensions against which the performance of BCUs will be measured. Alongside targets relating to crime reduction and investigation, police performance is to be judged in terms of public satisfaction and reassurance; suggesting that the management of public perceptions of crime and disorder is as significant as managing actual levels of offending behaviour. In addition, the National Policing Plan requires that chief officers incorporate various elements within the local policing plans they are required to produce. As well as requiring measures such as reducing the number of road traffic accidents and prioritising the policing of offences against children, chief officers must include measures to ensure local partnership working and to develop strong community relations. Along these lines, local policing plans are required to 'embed good practice for promoting community cohesion into all aspects of their work' and 'to take part in initiatives to empower communities to contribute directly to crime reduction' (Home Office, 2002b: 47).

Policing diversity: conceptual framework and implications

In many respects, the notion of 'policing diversity' appears to encapsulate and promote the principle of policing by consent that has informed the development of policing in Britain since the establishment of modern police forces in the first half of the nineteenth century. While the need for some of the policies outlined above appears to indicate that policing by consent has not been achieved in practice, as an organising principle it has featured fairly consistently for many decades. In the past 'consent' was understood as a relatively straightforward concept: if the police acted in a way broadly consistent with the expectations of the public, if they used minimal force, tackled crime with reasonable effectiveness and efficiency, and treated non-criminal members of the public with courtesy and respect, it was held that consent would be forthcoming – it would be conferred upon the police for a job well done. Reiner (2000: 50–8) argues that securing public consent for the police in the nineteenth century partly was the result of a deliberate set of policy decisions focusing on bureaucratic organisation, the rule of law, minimal force, non-partisanship, accountability, the service role and effectiveness.

The emphasis on policing diversity might be understood as a subtle renegotiation of this traditional principle, since it recognises that consent cannot be gleaned simply by treating all members of the public in the same manner: the public no longer have a consistent, or even a coherent, set of expectations for the police to fulfil. Given that society is increasingly diverse and culturally heterogeneous, the demands placed on the police are no longer straightforward, and it may be increasingly recognised that the police cannot satisfy all of the expectations with which they are faced. It might be that the development of 'policing diversity' is partly a response to the introduction of new managerialism, such that mission statements, targets and goals feature heavily in the commitments that police organisations make to their clients and customers. Recognition of the diverse requirements of the client base is a fairly fundamental principle of free-market provision, and in an age where the police service is increasingly understood as one provider of 'law and order' services among many, it is perhaps the case that retaining market share requires that the service attends more carefully to the varied needs of the community. While these broader trends might provide an important context that has encouraged the development of the principle of policing diversity, it is also clear that there has been a significant political agenda that has 'driven' the type of changes outlined in this chapter.

Police concern with community and race relations, prior to the Lawrence Report of 1999, was generally focused on ensuring that all ethnic groups received an equal level of service delivery. The notion of 'diversity' recognises that the needs and demands of ethnic groups differ, and so the provision of an identical service, one that was designed, unwittingly, for the majority ethnic population and assumed to be applicable to all, is no longer tenable. Delivery of an 'off the shelf' policing service to the public at large effectively means that those groups, whose priorities and concerns are divergent from the mainstream, receive a less than satisfactory service, even though it might be considered identical to that provided to all.

These conceptual concerns have underpinned the type of reforms outlined in this chapter and across the book more widely. However, it might be argued that the policies that have resulted represent a beginning and not the end of a process whereby social diversity is properly reflected in the service provided by the police. Almost without exception, policing diversity strategies are focused on meeting the needs of an ethnically heterogeneous society. Cultural diversity is conceived in terms of ethnic and racial differences, with gender and sexuality occasionally featuring in strategy documents and the like. For political reasons it might be that prioritising improvements in police relations with minority ethnic communities is understandable; pressure groups of various kinds have campaigned over police racism, racist violence and the like for decades and the Lawrence case certainly provided the major impetus for the renewed emphasis on policing diversity. Notwithstanding the *realpolitik* of recent developments in the United Kingdom, the concentration on ethnicity as the key to diversity strategy presents conceptual problems, since it implicitly downgrades other factors that shape diverse communities. While it is laudable to improve services provided to minority ethnic groups, and to seek to address a series of problems that have been of long-standing concern, it is unclear why this principle should not be extended to other groups who are marginalised according to other variables. To an extent, of course, this is already being done – as has been mentioned, the position of women and the lesbian, gay and transgender communities is incorporated, to some extent, in the measures briefly outlined above. Home Office (1998a: 3.52) guidelines suggested that the 'hard to reach' groups that ought to be included in consultation procedures included 'young men, the homeless, drug users, the gay community, members of ethnic minority communities, children, those who suffer domestic abuse and the elderly'. As was mentioned in earlier discussion of the debate surrounding hate crime legislation, Tatchell (2002) identified religion, sexual orientation, political opinion, disability, sex, medical condition, national or social origin, gender identity and physical appearance as factors that might aggravate criminal incidents and so provide specific needs that the police service ought to address. More recently an HMIC report (2003: 176) identified the following subjects that need to be included in the diversity agenda:

- race/ethnicity
- religion/faith
- sexual orientation
- social status
- poverty
- disability – physical
- age
- gender
- migrants
- asylum seekers
- travellers (including Roma)
- homelessness
- non-English speaking groups
- learning disabilities and mental health
- single parents
- unemployed
- students
- mixed heritage
- family status

The main focus though, in recent experience in Britain, has remained largely on issues relating to 'race': while it might be common, for example, to refer to police 'community and race relations', it seems that this usually pays considerably more attention to the latter than to the complexity of issues surrounding the former. Jones and Newburn (2001) noted the tendency for the term 'community' to be used as a synonym for 'minority ethnic' in discussion of police relations with the public. The specific recent context of British society might explain the focus on race and ethnicity, but it is not clear why this imbalance ought to remain, or why other minority groups ought not be more fully incorporated into the policing diversity rubric.

Once this principle is acknowledged, though, it is hard to identify where its consequences might end. As the various reports referred to above illustrate, it is not possible to produce a definitive list of those factors within the diversity umbrella that might require the police to provide a nuanced or specialist response of some kind. The tendency to perpetually extend the range of criteria might be inevitable once a greater number of groups are identified and entered into the framework. One tension that has resulted from this, from time to time, is that the need for the police service to address the post-Lawrence agenda relating to minority ethnic communities is seen by some groups to be under-mined and weakened by the embrace of a wider diversity agenda. Representatives from groups such as the Black Police Association, for example, have argued on occasion that the priority ought to continue to be about 'race' and ethnicity since these matters have been of grave concern for longer than other legitimate problems identified more recently. To be seen to move the agenda of reform into other areas runs the risk, it has been argued, of signalling that the problems identified by Macpherson have been resolved and that other topics can now be reviewed. Groups representing other interests have argued in response that their needs and rights in respect of policing are of equal validity and that the fundamental problems of stereotyping and prejudice are of general concern. Often competing arguments that stress the importance of recognising the true extent of the range of diversity and those that favour continued emphasis on 'race' and ethnicity lead to ambiguity at the policy level. One large force known to the author, for example, retitled its 'race relations training' programme as 'diversity training' in acknowledgement of the broader scope signalled by the latter. However, the actual content of the programme remained unaffected, and continued to address only matters relating to 'race' and ethnicity. Such ambiguity was also evident in the HMIC report referred to above, which argued that it was 'appropriate' for the focus to remain on race issues, while also recommending that 'wider diversity matters are also incorporated into all aspects of police training' (HMIC, 2003: 63).

While the need for the police to recognise the range and breadth of issues that might impact on the service that they deliver is clear, it continues to rely upon a relatively crude notion of 'community', which means that the diversity agenda advanced at a policy level is likely to remain difficult to apply in practice. A number of conceptual problems arise each of which are reviewed at greater length below. Firstly, there remains a tendency to conceive of communities in one-dimensional terms as being defined by one characteristic. Secondly, the characteristic seen to define each community becomes reified and understood as the most salient factor that determines the policing needs of that group. Thirdly, the communities tend to be regarded as relatively consensual and monolithic, with clearly identifiable leaders and forms of organisation. Fourthly, communities tend to be regarded in spatial terms, which do not encompass other patterns and forms of community. Fifthly, the conceptualisation of police–community relations continues to be predicated upon a majority–minority model, which regards the white community as normative and from which other groups are divergent.

Recent debates on the extent of and response to rural crime seem to indicate that rural communities have different policing needs to their urban counterparts. Other research suggests that minority ethnic communities living in rural areas experience different levels and forms of racism and discrimination compared with those in towns and cities (Chakraborti and Garland, 2003a, b). This might mean that minority ethnic communities living in rural areas have policing needs that are different from both their white neighbours and minority ethnic groups living in urban locations. Equally, the experience of the elderly, women, gays and lesbians suggests that still other sets of variables need to be factored into the equation when it comes to providing policing services that reflect the diversity of the community. In addition, those who are unemployed, have mental health problems, sleep rough, have problems relating to addictions of various kinds, are also likely to have certain specific requirements of the police. Much of the implicit conceptualisation surrounding policing diversity fails to recognise the complexity of communities, and that identity is not fixed and one-dimensional but transient and multi-faceted.

Closely related to this is a tendency to reify the characteristic seen to define communities included in policing diversity models such that it becomes the fundamental basis around which their policing needs are identified. A frequently observed response from police officers to the CRR training sessions outlined in Chapter 4 was that they sought from 'community speakers' a definitive understanding of what the Sikh or the black community, for example, wanted from the police service. That other factors, such as age, area of residence, poverty, and so on, might also need to be taken into account seems only to feature as a secondary consideration behind the key 'fact' of ethnic identity. Not only is this simplistic, it is also counterproductive in terms of the expressed purpose of policing diversity models in that it reinforces the apparent difference and separate identity of minority ethnic communities from an implied mainstream. While minority groups of different kinds are likely to have certain specific needs in relation to their disproportionate experience of certain types of crime, or because they need particular types of treatment from officers, it is not necessarily the case that this will extend into all aspects of the service that they might require from the police. Put simply, diverse groups are likely to have more in common than they do apart when it comes to the provision of police service in response to many incidents. Although minority groups, for example, might have specific cultural requirements in terms of the manner in which they are dealt with, the broad framework of their needs is likely to be fairly consistent with those of the 'mainstream'.

A third conceptual weakness that has undermined police relations with minority communities has been a tendency to conceive of them as cohesive groups with a conveniently hierarchical internal organisation that produces readily identifiable leaders with whom the service can enter into dialogue. The police service has often been reminded that communities cannot simply be accessed via established 'leaders' who act as gatekeepers to a wider public (HMIC, 1999b, 2003; Jones and Newburn, 2001). Nonetheless, it remains the case, perhaps for organisa- tional reasons, that processes of dialogue and consultation more easily incorporate 'community leaders' affiliated to religious and cultural groups and find it harder to access the marginalised. That the police service relied upon co-opting nominal 'community leaders' in order to develop dialogue in the early 1970s is indicative of the lack of widespread channels of communication with minority ethnic individuals more generally. As was discussed in Chapter 2, an advantage, it is believed, of increasing the number of minority ethnic recruits to the service is that this will generate more effective and routine engagement. While it might be recognised that continuing to rely upon this approach offers only a limited basis for communication, the absence of clear alternatives is evident from recent advice on contacting 'hard to reach' groups (Jones and Newburn, 2001). Debate about the terminology used to describe these is revealing, since it has been argued that marginalised sections of society are not 'hard to reach', in the sense that they are remote or uncooperative, but instead 'hard to hear', since the police service has not heeded their perspectives in the past (HMIC, 2003).

The fourth limitation of recent attempts to engage communities in policing diversity relates to a narrow understanding of what constitutes a 'community' and to the structural organisation of the police service. Simply put, communities whose diverse needs the police service seeks to address continue to be understood in geographical terms. Partly this reflects the way in which the term community has been used more generally to imply a level of proximity: a *local* community, distinct in certain ways from the general population at large. This use of the term 'community' is consistent with what Trojanowicz and Moore (1988) suggest is the original use of the concept. They argue that the 'community' denoted those resident in a geographically distinct area, which could be anything from a small village to an urban neighbourhood. It described a social unit larger than the family, and provided a way of explaining how elements of simple, often rural, societies, characterised by close kinship ties, a homogeneous culture and traditional customs and practices, were retained in industrial urban settings. This geographically centred use of the term 'community' is consistent with the spatial organisation of policing: focused as it is on the provision of services to a bounded area, be it a basic command unit, a sector, an area or a constabulary. In the light of this it is has generally been straightforward to suggest that the community refers to those within a certain territory on whose behalf the police service of that area operates.

There are two reasons, though, why this framework of community policing is beginning to unravel. The first relates to the process of *distantiation* whereby the routines and organising principles of everyday life are increasingly divorced from the territory in which individuals are based (Giddens, 1990). If the space in which individuals are located is increasingly less important in the shaping of their identity, then the centrality of territory as an organising principle of community policing is also undermined. This poses practical as well as conceptual problems for the police since their performance is now measured, under the terms of the National Policing Plan (Home Office, 2002b), in part on the basis of public reassurance, a subjective perception that may bear only limited connection with the activity of the police service local to their area. The impact of the media on public perceptions of their risk of crime is such that the extent to which incidents are feared is not wholly determined by factors within the control of local police services. While the notion that locality has been divorced from creating and sustaining identity has been questioned by those who point to the continued role that space and place play, particularly in terms of crime and disorder (Keith, 1993; Sparks, 2001), it is clear that these processes are more complex and fractured than have usually been conceived in debate of police community relations. The implications of this are recognised by Trojanowicz and Moore (1988) when they argue that the traditional conceptualisation of community requires further development because:

The three major technological changes, mass transportation, mass communication, and mass media, have played a great role in the divorce between geography and community. And while some researchers have touched on the effects of one or more of these factors, it is almost impossible to overstate the impact this trio has wrought.

The second reason why the traditional framework of community policing appears to be breaking down takes this discussion back to the issue of diversity. As currently enacted in the British context, as has been shown, the notion of diversity is primarily concerned with questions of 'race' and ethnicity. It has been argued here that this focus ought to be broadened and that other variables ought to be more centrally considered under the mantle of 'policing diversity'. In any case, these factors are not usually organised along spatial lines in the same manner as policing in general; particularly community policing. Whereas policing structures have traditionally been determined by territory, many of the communities that might be incorporated in 'policing diversity' are predicated upon other factors, be it ethnicity, gender, sexual orientation, age, or whatever. As Johnston (2000: 54–5) argued:

> Nowadays, the singularity of 'community' has given way to the plurality of communities: moral communities (religious, ecological, gendered); lifestyle communities (of taste and fashion); communities of commitment (to personal and non-personal issues); contractual communities (consisting of subscribing consumers); virtual communities (joined together in cyberspace); and so on. Such communities, far from being homogenous, are diverse, overlapping, pragmatic, temporary, and, frequently, divided from one another.

Many of these emerging forms of communities tend to rely on self-ascription, whereby individuals choose to associate with others rather than simply having their identity assigned to them. One implication of this is that individuals belong to many communities: based on residence, but also employment, ethnicity, religion, leisure pursuits, health problems, and so on. Recent British discourse on policing diversity has not begun to get to grips with this proliferation of communities; the overwhelming focus on ethnicity as a source of identification serves to obscure other dimensions that might prove to be of equal significance. Furthermore, the whole territorial basis of contemporary and historical policing systems seems ill-suited to an emerging era in which geography and space are of relatively declining importance.

The fifth conceptual weakness surrounding the policing diversity agenda arises from those identified above and reflects what Keith (1988) described as the 'fallacious' notion of community that he felt undermined consultation processes in the 1980s, but seems to continue to be relevant in the post-Lawrence era. Keith (1988: 65) criticised the prevailing conception of communities, particularly 'the assumption . . . that there is, out there in the real world, a natural series of geographic, ethnic and religious groupings, hierarchically structured and answerable to individuals who assume readily identifiable positions of leadership'.

Although the policing diversity agenda appears to embrace legitimate differences in the nature of the police service offered to a fragmented postmodern society, it continues to rely upon a model at the heart of which is a coherent majority. Recognising that certain communities – of whatever composition – have particular needs that the police service ought to meet is clearly appropriate in some contexts, such as in response to racist violence. However, the particular benefits that this might bring become more difficult to imagine if the list of salient characteristics is as exhaustive as that, for example, noted above, which contained nineteen categories including such broad issues as 'poverty' or 'family status'. Quite how such factors are to inform operational policing remains unclear. The risk is that in the absence of any clear means of applying this extended agenda of policing diversity, police officers will revert to associating it purely with relations with minority ethnic communities. Just as 'community relations' became synonymous with police dealings with minority ethnic groups, policing diversity is likely to be applied in one-dimensional terms that effectively reinforce a sense of marginalisation and separation from a mainstream: a mainstream that itself does not exist in any coherent sense.

Chapter 9

Conclusion

An underlying theme of this book has been to explore the extent to which the agenda for police reform set out in the Lawrence Report has had an impact on relations between the police and minority ethnic communities. At the time of the publication of the report, many of those vociferous in demanding change expressed reservations that the recommendations it contained would not be properly implemented and that real reform would not be forthcoming. That much of the broader social and policing agenda outlined in the earlier Scarman Report had not been fulfilled produced some scepticism about the impact that the Lawrence Inquiry findings might have. While many elite voices claimed that Macpherson's Report amounted to a 'watershed' in British race relations (Solomos, 1999), it was noted by others that had Scarman's vision been realised, the failings uncovered in relation to the murder of Stephen Lawrence might never have occurred. During the parliamentary debate that followed publication of the report, Bernie Grant, MP for Tottenham who had became a controversial critic of the police in the wake of the Broadwater Farm disorders in 1985, observed (*Hansard*, 24 Feb 1999: Column 399):

> We have been here before. I remember being very optimistic in 1981, after the Scarman inquiry. We thought that it was a watershed and that things would change, but 18 years later – I have read both reports – we are back to almost the same recommendations that the Scarman inquiry made. This is a last chance for British society to tackle racism and to push for racial equality. The black community is giving British society a last chance.

Perhaps it was in anticipation of such concerns that publication of the Macpherson Report was immediately followed by an outline of the

Home Secretary's response, which detailed how each of the Report's recommendations would be developed, and that 60 of the recommendations were accepted, three partially accepted, and seven would be subject to further consideration (Home Office, 1999b). A steering group comprising the range of agencies involved in police governance, but also organisations such as the CRE and the BPA, was established to oversee implementation of the post-Lawrence agenda and to report annually on progress made. The clear emphasis of the immediate political response to the Macpherson Inquiry was that this was a report that would occasion wide-ranging reform of the police service and other public institutions. Given the political capital that the Home Secretary had invested in establishing the inquiry soon after achieving office, it is perhaps not surprising that the findings were so readily embraced. As O'Byrne (2000) has noted, an important distinction between the Scarman and Macpherson reports is that the former was delivered into a broadly hostile political climate while the latter reported against a context in which central government was positively predisposed to its key findings. It is argued below that this favourable context has receded somewhat five years after publication of the Macpherson Report as racialised debates about crime and the politics of asylum have created a more difficult climate for anti-racism.

As has been outlined in previous chapters, though, the development of a programme of reform was more than a short-term political expediency. A very considerable range of sustained activity has been outlined in these pages, and many others beside have been implemented. By 2003 the Home Office had published four annual reports outlining the initiatives taken to apply Macpherson's recommendations. The Metropolitan Police Racist and Violent Crime Taskforce outlined more than 100 measures that had been introduced in London under the rubric of Operation Athena in the year after publication of the Lawrence Report (Metropolitan Police, 2000). These initiatives included the development of procedures to establish lay advisors to critical incident investigations, improving the training and organisation of family liaison officers, and broader community consultations with those affected by hate crime. In addition, of course, there have been numerous action plans and programmes developed in other police services – such as Operation Catalyst implemented by Greater Manchester Police, only a small proportion of which has been outlined in earlier chapters of this book. The impact of the Lawrence Report extended beyond the police to the public sector more generally: local authorities, education providers and churches have expressed commitment to tackling racism, and under the terms of the 2000 Race Relations (Amendment) Act are required to devise anti-racist strategies. The extent of the challenge that the Lawrence Report posed to British society was widely noted at the time of publication and support, as Loader and Mulcahy (2003: 136) observed, came from unlikely champions of liberal causes, such as the *Daily Telegraph* and the Police Federation. A year after publication of the Lawrence Report, the journalist, Gary Younge, argued that one reason why the report's analysis and agenda proved so resonant across society lay in the very processes by which the inquiry was established (*Guardian*, 2002):

> In the past, to get a report written about the state of race relations in Britain, black people either had to take on the police (the Scarman report) or defend themselves against white thugs (the Salmon report). But Macpherson emerged from an incident prompted by a group of white racist louts, bungled by an overwhelmingly white police force, which sparked an investigation presided over by a white lord. This in itself was a seminal moment in British race relations. This was no longer a debate about how to contain the problems that black people cause by their very presence. This was white people talking to other white people about the problems engendered by their racism.

If questions about the extent to which the promise of the Macpherson Report – a 'seminal moment in British race relations' – had led to genuine transformation in the policing service delivered to minority ethnic communities could be answered by reference to the efforts expended in terms of policy and programme development, then it would be clear that much had been achieved. A characteristic feature of police leadership is the value placed on action and the ability to 'get things done' (Adlam and Villiers, 2003). That this dynamism effectively marginalises opportunities for rigorous analysis and strategic development is a significant disadvantage of a policing and political culture that requires immediate solutions to identified problems. The Home Secretary's Action Plan and the myriad programmes compiled by police services and other public bodies across the country reflected the widespread contrition and acceptance of the central criticisms made by Macpherson. Senior officers such as the Chief Constable of Greater Manchester Police, David Wilmot, and the Metropolitan Police Commissioner, Paul Condon, acknowledged that institutional racism existed in their respective forces. In April 1999 Wilmot launched Operation Catalyst to implement the recommendations laid out in the Lawrence Report, a title redolent with connotations of dynamic intervention and fast reaction. No doubt the familiar scepticism with which official reports, policy innovations and commitments to organisational change are often greeted, encouraged those who manage and lead the police service to establish a programme of action that would operationalise the

Lawrence Report and ensure it did not 'sit on a shelf gathering dust', as the complaint often goes. An increasingly lengthy catalogue of reports outlining the need for the service to improve community and race relations has developed, many of which are critical of the failure to properly implement those that have gone before (HMIC, 2003).

The collective response to the Macpherson Report proclaimed that reform would be stifled no longer, and a raft of targets, pledges and activity pointed to the process by which public 'trust and confidence' would be secured. The primacy of demonstrating an active response to the Lawrence Report findings reflects the culture of police leadership in general and the particular political context of the period in which the report was released: a cynical analysis might note that the report's criticisms of police leadership (described by Macpherson as 'failed') were largely overlooked while public debate focused on the origins and dynamics of institutional racism, and that this was a process that senior police officers had an interest in sustaining. However, one consequence of this has been that the concept of institutional racism – poorly outlined in the Macpherson Report itself, as was argued in the first chapter of this book – has not been properly reflected in the reforms that have been made. This point is further developed in the final section of this chapter.

As several earlier chapters have outlined, however, it remains unclear to what extent the flurry of development at the level of policy has been matched by improved service delivery 'on the ground'. Answering the question that provides an organising theme for this book – 'what has changed since Macpherson?' – remains a difficult and ultimately inconclusive task. The complexities that prevent a definitive answer to this question are outlined in what follows; and a number of factors that have inhibited change will be reviewed. In the final sections of this chapter, the broader context in which the police have developed in the post-Lawrence era will be examined and their impact considered. Finally, it is argued that Macpherson's central finding of institutional racism has not been properly addressed and that the structural position of the police in British society suggests that the promise of an anti-racist police service seems unlikely to be properly fulfilled.

The complexities of change

Given that it promised fundamental reform, it is understandable that definitive judgement is sought on the impact that the Macpherson Report has made since it was published. Since politicians and senior police officers paraded their commitment to reform and maintained that cynics ought to remain silent until such time as the police could be fairly judged on performance, it seems reasonable to call them to account. Nonetheless, a straightforward answer remains elusive, and attempts to provide one betray a simplistic understanding of the complex process that has shaped police relations with minority ethnic communities in Britain for decades. The prevalence of performance indicators and targets might provide a sound basis for measuring some of the activity that has occurred in the post-Lawrence Report period, but they reveal relatively little about the lived realities of policing as experienced by minority ethnic and other communities. The extent of racism and the possible impact of measures to confront it cannot be reduced to entries on a balance sheet that might provide conclusive or convincing judgement on police reform. Quantitative measures of performance shed little light on qualitative issues such as public trust and confidence in the police. While it is clear that there has been a plethora of initiatives with the stated aim of implementing the Lawrence agenda, it is far more difficult to determine the effect that these have, or have not had, on the street or in the police station. Although evaluation has become a central component of administrative criminological attempts to identify 'what works' and is applied routinely to crime prevention and policing strategies, such verification is elusive in the context of relatively nebulous and subjective matters such as those that underpin the Lawrence Report. Even if mechanisms are devised to measure public trust and confidence in the police, incorporating, for example, public opinion poll data, the number of incidents reported to the police or the extent of other routine interactions between officers and the public, making connections between such findings and particular initiatives or programmes is inherently difficult (Pawson and Tilley, 1997).

That racism continues to shape relations between the police and minority ethnic communities might lead to the conclusion that 'nothing has changed' since 1999, and that the policies and strategies analysed in this book amounted to either political expediency or a 'politically correct' distraction from the 'real business' of policing. Certainly some have used continuing concerns about high levels of street crime, as outlined below, as a basis for arguing that an over-emphasis on police racism has 'paralysed' officers who fear that their efforts to enforce the law will bring them into conflict with senior managers who are more interested in pursuing political goals. Efforts to evaluate the extent to which reform has been achieved should not overlook the fact that for sections of the public the fulfilment of the Lawrence agenda would represent further deviation from 'traditional' policing, accelerating a broader trend that has been underway for decades. Loader and Mulcahy (2003) record the centrality of the police to popular cultural representations of England as a stable ordered society in the 1950s, and the manner in which the development of a multi-cultural, multi-ethnic nation articulates with a sense of decline and loss. In these terms the post-Lawrence agenda represents something quite distinct, described by Loader and Mulcahy (2003: 147) as:

> A tendency to attribute the police's perceived failings and misplaced priorities to the undue pressures brought to bear on them by judges, politicians, liberal elites, and, of especial importance in this context, the 'race relations industry' (a pejorative coinage that almost always functions in English public discourse as code for opposition to organized forms of anti-racism).

The sense of a – real or perceived – conflict between 'street' and 'management' police officers (Ianni and Ianni, 1983) and the impact that this might have had on the post-Lawrence agenda is considered further in the following section. That the extent of reform is difficult to determine is further illustrated by the comments of a senior police officer and a political advisor reflecting on the state of police relations with minority ethnic communities and the post-Lawrence Report experience. Perhaps contrary to expectation, the senior police officer, Commander Cressida Dick, head of the Met's Diversity Directorate, remarked at the time of the tenth anniversary of the murder of Stephen Lawrence that the service was still institutionally racist – notwithstanding the considerable reforms that had been undertaken or the improvements achieved (*Independent*, 2003a). This view contrasts somewhat with that of Lee Jasper, advisor to the Mayor of London and sometime critic of the police, who suggested that the black community cooperates more readily with the police because levels of trust and confidence have increased post-Lawrence. Jasper suggested that many within minority ethnic communities had been encouraged by the apparent willingness of the police to recognise the extent of racism, arguing that 'because the police accepted that they could be in the wrong, people who lived in fear are coming forward' (Cohen, 2003). It is an indication of the changing terrain of debates about racism and policing that a senior officer points to a continuing problem of institutional racism, while a political activist emphasises improving relations between the police and the black community.

As these extracts suggest, any answer to the question of whether the Lawrence Report has 'made a difference' requires clarification of a whole series of supplementary issues about the terms of that difference and from which perspective the question ought to be addressed. Some police officers interviewed in the preparation of this book suggested that the Lawrence Report brought a painful but necessary period of self-examination and created a basis from which relations with the community could be strengthened. Others suggested that senior officers' acceptance of the charge of institutional racism was at worst a gross betrayal and at best a political expedient that would ultimately make little difference to their working practices. Others, as has been mentioned above and in an earlier discussion of stop and search, have claimed that fear of being labelled racist has prevented officers from dealing effectively with crime. Similar differences of opinion can be identified among observers from outside the police service, such as Michael Eboda, the media executive critical of the police use of stop and search against black people, as mentioned in Chapter 4, or the poet Benjamin Zephania who, as noted in Chapter 2, refused to allow the Met to use his work in a recruitment campaign. Perhaps most notably, Doreen Lawrence argued, on the tenth anniversary of her son's murder, that the attitudes of many junior officers had been largely unaffected by the Macpherson Report (*Guardian*, 2003a). Concern that racism in the police service continued in the post-Lawrence Report era resurfaced in October 2003, following a TV documentary which exposed extreme racist attitudes among several police recruits at a training school near Warrington (BBC, 2003). On the other hand, as Lee Jasper's comments above illustrate, have been those in the black community who have argued that relations with the police have been improving. That media reports have continued to highlight racist attitudes among some police officers clearly indicates that the problem of racism has not been eradicated from the service, and that efforts to tackle it are still needed. Such reports, however, do not necessarily demonstrate that the Lawrence agenda has 'failed' or that 'nothing has changed' in its wake.

In many ways it is unsurprising that opinions vary about the state of police relations with minority ethnic communities several years after the Lawrence Report was published: a range of views is common on contentious issues. The quantitative evidence also suggests a mixed picture, however. Stone and Pettigrew's (2000) research suggested that all sections of the community, including minority ethnic respondents, broadly supported the powers of the police to stop and search people on the street, providing this was done with good reason and with courtesy. This seems to suggest residual support for the police. Additionally, some comfort might be drawn from the increasing number of racist incidents reported to the police, since this suggests that those experiencing such events are more confident that the authorities will take them seriously. It may also reflect a greater recognition among officers that such incidents need to be recorded in the proper manner and that the racist element of any offence is not to be marginalised or dismissed altogether. These empirical indications of public confidence in the police are not reflected, though, in the number of minority ethnic officers being appointed. As was outlined in Chapter 1, this remains low relative to the presence of minority ethnic people in the overall population and below the targets established for the police service in the aftermath of the

Lawrence Report. The quantitative evidence remains as mixed as the qualitative information concerning the question 'what has changed since Macpherson?'.

Dynamics of police reform

One obstacle to police reform that has been identified in other studies is the ability of relatively junior ranks within the service to inhibit changes that their superiors within and without the service wish to implement. As has been discussed in relation to police subculture in Chapter 2, it has often been noted that the lower ranks within the service are able, by virtue of the discretionary powers available to them, to frustrate programmes of organisational change. It has been illustrated at various stages in this book that many police officers have felt personally offended by the term 'institutional racism' and have felt that the post-Lawrence agenda for change has been a 'politically correct' distraction from their core task. If this represents the view of even a minority within the service, there might be scope for the programme of reform to be derailed. As Brogden and Shearing (1993) argued, in circumstances where the rules and regulations surrounding police work are tightened in ways that do not coincide with prevailing interpretations and views of the world, officers have considerable scope to apply new frameworks selectively in order that they comply with dominant perspectives. Chan (1997) noted that this ability of junior ranks to resist reform from above explained the apparent success of anti-corruption campaigns in policing in Australia and the relative failure of those to tackle racism. Put simply, Chan suggested that the former chimed with prevailing cultures of policing in their broader social context while the latter did not.

Although examination of policing in Britain during the post-Macpherson period bears out concern about resistance to reform, the position of more senior officers must also be considered. The ability of junior staff to impede change might be partly explained by the nature of police work but it also reflects an often-cited failure of management and leadership. It is worth noting that the Macpherson Report placed considerable emphasis on the collective failure of leadership and that many recent studies have pointed to an organisational crisis whereby prevailing cultures and styles of management are increasingly inappropriate and ineffective in terms of contemporary demands on the service (Adlam and Villiers, 2003). Many have argued that the quasi-militaristic nature of police leadership, based upon rank and hierarchy, delivers decreasing returns. Indeed, it has been noted that the militaristic model has been replaced within the armed services even while it has remained evident in policing (Panzarella, 2003). Given that the diverse and competing demands placed on the service increase the scope of discretion available to junior officers, a command-and-control approach to management within the service is increasingly untenable. There is widespread agreement that police leadership has been a cause of many of the problems identified within the service, as expressed by Macpherson, and needs rethinking (Adlam and Villiers, 2003; Long, 2003). However, the form that a rejuvenated contemporary approach to police leadership might assume remains unclear. While many advocate the development of a transformational style of leadership, which places emphasis on inspiring junior officers and respecting their professional competence and autonomy, the prospect of achieving this in an environment in which the fundamental aims and objectives of the service remain poorly defined is problematic (Miller and Palmer, 2003). Furthermore, the scope for transformational leadership seems limited in an environment in which performance indicators greatly proscribe the ability of BCU commanders to act with autonomy.

While it seems highly likely that some degree of internal resistance has inhibited the implementation of the post-Lawrence Report agenda, the inadequacy of leadership within the service, which has failed to overcome the prevarication and obstruction from some junior ranks, must also be addressed. However, it is also apparent that senior ranks within the service have also become increasingly subjected to performance indicators and management targets emanating from the Home Office that circumscribe their ability to provide a style of transformational leadership often held to be more progressive and effective than traditional approaches. For this reason the broader context of social and political concern about crime and policing, which has continued to rely on racialised themes, needs to be understood in order to appreciate the limited impact that the Macpherson agenda has had.

The social context of policing

Most of the initiatives and programmes outlined in this book have related to the internal working practices of the police and the impact that these have on the communities they serve. The strengths and weaknesses of these various initiatives have been identified and discussed; however, attention also needs to be paid to the more fundamental role of the police service in British society and the political context against which policing in the post-Macpherson era has been conducted. Whatever the strengths of individual programmes or the undoubted commitment of those who seek to apply them, it must be recognised that the stated aim of developing an anti-racist police service would require overturning the historical structural basis of policing which has been about controlling the streets and 'managing' the marginalised (Brogden, 1982; Reiner, 2000). During the period since the publication of the Lawrence Report, a series of law-and-order 'crises' that have related to minority ethnic communities have reiterated the supposed connection between 'race' and crime. Since the 'mugging panics' of the 1970s, which created the folkloric image of the aggressive black mugger preying on white society, as documented by Hall *et al.* (1978), the racialisation of crime in Britain has taken various forms and continues in the post-Lawrence era. Loader and Mulcahy (2003) have shown how the nostalgic reconstruction of the 'golden age' of British policing – when the bobby on the beat was more authoritative and effective than his contemporary counterpart – refers to a period prior to the development of a multi-ethnic society. While this narrative might be at odds with some of the contemporaneous evidence from the immediate post-war period that has highlighted police corruption and violence during the 'golden age', it remains a powerful organising theme against which the police service in the post-Lawrence era is found wanting. The corollary of this reading of recent British police history is that the tarnishing of the golden era has accompanied the transition into a multi-cultural and multi-ethnic society. There are a number of ways in which this perspective is flawed and yet it remains evident among 'elite' discourse on policing, as has been shown, for example, in earlier discussions in Chapter 4 that claimed the ability of the police to tackle street crime was curtailed by 'politically correct' post-Lawrence interference.

Since the 'race-crime' debate developed in the 1970s it has incorporated various themes and ethnic groups. For much of the period since, it has tended to focus on the alleged criminality of sections of the black community, initially in terms of street robbery, but also in respect of the urban unrest of the 1980s that was widely explained in terms of the cultural proclivities of the black community who were unable to exercise necessary control over youths predisposed to violence (Gilroy, 1987; Solomos, 1991). That this interpretation of public disorder could not explain the widespread involvement of white people in the unrest, nor recognise any formative role that policing or socio-economic factors might have played, did not prevent it from forming the dominant explanatory framework. One reason why this racialised discourse proved so resonant was that it spoke to a broader theme in the imagination of the nation, which is that a defining characteristic of the English people is respect for and obedience to the law. That this is a largely invented tradition, ignorant of a lengthy history of unrest and rebellion, matters little (Pearson, 1983; Thompson, 1968). Collective violence of the sort witnessed in many inner cities in the 1980s assumed a wider symbolic importance during a period in which national identity was heavily contested between New Right attempts to reformulate and reassert former glories and those keen to establish a post-colonial multi-culturalism. In such circumstances the police embodied the 'thin blue line' protecting the mainstream law-abiding community from threatening interlopers.

Some of those who located the cause of the 1980s disturbances in the cultural dysfunctionalism of the black community contrasted the problem with imputed strengths in other minority ethnic groups, often doing so in order to claim that their analysis could not therefore be racist in nature. Along these lines, other minorities, most often Asian and Jewish communities, were held to be model additions to English society characterised by the value that they placed on the integrity of the family, the benefits of hard work and self-reliance and respect for the law. That these groups did not resort to collective violence in response to social and economic privations reinforced the culpability of those – the black community – that did. Subsequent urban unrest in Bradford, Oldham, Burnley and elsewhere during the early 1990s and again in 2001 that did involve sections of the Asian community required the reformulation of connections between 'race' and national identity, but retained the theme that it was the cultural properties of those communities that led to violence. In particular, it was asserted that irreconcilable tensions between different generations of the Asian community placed Asian youth in a moral vacuum that pitched them into conflict (Rowe, 2003). The Chief Constable of West Yorkshire Police analysed the disorders in terms that problematised the Asian community (*The Times*, 1995):

> What we are dealing with here is young men, Bradford-born, brought up and educated. They have lost in some way their ties with their old religion and their country, yet they feel themselves alienated within Western culture. Then you have this tremendous powder keg within them. The frustration and anger which they vent on the police, they are also venting on their own community.

Claims of a cultural crisis amid the Asian population have been supplemented by more recent concerns about Islamic fundamentalism and an apparent irreconcilability of British and Muslim identities. While these debates have not been primarily focused on the apparent criminality of the Asian community (although issues such as drug dealing have certainly featured), they do rely on the notion of a relatively homogenous mainstream of society and a marginal but threatening danger: an emerging 'enemy within'.

While processes of racialising crime, disorder and policing have broadened since the focus on the black community of the 1970s and 1980s, various concerns during the post-Lawrence era have continued to reiterate these long-established themes. A variation on the problem of mugging emerged in 2001 when media, policing and political attention focused on 'taxing' and the theft of mobile phones. Although discussion of these problems may not have reflected the crude racist imagery of constructions of the 'race-crime' debate of earlier periods, such themes were often implicit. Hall *et al.* (1978) noted the discursive power of places associated with minority ethnic communities in the context of discussion of street crime, law and disorder. Mention of these symbolic locations invokes association with minority ethnic communities and reiterates images of criminality even in the absence of explicit labelling of the particular problem as one related to a certain ethnic group. Media coverage of mugging in the 1970s or urban unrest in the 1980s often explicitly identified the black community as responsible. Such connotations may have become less overt in response to more recent concerns about the theft of mobile phones, but a similar effect can be achieved more subtly by drawing upon the symbolic power of locations. A recent example of the discursive work done by referring to symbolic locations occurred in press reporting of gun crime, which suggested that the problem was developing to such proportions in urban Britain that 'some parts of London are now said to be more dangerous than Soweto [and] parts of Birmingham have acquired a sinister atmosphere reminiscent of the worst quarters of Los Angeles' (*Sunday Telegraph*, 2003). Invocations of locales that conjure up broader associations of black unrest and rebellion reinforce the relation, not explicitly stated in this article, between ethnicity, crime and disorder. Against this background, and as discussed in Chapter 4, government pressure on the police to tackle street crime in the post-Lawrence era continues established processes of racialisation that have remained relatively unaffected by efforts to more closely monitor and regulate the application of stop-and-search powers. Suggestions that the process of police reform in the post-Lawrence era has had limited impact need to recognise the perpetuation of these processes of racialisation, which cannot be addressed by a relatively narrow range of initiatives that focus primarily on the actions of individual officers.

While debates surrounding street robberies in recent years have seen a continuation of well-established processes of racialisation, an apparent rise in gun crime has led to unprecedented developments that have been explicitly related to an apparently 'new era' in police relations with minority ethnic communities brought about by the Macpherson Report. The shooting of two black teenagers in the early hours of New Year's Day 2003 in Birmingham was followed by intense media discussion about the apparently increasing prevalence of gun use in Britain and the role of garage music and gangsta rap in influencing a generation of black youth towards a ghetto culture centring on violence, machismo and drugs. In the wake of the shootings in Birmingham and official statistics that indicated a 35 per cent increase in gun-related crime in the preceding year, a 'summit' of senior police officers, prosecutors and the intelligence services was convened in January 2003 to develop a 'tougher' strategy. Senior police officers and politicians clearly related escalating violence with the culture of sections of the black community. The Assistant Commissioner of the Met, Tariq Ghaffur, suggested that rap music formed a backdrop against which violence was normalised, and the culture minister, Kim Howells, argued (*Guardian*, 2003b):

> The events in Birmingham are symptomatic of something very, very serious. For years I have been very worried about these hateful lyrics that these boasting macho idiot rappers come out with. It is a big cultural problem. Lyrics don't kill people but they don't half enhance the fare we get from videos and films. It has created a culture where killing is almost a fashion accessory.

Similarly, an editorial in the *Mail on Sunday* (2003) argued that research was needed to determine the link between violent computer games and other forms of media 'which may have played a potent role in spreading the toxic gangster culture that infects so many parts of Britain'. In addition, the paper argued:

> the police must understand that they need to re-establish themselves in ethnic minority areas. There need to be more black officers, not for public relations' purposes but to penetrate the unpoliced parts of society where armed disorder is rapidly becoming endemic.

While the suggestion that aspects of popular culture are criminogenic, infectious, and morally damaging, seem to recur at least once each generation, what has been noteworthy in the wake of these recent developments have been the voices from within the black community, and the music industry, that have argued that some aspects of youth cultures were having a damaging effect. Some suggested that the problem of gun crime within the black community could not simply be attributed to rap music but had more complex origins. Among these was Lee Jasper, advisor to the Mayor of London, who identified 'high unemployment and educational failure as the primary causes that give rise to lots of young people being seduced into a gangster lifestyle' (*Independent*, 2003b).

While arguments continued between those who attribute the problem to the malign influence of popular culture and others who point to broader issues of social, economic and political marginalisation, the association between ethnicity, violence, crime and culture tended to be regarded as axiomatic. Some of the questionable assumptions reflected in this dominant understanding are illustrated by the critical perspectives expressed below, that were contained in one of few articles in the mainstream press following the shootings in Birmingham that diverged from the broad consensus outlined above. The first paragraph contains the view of Kwaku, presenter of a pirate radio programme in London, and the second Elaine Sihera, founder of the British Diversity Awards (*Observer*, 2003):

> There aren't any black countries that make guns, and we don't own any gun factories in England . . . someone outside the community provides them. It's the gun trade that must be stopped, and not the black community blamed for it. When football hooligans go abroad, the papers don't blame the entire British population, just a small segment. So why do they blame the entire community for the work of a few criminals?

> The media never report 'white-on-white' crime . . . guns are carried by all types of people, white and black, but the reporting creates a perception that a higher proportion of black people carry guns.

The coupling of concerns about street and gun crime, and the racialisation that has entwined these debates in the period since the Lawrence Report, reflects the continuation of a long-term process. Emerging themes in contemporary policing relating to antisocial behaviour and public reassurance are more recent developments that might also frustrate efforts to improve minority ethnic communities' trust and confidence in the police. While there have been successive falls in both annual recorded crime in England and Wales and the British Crime Survey estimates of offending, it is clear that public fear of crime has not been reduced. Individual perceptions about the risk of victimisation or about the general state of the crime problem continue to be out of kilter with the statistical reality, creating a 'reassurance gap' which means that apparent success in reducing crime levels has not permeated public attitudes about personal safety and risk. One reason for the disparity between the objective 'reality' of crime rates and risks and subjective perceptions might be that factors which generate feelings of insecurity are not criminal offences in any legal sense. Incivilities and antisocial behaviour are forms of low-intensity public disorder that traditionally have not been a high priority for the police service. While the 1998 Crime and Disorder Act underlined the importance of responding to such problems, the need to tackle antisocial behaviour was subsequently reinforced by the National Policing Plan and by an Anti-Social Behaviour Bill published in 2003. Plans to introduce antisocial behaviour 'task forces' to deal with problem areas and action lines to encourage the public to report unacceptable behaviour were announced by the Home Secretary in October 2003. Among the Best Value Performance Indicators against which the performance of basic command units is judged are those measuring the 'fear of crime' and 'public reassurance and quality of life' (Home Office, 2002). As outlined in Chapter 6, such provisions might provide a framework for tackling those common forms of persistent racist violence and harassment that have often not featured high on police agendas. However, it also seems likely that attempts at public reassurance will lead to further policing of those marginalised groups regarded in the public imagination as threatening and inimical to the quality of life. Police efforts to reassure the public will, on occasion, reinforce enduring processes of racialisation and criminalisation in ways that endanger the Lawrence Report's priority of increasing minority ethnic communities' trust and confidence in the police.

The individuation of institutional racism

That the post-Lawrence reforms intended to tackle police racism may be undermined by the broader socio-political context in which the service operates illustrates a significant limitation of the measures outlined in this book. While the concept of institutional racism proved the most controversial issue in the immediate period after publication of the Lawrence Report and senior officers went out of their way to publicly acknowledge that they accepted that the police service was institutionally racist, it is unclear whether the structural aspects of the problem have been adequately addressed. The conceptual development of the idea of institutional racism was described at some length in the introduction to this book, and some of the confusion that has surrounded the application of the Lawrence Report's recommendations might be attributed to the lack of clarity about what the term actually means.

Although the Lawrence Report has clearly been instrumental in placing racism at the top of the political and policing agenda and has developed an impetus for a substantial programme of activity, only some of which has been outlined in this book, it is hard to discern particular responses that are qualitatively distinct from previous efforts to tackle racism. While earlier attempts to combat racism in the police service might have been piecemeal and partial in comparison with the programme that the Macpherson Report engendered, most of the individual actions undertaken since 1999 are in keeping with established methods to tackle racism in the service. The broader structural focus that the concept of institutional racism invokes has not been evident in much of the programme of anti-racist action developed since the Lawrence Report endorsed it so powerfully. Most of the activity reviewed in earlier chapters of this book would be appropriate responses to earlier models of racism that associated the problem with the properties of recalcitrant individuals. Efforts to recruit more minority ethnic officers, to train staff to recognise the nature and impact of personal values and attitudes, or to monitor more closely the practice of stop-and-search powers – important and worthy though each may be – do little to address the institutional aspects of racism identified in the Lawrence Report. It seems that the model of racism that underpins the analysis and recommendations contained in the report is not properly reflected in the reforms that have developed in its wake and that racism continues to be conceived at an individual level.

Since the report is itself unclear about what actually constitutes institutional racism, it is unsurprising that the police service, and those responsible for its governance, has often reverted to a model of racism that offers only slight variant on the 'rotten apples' approach outlined earlier in the Scarman Report: in more recent discourse on police racism the problem is caused not just by a small minority intent on infecting an otherwise healthy organism but also by the unintended acts of omission or misunderstanding of many individuals. What seems to have changed most is that the individuals responsible for allowing racism to 'infect' the police service are no longer held to be personally culpable – their shortcomings are likely to be 'unwitting or unknowing', as Macpherson described aspects of institutional racism. Nonetheless, the institutional dimensions of police racism are understood as the aggregation of the activities and attitudes of individuals.

Many of the efforts to tackle racism within the police service have been predicated on an interpretation of institutional racism that regards the problem as one that has developed in an organisation that has been staffed by and servicing the needs of white people. While problems of staffing and service provision need to be addressed, and earlier chapters have outlined ways in which this has commenced, they do little in terms of reviewing the structural role of the police; which has been to control territory and sections of the population construed as threatening to the mainstream. While police organisations might have adopted the language and terminology of the service industry, the role of enforcement and control – associated with a police force – has clearly not been relinquished. For those minority ethnic communities who are not socially, economically or politically marginalised, future relations with the police might be brighter as a result of the Macpherson Report. However, concerns about street crime outlined above are only the most recent manifestation of recurrent themes that bode very badly in terms of future relations between the police service and marginalised minority ethnic communities.

In the absence of a fundamental programme of reform that addresses the institutional role of the police and confronts racism in all of its guises, it is clear that the agenda outlined in the Macpherson Report and the significant efforts that many in the police service have made will not rewrite the 'tale of failure' of police relations with minority ethnic communities that Scarman identified in 1981. To suggest that this might mean that 'another Lawrence' or 'another Macpherson' is likely to occur misses the point, since there have been and continue to be racist attacks, including murders, in British society. The Lawrence murder was not the last of its kind, but it seems likely that – on balance – the police are better placed to respond effectively to such crimes than once they were. The steps necessary to address the broader structural conditions that led to the kind of incident that occurred in Eltham on 22 April 1993 can only be undertaken at the societal level. The continuing racialisation of debates surrounding crime, national identity and migration suggest that the transformation of Britain into a society confidently diverse and securely multi-ethnic and multi-cultural – the kind of society in which racist violence is very much reduced – has yet to be achieved. Against such a background it is inevitable that the bold promises of reform that greeted the Lawrence Report have yet to be fully realised.

References

Adlam, R. and Villiers, P. (eds) (2003) *Police Leadership in the Twenty First Century: Philosophy, Doctrine and Developments*, Winchester: Waterside Press.

Adorno, T.W., Frenkel-Brunswick, E., Levinson, D.J. and Sanford, R.N. (1950) *The Authoritarian Personality*, New York: Harper & Bros.

Alderson, J. (1979) *Policing Freedom*, Plymouth: Macdonald and Evans.

Association of Chief Police Officers (undated) *Policing Diversity Strategy*, London: ACPO.

Association of Chief Police Officers (2000) *Guide to Identifying and Combating Hate Crime*, London: ACPO.

Association of Police Authorities (2001) *Police Stops: Consulting Communities, Association of Police Authorities Report to the Lawrence Steering Committee*, London: Association of Police Authorities.

Audit Commission (2002) *Community Safety Partnerships*, London: Audit Commission.

Banton, M. (1967) *Race Relations*, New York: Basic Books.

Bauman, Z. (2001) *Community: Seeking Safety in an Insecure World*, Cambridge: Polity.

BBC (2000) 'The right stuff', Radio 4, *File on Four*, 24 and 31 January.

BBC (2001) *File on 4*, Radio 4, 25 September.

BBC (2003) *The Secret Policeman*, BBC 1, 21 October.

Bennett, T. (1994) 'Recent developments in community policing', in Stephens, M. and Becker, S. (eds) *Police Force, Police Service*, London: Macmillan, pp. 107–30.

Benyon, J. (1986) *A Tale of Failure: Race and Policing*, Policy Papers in Ethnic Relations No. 3, Warwick: Centre for Research in Ethnic Relations.

Bethnal Green and Stepney Trades Council (1978) *Blood on the Streets*, London: Bethnal Green and Stepney Trades Council.

Blagg, H., Pearson, G., Sampson, A., Smith, D. and Stubbs, P. (1988) 'Inter-agency co-operation: rhetoric and reality' in Hope, T. and Shaw, M. (eds) *Communities and Crime Reduction*, London: HMSO.

Bourdieu, P. (1990) *In Other Words: Essay Towards a Reflexive Sociology*, Cambridge: Polity Press.

Bourdieu, P. (1990) *The Logic of Practice*, Cambridge: Polity Press.

Bowling, B. (1998) *Violent Racism: Victimisation, Policing and Social Context*, Oxford: Clarendon Press.

Brogden, M. (1982) *The Police: Autonomy and Consent*, New York: Academic Press.

Brogden, M. and Shearing, C. (1993) *Policing for a New South Africa*, London: Routledge.

Brogden, M., Jefferson, T. and Walklate, S. (1988) *Introducing Policework*, London: Unwin Hyman.

Brown, J. (1997) 'Equal opportunities and the police in England and Wales: past, present, and future possibilities', in Francis, P., Davies, P., and Jupp, V. (eds) *Policing Futures: the Police, Law Enforcement and the Twenty-First Century*, Basingstoke: Macmillan, pp. 20–50.

Bunyard, R. (2003) 'Justice, integrity and corruption: lessons for police leadership', in Adlam, R. and Villiers, P. (eds) *Police Leadership in the Twenty-First Century: Philosophy, Doctrine and Developments*, Winchester: Waterside Press, pp. 86–104.

Burney, E. and Rose, G. (2002) *Racist Offences: How is the Law Working? The Implementation of the Legislation on Racially Aggravated Offences in the Crime and Disorder Act 1988*, Research Study 244, London: Home Office.

Burrows, J., Tarling, R., Mackie, A., Lewis, R. and Taylor, G. (2000) *Review of Police Forces' Crime Recording Practices*, Research Study 204, London: Home Office.

Butler, A.J.P. (1982) *An Examination of the Influence of Training and Work Experience on the Attitudes and Perceptions of Police Officers*, Bramshill: Police Staff College.

Carmichael, S. and Hamilton, C. (1967) *Black Power: The Politics of Liberation in America*, New York: Vintage Books.

Cashmore, E. (2000) *Ethnic Minority Police Officers: Final Report*, Stoke: Staffordshire University Press.

Cashmore, E. (2001) 'The experiences of ethnic minority police officers in Britain: under-recruitment and racial profiling in a performance culture', *Ethnic and Racial Studies*, 24(4), July: 642–59.

Cathcart, B. (2000) *The Case of Stephen Lawrence*, London: Penguin.

Chakraborti, N. and Garland, J. (2003a) 'An "invisible" problem? Uncovering the nature of racist victimisation in rural Suffolk', *International Review of Victimology*, 10: 1–17.

Chakraborti, N. and Garland, J. (2003b) 'Under-researched and overlooked: an exploration of the attitudes of rural minority ethnic communities towards crime, community safety and the criminal justice system', *Journal of Ethnic and Migration Studies*.

Chan, J. (1996) 'Changing police culture', *British Journal of Criminology*, 36(1): 109–34.

Chan, J. (1997) *Changing Police Culture*, Sydney: Cambridge University Press.

Clancy, A., Hough, M., Aust, R. and Kershaw, C. (2001) *Crime, Policing and Justice: the Experience of Ethnic Minorities: Findings from the 2000 British Crime Survey*, Research Study 223, London: Home Office.

Clarke, J. (1996) 'Crime and social order: interrogating the detective story', in Muncie, J. and McLaughlin, E. (eds) *The Problem of Crime*, London: Sage, pp. 65–100.

Cochrane, R. and Butler, A.J.P. (1980) 'The values of police officers, recruits and civilians in England', *Journal of Police Science and Administration*, 8: 73–88.

Cohen, N. (2003) 'Dancing to the same tune', *Observer*, 10 August.

Colman, A. and Gorman, L. (1982) 'Conservatism, dogmatism and authoritarianism in British police officers', *Sociology*, February.

Commission for Racial Equality (1996) *Race and Equal Opportunities in the Police Service – a Programme for Action*, London: Commission for Racial Equality.

Commission for Racial Equality (2002) *The Duty to Promote Race Equality: Performance Guidelines for Police Forces and Authorities*, London: Commission for Racial Equality.

Crown Prosecution Service (2001) *RIMS Annual Report, 1999–2000*, London: Crown Prosecution Service.

Dixon, D. (1997) *Law in Policing: Legal Regulation and Police Practices*, London: Clarendon Press.

Eboda, M. (2003) 'When being black and driving a Jaguar makes you a criminal', *Observer*, 23 February, p.3.

Edwards, A. and Benyon, J. (2000) 'Community governance, crime control and local diversity', *Crime Prevention and Community Safety: an International Journal*, 2(3): 35–54.

Emsley, C. (1983) *Policing and Its Context, 1750–1870*, London: Macmillan.

Emsley, C. (1987) *Crime and Society in England 1750–1900*, London: Longman.

Emsley, C. (1996) *The English Police* (2nd edn), London: Harvester Wheatsheaf.

FitzGerald, M. (1999) *Searches in London Under S1 of the Police and Criminal Evidence Act*, London: Metropolitan Police.

FitzGerald, M. and Sibbit, R. (1997) *Ethnic Monitoring in Police Forces: a Beginning*, Research Study 173, London: Home Office.

Forbes, D. (1988) *Action on Racial Harassment: Legal Remedies and Local Authorities*, London: Legal Action Unit and London Housing Group.

Gadher, D., Ludlow, M. and Lepperd, D. (2003) 'Silenced by the rule of the gun', *Sunday Times*, pp.12–13.

Garland, J. and Rowe, M. (2001) *Racism and Antiracism in Football*, Basingstoke: Palgrave.

Giddens, A. (1990) *The Consequences of Modernity*, Cambridge: Polity Press.

Gilroy, P. (1987) 'The myth of black criminality', in Scraton, P. (ed.) *Law, Order, and the Authoritarian State*, Milton Keynes: Open University Press, pp. 107–20.

Gilroy, P. (1990) 'The end of anti-racism', in Ball, W. and Solomos, J. (eds) *Race and Local Politics*, London: Macmillan.

Glass, R. (1960) *The Newcomers*, London: Centre for Urban Studies.

Goldstein, H. (1964) 'Police discretion: the ideal versus the real', *Public Administration Review*, 23: 140–8.

Goldstein, H. (1979) *Problem-Oriented Policing*, New York: McGraw-Hill.

Goldstein, J. (1960) 'Police discretion not to invoke the criminal process: low-visibility decisions in the administration of justice', *Yale Law Journal*, 69: 543–94.

Gordon, P. (1986) *Racial Violence and Harassment*, London: Runnymede Trust.

Gordon, P. (1990) *Racial Violence and Harassment* (2nd edn), London: Runnymede Trust.

Graef, R. (1989) *Talking Blues*, London: Collins.

Greaves, G. (1984) 'The Brixton disorders', in Benyon, J. (ed) *Scarman and After – Essays Reflecting on Lord Scarman's Report, the Riots and their Aftermath*, Oxford: Pergamon Press, pp. 63–72.

The Guardian (2001) 'Met invitation leaves poet lost for words', 3 July.

The Guardian (2002) 'A year of reckoning', 21 February.

The Guardian (2003a) 'Police hit by fresh claims of racism', 29 October.

The Guardian (2003b) 'Met reinstates Ali Dizaei after £7m inquiry fiasco', 31 October.

The Guardian (2003c) 'Met's "black bounty" recruitment plan shelved', 20 May.

The Guardian (2003d) 'Momentum in fight against racism "wanes" ', 19 April.

The Guardian (2003e) 'Minister labelled racist after attack on rap "idiots"', 6 January.

The Guardian (2003f) 'Met faces boycott in race row', 16 September.

Hague, W. (2000) 'Where was Jack Straw when Damilola died?', *Sunday Telegraph*, 17 December.

Hall, S., Critcher, C., Jefferson, T., Clarke, J. and Roberts, B. (1978) *Policing the Crisis: Mugging, the State, and Law and Order*, London: Macmillan.

Hall, T. (1988) 'Race relations training: a personal view', in Southgate, P. (ed) *New Directions in Police Training*, London: Home Office.

Hare, I. (1997) 'Legislating against hate: the legal response to bias crimes', *Oxford Journal of Legal Studies*, 17(3): 415–39.

Her Majesty's Inspectorate of Constabulary (1996) *Developing Diversity in the Police Service*, London: Home Office.

Her Majesty's Inspectorate of Constabulary (1997) *Winning the Race: Policing Plural Communities*, London: Home Office.

Her Majesty's Inspectorate of Constabulary (1999a) *Managing Learning: a Thematic Inspection of Police Training*, London: Home Office.

Her Majesty's Inspectorate of Constabulary (1999b) *Winning the Race: Policing Plural Communities – Revisited*, London: Home Office.

Her Majesty's Inspectorate of Constabulary (2000) *Policing London: 'Winning Consent'*, London: Home Office.

Her Majesty's Inspectorate of Constabulary (2001) *Winning the Race: Embracing Diversity*, London: Home Office.

Her Majesty's Inspectorate of Constabulary (2003) *Diversity Matters*, London: Home Office.

Hesse, B., Rai, D.K., Bennett, C. and McGilchrist, P. (1992) *Beneath the Surface: Racial Harassment*, Aldershot: Avebury.

Hinsliff, G., Bright, M. and Burke, J. (2003) 'Pop industry makes guns glamorous, say police', *Observer*, 5 January, p.1.

Holdaway, S. (1996) *The Racialisation of British Policing*, Basingstoke: Macmillan.

Holdaway, S. (1999) 'Police, race relations', position paper for The Commission on the Future of Multi-Ethnic Britain, London: Runnymede Trust.

Holdaway, S. and Baron, A.M. (1997) *Resigners? The Experience of Black and Asian Police Officers*, London: Macmillan.

Home Office (1998a) *Crime and Disorder Act 1998: Guidance on Crime and Disorder Reduction Partnerships*, London: Home Office.

Home Office (1998b) *Introductory Guide to the Crime and Disorder Act*, London: Home Office.

Home Office (1999a) *Dismantling Barriers to Reflect the Community We Serve – the Recruitment, Retention and Progression of Ethnic Minority Officers*, London: Home Office.

Home Office (1999b) *Stephen Lawrence Inquiry: Home Secretary's Action Plan*, London: Home Office.

Home Office (2000a) *Statistics on Race and the Criminal Justice System*, London: Home Office.

Home Office (2000b) *Statistics on Women and the Criminal Justice System*, London: Home Office.

Home Office (2000c) *Police Stops and Searches: Lessons from a Programme of Research*, London: Policing and Reducing Crime Unit, Home Office.

Home Office (2000d) *Auditing Organisational Culture Within the Police Service*, Home Office Circular 14/2000, London: Home Office.

Home Office (2001) *Specialist Support in Police Community Relations*, Home Office Circular 6/2001, London: Policing and Reducing Crime Unit, Home Office.

Home Office (2002a) *PACE Review: Report of the Joint Home Office/Cabinet Office Review of the Police and Criminal Evidence Act 1984*, London: Home Office.

Home Office (2002b) *The National Policing Plan, 2003–2006*, London: Home Office.

Home Office (2003) *Race Equality: The Home Secretary's Employment Targets*, London: Home Office.

Hope, R. (1995) 'Copper and black', *Policing*, 11: 36–45.

House of Commons Home Affairs Select Committee (1982) *Racial Attacks, second report*, London: HMSO.

House of Commons Home Affairs Select Committee (1997) *Police Complaints and Disciplinary Procedures*, HC 258, London: House of Commons.

House of Commons Home Affairs Select Committee (1998) *Confidentiality of Police Settlements of Civil Claims*, HC 894, London: House of Commons.

Hughes, G. (1994) 'Talking cop shop? A case study of police community consultative groups in transition', *Policing and Society*, 4: 253–70.

Ianni, E.R. and Ianni, R. (1983) 'Street cops and management cops: the two cultures of policing', in Punch, M. (ed) *Control in the Police Organisation*, Cambridge, MA: MIT Press.

Iganski, P. (1999) 'Why make hate a crime?', *Critical Social Policy*, 19(3): 386–95.

Iganski, P. (2001) 'Hate crimes hurt more', *American Behavioral Scientist*, 45(4): 626–38.

Iganski, P. (ed.) (2002) *The Hate Debate: Should Hate be Punished as a Crime?*, London: Institute for Jewish Policy Research.

Imbert, P. (1991) 'Preparing police to deal with a multicultural society', *International Contemporary Police Review*, March–April: 2–8.

Independent (1999) ' "Institutional Racism" – the official meaning', 25 February.

Independent (2003a) 'We are still racist, police chief admits', 22 April.

Independent (2003b) 'Reformed gangsters should give gun talks in school', 8 January.

Institute of Race Relations (1979) *Police Against Black People, Evidence Submitted to the Royal Commission on Criminal Procedure*, London: Institute of Race Relations.

Jacobs, J. and Potter, K. (1998) *Hate Crimes: Criminal Law and Identity Politics*, New York: Oxford University Press.

Jason-Lloyd, L. (2000) *An Introduction to Policing and Police Powers*, London: Cavendish Publishing.

Jefferson, T. and Grimshaw, R. (1984) *Controlling the Constable: Police Accountability in England and Wales*, London: Muller.

Jencks, C. (1992) *Rethinking Social Policy*, Cambridge, MA: Harvard University Press.

Jenkins, R. and Solomos, J. (eds) (1987) *Racism and Equal Opportunity in the 1980s*, Cambridge: Cambridge University Press.

Jenness, V. (2002) 'Contours of hate crime politics and law in the United States', in Iganski, P. (ed) *The Hate Debate: Should Hate be Punished as a Crime?*, London: Institute for Jewish Policy Research.

Johnston, L. (2000) *Policing Britain: Risk, Security and Governance*, Harlow: Longman.

Jones, T. and Newburn, T. (2001) *Widening Access: Improving Police Relations with Hard to Reach Groups*, Police Research Series 138, London: Home Office.

Katz, J. (1978) *White Awareness: Handbook for Anti-racism Trainers*, Oklahoma: Oklahoma University Press.

Keith, M. (1988) 'Squaring circles? Consultation and "inner city" policing', *New Community*, 15(1): 63–77.

Keith, M. (1991) 'Policing a perplexed society?: No-go areas and the mystification of police-black conflict', in Cashmore, E. and McLaughlin, E. (eds) *Out of Order? Policing Black People*, London: Routledge, pp. 189–214.

Keith, M. (1993) *Race, Riots and Policing: Lore and Disorder in a Multiracist Society*, London: UCL Press.

Kirkpatrick, D. (1998) *Evaluating Training Programs*, San Francisco: Berrett-Koehler.

Knights, E. (1988) 'Foreword', in Southgate, P. (ed) *New Directions in Police Training*, London: Home Office.

Langmead-Jones, P. (1999) *On a Course: Reducing the Impact of Police Training on Availability for Ordinary Duty*, Police Research Series Paper 111, London: Home Office.

Lea, J. and Young, J. (1984) *What is to be Done About Law and Order?*, Harmondsworth: Penguin.

Leigh, A., Johnson, G., and Ingram, A. (1998) *Deaths in Police Custody: Learning the Lessons*, Police Research Series Paper 26, London: Home Office.

Leigh, A., Read, T., and Tilley, N. (1996) *Problem Oriented Policing: Brit Pop*, Crime Detection and Prevention Series Paper 75, London: Home Office.

Leigh, A., Read, T. and Tilley, N. (1998) *Brit Pop II: Problem-Oriented Policing*, Police Research Series 93, London: Home Office.

Leinen, S. (1984) *Black Police: White Society*, New York: New York University Press.

Loader, I. and Mulcahy, A. (2001) 'The power of legitimate naming: Part II – Making sense of the elite police voice', *British Journal of Criminology*, 41: 252–65.

Loader, I. and Mulcahy, A. (2003) *Policing and the Condition of England: Memory, Politics and Culture*, Oxford: Oxford University Press.

Long, M. (2003) 'Leadership and performance management', in Newburn, T. (ed) *Handbook of Policing*, Cullompton: Willan Publishing, pp. 628–54.

Luthra, M. and Oakley, R. (1991) *Combating Racism Through Training: A Review of Approaches to Race Training in Organisations*, Policy Paper in Ethnic Relations No. 22, University of Warwick: Centre for Research in Ethnic Relations.

Macpherson, Sir W. (1999) *The Stephen Lawrence Inquiry*, London: HMSO.

Maguire, M. (1994) 'Crime statistics, patterns and trends: changing perceptions and their implications', in Maguire, M., Morgan, R. and Reiner, R. (eds) *The Oxford Handbook of Criminology*, Oxford: Clarendon Press, pp. 233–91.

Mail on Sunday (2003) 'Gun crime requires clear thinking, not just token gestures', 5 January.

Mark, R. (1977) *Policing a Perplexed Society*, London: George and Allen Unwin.

Marlow, A. and Loveday, B. (eds) (2000) *After Macpherson: Policing after the Stephen Lawrence Inquiry*, London: Russell House Publishing.

Maynard, W. and Read, T. (1997) *Policing Racially Motivated Incidents*, Crime Detection and Prevention Series Paper 84, London: Home Office.

McLaughlin, E. (1991) 'Police accountability and black people: into the 1990s', in Cashmore, E. and McLaughlin, E. (eds) *Out of Order? Policing Black People*, London: Routledge, pp. 109–33.

McLaughlin, E. (1996) 'Police, policing and policework', in McLaughlin, E. and Muncie, J. (eds) *Controlling Crime*, London: Sage, pp. 51–106.

McLaughlin, E. and Johansen, A. (2002) 'The prospects for applying restorative justice to citizen complaints against the police in England and Wales', *British Journal of Criminology*, 42: 635–53.

McLaughlin, E. and Murji, K. (1997) 'The future lasts a long time: public policework and the managerialist paradox', in Francis, P., Davies, P. and Jupp, V. (eds) *Policing Futures: The Police, Law Enforcement and the Twenty-First Century*, London: Macmillan.

Metropolitan Police (undated) *Protect and Respect: Diversity Strategy*, London: Home Office.

Metropolitan Police (2000a) *Policing London – Winning Consent: A Review of Murder Investigation and Community and Race Relations Issues in the Metropolitan Police Service*, London: Home Office.

Metropolitan Police (2000b) *Operation Athena: Action Plan Update*, London: Metropolitan Police.

Miles, R. (1989) *Racism*, London: Routledge.

Miles, R. (1993) *Racism After 'Race Relations'*, London: Routledge.

Miller, J., Quinton, P. and Bland, N. (2000) *Police Stops and Searches: Lessons from a Programme of Research*, Police Research Series, Papers 127–32, London: Home Office.

Miller, S. and Palmer, M. (2003) 'Authority, leadership and character', in Adlam, R. and Villiers, P. (eds) *Police Leadership in the Twenty First Century: Philosophy, Doctrine and Developments*, Winchester: Waterside Press, pp. 105–18.

Mooney, J. and Young, J. (2000) 'Policing ethnic minorities: stop and search in North London', in Marlow, A. and Loveday, B. (eds) *After Macpherson: Policing After the Stephen Lawrence Inquiry*, Lyme Regis: Russell House Publishing, pp. 73–87.

Morgan, R. (1992) 'Talking about policing', in Downes, D. (ed) *Unravelling Criminal Justice*, London: Macmillan.

Morris, L. (1994) *Dangerous Classes: the Underclass and Social Citizenship*, London: Routledge.

Morsch, J. (1991) 'The problem of motive in hate crimes: the argument against presumptions of racial motivation', *Journal of Criminal Law and Criminology*, 82(3): 659–89.

Mulraney, S. (2002) 'Senior officer warns that one million stops could be recorded', *Police Review*, 22 November, p. 6.

MVA and Miller, J. (2000) *Profiling Populations Available for Stops and Searches*, Police Research Series Paper 131, London: Home Office.

Oakley, R. (1989) 'Community and race relations training for the police: a review of developments', *New Community*, 16(1): 61–79.

Observer (2003) 'It's no longer a black-on-black problem', 5 January.

O'Byrne, M. (2000) 'Can Macpherson succeed where Scarman failed?', in Marlow, A. and Loveday, B. (eds) *After Macpherson: Policing After the Stephen Lawrence Inquiry*, London: Russell House Publishing, pp. 107–12.

PA News (1998) Commissioner Sir Paul Condon, Evidence to the Lawrence Inquiry, 31 October.

Panzarella, R. (2003) 'Leadership myths and realities', in Adlam, R. and Villiers, P. (eds) *Police Leadership in the Twenty First Century: Philosophy, Doctrine and Developments*, Winchester: Waterside Press, pp. 119–33.

Pawson, R. and Tilley, N. (1997) *Realistic Evaluation*, London: Sage.

Pearson, G. (1983) *Hooligan – a History of Respectable Fears*, London: Macmillan.

Phillips, M. (2002) 'Hate crime: the Orwellian response to prejudice', in Iganski, P. (ed.) *The Hate Debate: Should Hate be Punished as a Crime?*, London: Institute for Jewish Policy Research.

Police Review (2001a) 'President delivers race relations warning to BCU commanders', 16 February, p. 6.

Police Review (2001b) 'Diversity drive "not motivated" by human rights', 27 April, p. 14.

Police Review (2001c) ' "Changing" Met must reach out to minorities', 27 April, p.15.

Police Review (2002a) 'Fewer stops but imbalance still exists for ethnic minorities', 30 August, p. 7.

Police Review (2002b) 'Force hopefuls', 30 August, p. 6.

Police Review (2002c) 'Course aims to boost black officers' promotion prospects', 30 August, p. 6

Police Review (2002d) 'Plan to increase ethnic officers in specialisms', 17 May, p. 13.

Police Training Council (1983) *Community and Race Relations Training for the Police: Report of the PTC Working Party*, London: Home Office.

Reiner, R. (1978) *The Blue Coated Worker*, Cambridge: Cambridge University Press.

Reiner, R. (1992) *The Politics of the Police* (2nd edn), London: Harvester Wheatsheaf.

Reiner, R. (1994) 'Policing and the police', in Maguire, M., Morgan, R. and Reiner, R. (eds) *The Oxford Handbook of Criminology* (1st edn), Oxford: Oxford University Press, pp. 705–72.

Reiner, R. (1995) 'The perfidy of the paramour: how the police fell out of love with the Conservatives', *Times Literary Supplement* (4822), 1 Sept., pp. 9–10.

Reiner, R. (2000) *The Politics of the Police* (3rd edn), Oxford: Oxford University Press.

Reith, C. (1956) *A New Study of Police History*, London: Oliver and Boyd.

Rowe, M. (1995) 'The police and stereotypes of ethnic minorities', in Shelley, L. and Vigh, J. (eds) *Social Change, Crime and the Police*, Reading: Harwood Academic Publishers, pp. 130–43.

Rowe, M. (1998) *The Racialisation of Disorder in Twentieth Century Britain*, Aldershot: Ashgate.

Rowe, M. (1999) 'Institutional racism', *Politics Review*, 9(2): 32–4.

Rowe, M. (2002a) 'Policing diversity: themes and concerns from the recent British experience', *Police Quarterly*, 5(4): 424–46.

Rowe, M. (2002b) 'The changing politics of race and ethnicity', *Politics Review*, 12(1): 32–3.

Rowe, M. (2003) ' "To think this is England": culture, "racial difference" and law and order in Britain', in Melossi, D. (ed.) *Migrations, Interactions and Conflicts in the Making of European Democracy*, Bolgna: Giuffrè, pp. 1041–62.

Saggar, S. (ed.) (1998) *Race and British Electoral Politics*, London: UCL Press.

Sampson, F. (2001) *Blackstone's Police Manual, General Police Duties, Human Rights Edition*, London: Blackstone Press.

Saulsbury, W.E. and Bowling, B. (1991) *The Multi-Agency Approach in Practice: the North Plaistow Racial Harassment Project*, Home Office: Research and Planning Unit Paper 64, London: HMSO.

Savage, S. (1984) 'Political control or community liaison?', *Political Quarterly*, 55(1): 48–59.

Scarman, Lord (1981) *The Brixton Disorders: 10–12 April 1981 – Report of an Inquiry by the Rt Hon Lord Scarman, OBE*, London: HMSO.

Scraton, P. (1985) *The State of the Police*, London: Pluto Press.

Scraton, P. (ed.) (1987) *Law, Order, and the Authoritarian State*, Milton Keynes: Open University Press.

Scripture, A.E. (1997) 'The sources of police culture: demographic or environmental variables?', *Policing and Society*, 7: 163–76.

Select Committee on Race Relations and Immigration (1972) *Police/Immigrant Relations*, London: HMSO.

Sherman, L.W. (1983) 'After the riots: police and minorities in the United States, 1970–1980', in Glazer, N. and Young, K. (eds) *Ethnic Pluralism and Public Policy*, London: Heinemann, pp. 212–35.

Sim, J. (1982) 'Scarman: the police counter attack', *The Socialist Register*, London: The Merlin Press, pp. 57–77.

Singh, G. (2000) 'The concept and context of institutional racism', in Marlow, A. and Loveday, B. (eds) *After Macpherson — Policing After the Stephen Lawrence Inquiry*, Lyme Regis: Russell House, pp. 29–40.

Sivanandan, A. (1985) 'RAT and the degradation of the black struggle', *Race and Class*, 26(4): 1–33.

Skolnick, J. (1966) *Justice Without Trial: Law Enforcement in a Democratic Society*, New York and London: Wiley.

Skolnick, J. (1969) *The Politics of Protest*, New York: Simon and Schuster.

Skolnick, J.H. (1975) 'Why police behave the way they do', in Skolnick, J.H. and Gray, T.C. (eds) *Police in America*, Boston: Little Brown and Company.

Small, C. (2001) *Towards an Understanding of Resilience of Police Organizational Culture*, Unpublished MSc dissertation, Leicester: Scarman Centre, University of Leicester.

Smith, D.J. (1983) *A Survey of Police Officers*, London: Policy Studies Institute.

Smith, D.J. (1994) 'Race, crime and criminal justice', in Maguire, M., Morgan, R. and Reiner, R. (eds) *The Oxford Handbook of Criminology*, Oxford: Clarendon Press, pp. 1041–117.

Solomos, J. (1991) *Black Youth, Racism and the State: the Politics of Ideology and Policy*, Cambridge: Cambridge University Press.

Solomos, J. (1993) *Race and Racism in Britain* (2nd edn), London: Macmillan.

Solomos, J. (1999) 'Social research and the Stephen Lawrence Inquiry', *Sociological Research Online*, 4(1).

Southgate, P. (1982) *Police Probationer Training in Race Relations*, Research and Planning Unit Paper 8, London: Home Office.

Sparks, R. (2001) ' "Bringing it all back home": populism, media coverage and the dynamics of locality and globality in the politics of crime control', in Stenson, K. and Sullivan, R.R. (eds) *Crime, Risk and Justice – The Politics of Crime Control in Liberal Democracies*, Cullompton: Willan, pp. 194–213.

Steedman, C. (1984) *Policing the Victorian Community: the Formation of English Provincial Police Forces 1856–80*, London: Routledge and Kegan Paul.

Stephens, M. (1988) *Policing: the Critical Issues*, London: Harvester Wheatsheaf.

Stone, V. and Pettigrew, N. (2000) *The Views of the Public on Stops and Searches*, Police Research Series Paper 129, London: Home Office.

Stone, V. and Tuffin, R. (2000) *Attitudes of People from Minority Ethnic Communities Towards a Career in the Police Service*, Police Research Series Paper 136, London: Home Office.

Storch, R.D. (1975) 'The policeman as domestic missionary: urban discipline and popular culture in Northern England, 1850–1880', *Journal of Social History*, 9: 481–509.

Sunday Telegraph (2003) 'The bloody streets of Birmingham', 5 January, p. 18.

Tatchell, P. (2002) 'Some people are more equal than others', in Iganski, P. (ed) *The Hate Debate: Should Hate be Punished as a Crime?*, London: Institute for Jewish Policy Research.

The Times (1995) 'Police blame cultural gap for rioting', 12 June.

The Times (1997) 'Lawrence family to sue men cleared of racist murder', 14 February.

Thompson, E.P. (1968) *The Making of the English Working Class*, Harmondsworth: Penguin.

Thompson, G., Frances, J., Levacic, R. and Mitchell, J. (eds) (1993) *Markets, Hierarchies and Networks – the Coordination of Social Life*, London: Sage.

Trojanowicz, R.C. and Moore, M.H. (1988) *The Meaning of Community in Community Policing*, Michigan State University: the National Center for Community Policing.

Waddington, P.A.J. (1999a) 'Police (canteen) sub-culture: an appreciation', *British Journal of Criminology*, 39(2): 287–309.

Waddington, P.A.J. (1999b) *Policing Citizens*, London: UCL Press.

Walklate, S. (1996) 'Equal opportunities and the future of policing', in Leishman, F., Loveday, B., and Savage, S. (eds) *Core Issues in Policing*, London: Longman.

Westmarland, L. (2001) *Gender and Policing. Sex, Power and Police Culture*, Cullompton: Willan.

Williams, C. (2003) *Rotten Boroughs? How the Towns of England and Wales Lost their Police Forces in 1964*, paper presented to Urban History Workshop, University of Durham.

Young, J. (1994) *Policing the Streets: Stop and Searches in North London*, Middlesex: Centre for Criminology, Middlesex University.

Young, M. (1991) *An Inside Job: Policing and Police Culture in Britain*, Oxford: Oxford University Press.

Index

Acourt, Jamie 5, 6
Acourt, Neil 5, 6
Adams, Rolan 4
Adlam, R. 155, 160, 161
Adorno, T.W. 49
Age 72, 83, 146, 148, 151
Alderson, J. 139
Antisocial behaviour 108,
    115–6, 118, 166
Association of Chief Police
    Officers (ACPO) 13, 21,
    34, 44, 107, 125, 130,
    139, 141, 143
Association of Police
    Authorities 34, 93
Asylum seekers 146, 154,
    169
Audit Commission 127, 128

Banton, M. 10
Barron, A.M. 29, 41
Bauman, Z. 139
BBC 1, 32, 159
Benefield, Stacey 4
Bennett, T. 51
Benyon, J. 92, 127
Bethnal Green and Stepney
    Trades Council 100
Bhangal, Gurdeep 4
Birmingham 96, 164, 166
Black Police Association 13,
    15, 25, 32, 41, 43, 56,
    58–60, 147, 154
Black Power 10
Blagg, H. 100
Blair, Sir Ian 37
Blair, Tony 97
Blunkett, David 97
Bourdieu, P. 53, 58
Bowie, PC 32
Bowling, B. 100, 108, 115

British Crime Survey 91,
    104, 108–9, 112, 114,
    116, 117, 166
British Diversity Awards
    166
Brogden, M. 123, 160, 162
Brooks, Duwayne 4, 44
Brown, J. 41
Brunel University 64
Bunyard, R. 57
Burney, E. 114, 116, 118
Burrows, J. 108
Butler, A.J.P. 50

Carmichael, S. 10
Cashmore, E. 29, 98
Cathcart, B. 4, 5, 6, 8
Centrex 32
Chakraborti, N. 109, 115,
    136, 148
Chan, J. 15, 53, 58, 75, 98,
    131, 160
Christian Police Association
    59
Civil Rights 106
Clancy, A. 92, 104, 105, 117,
    118
Clarke, J. 51
Cochrane, R. 50
Cohen, N. 158
Colman, A. 50
Commission for Racial
    Equality 7, 21, 34, 154
Community, concept of 19,
    39, 64, 128, 136, 145,
    148–52
Condon, Sir Paul 7, 9, 59,
    155
Coroner's Court 6
Crime and criminal
    behaviour 17, 78–80,

82, 90, 94, 97, 108–9,
    112–5
Crime and Disorder Act
    1998 17, 18, 99–100,
    101–2, 106–7, 108, 115,
    116, 127, 166
Crime prevention and
    community safety 34,
    83, 100, 127, 135, 144
Criminal Justice Act 1991
    103
Criminal Justice and Public
    Order Act 1994 17,
    95–6
Criminal justice system 22,
    53, 62, 99, 103, 133
Criminalisation 13, 47,
    78–80, 90, 97, 161–7
Crown Prosecution Service
    5, 18, 103, 109, 111,
    133
Curtis, Les 2

D Ashley 97
Daily Mail 6
Daily Telegraph 155
Demographics 21, 34, 36,
    40, 41, 51, 78, 86, 126
Dick, Cressida 158
Disability 72, 105, 146
Diversity and policing 19,
    37, 46, 61, 72, 137–152
Dixon, D. 36, 50, 131
Dizaei, Ali 3, 25
Dobson, Gary 5, 6
Douglas, Brian 133
Drug-related crime 13, 19,
    84, 96–8, 163, 164–5
Duggal, Rohit 4

Eboda, M. 96

Education 34, 90, 138, 154, 165
Edwards, A. 127
Employment Tribunals 32, 33, 60
Emsley, C. 40, 49, 78, 79, 123, 138
Equal opportunities 21, 41, 141
Equalities Associates 65
Ethnic monitoring 82, 84, 85, 86, 93
Europe 52

Far-right groups
British National Party 4
Ku Klux Klan 2
National Front 128
National Socialist Movement 23
Fernandes, John 49
FitzGerald, M. 85, 86, 88, 90, 91, 94
Forbes, D. 100
Franklin, Mike 60

Gadher, D. 97
GALOP 130
Gangsta rap 164–5
Garage music 164–5
Gardner, Joy 133
Garland, J. 56, 109, 115, 136, 148
Gender 72, 105, 145–6, 148, 150
Ghaffur, Tariq 165
Giddens, A. 150
Gilroy, P. 74, 81, 162
Glass, R. 10
Goldstein, H. 85, 116
Goldstein, J. 85
Gordon, P. 100, 116
Gorman, L. 50
Graef, R. 46, 50, 52
Grant, Bernie 153
Greater London Authority Act 1999 121
Greater London Council 121, 125
Greater London Magistrates Court Authority 121

Grimshaw, R. 140
Guardian 3, 25, 27, 28, 41, 155, 165
Gun-related crime 13, 19, 84, 96–8, 164–5

Hague, W. 86
Halford, Alison 57
Hall, S. 48, 81, 162
Hall, T. 68, 69, 71
Halliday, William 32
Hamilton, C. 10
Harris, Lord 41
Hate crime 18, 99–119, 154
Health services 34, 138
Her Majesty's Inspectorate of Constabulary (HMIC) 20, 21, 22, 24, 25, 28, 31, 33, 34, 44, 60, 63, 68, 70, 72, 75, 76, 77, 85, 88, 128, 134, 140, 143, 146, 147, 149, 156
Herbert, Peter 37
Hesse, B. 100, 116
Heterosexism 106
Hinsliff, G. 97
Holdaway, S. 27, 29, 30, 32, 39, 41, 56, 59
HOLMES (Home Office Large Major Enquiry System) 8
Home Office 13, 17, 21, 22, 23, 24, 34, 35, 37, 50, 62, 63, 86, 87, 89, 93, 102, 105, 110, 121, 124, 130, 134, 143, 144, 146, 150, 154, 155, 167
Homelessness 146
Hope, R. 58
House of Commons Home Affairs Select Committee 100, 130
House of Commons Home Affairs Select Committee on Race Relations and Immigration 1972 24
Housing Act 1996 100
Howells, Kim 165
Hughes, G. 126, 129
Human Rights Act 2000 103
Hussain, Ishfaq 3

Ianni, E.R. 50
Ianni, R. 50
Iganski, P. 103, 104, 105, 106, 107
Independent 158, 165
Independent Police Complaints Commission 18, 121, 131–2
India 53
Inquest 130, 133
Institute of Race Relations 82, 99
Institutional racism 3, 7, 9, 10–12, 15, 16, 19, 33, 34, 45, 53, 55, 65, 66, 71, 73, 75, 156, 158, 160, 167–9
Ionann Management Consultants 63, 65, 67
Irish community 16, 78, 138
Islam 28, 29, 163

Jacobs, J. 103
Jamaica 97
Japan 53
Jason-Lloyd, L. 83
Jasper, Lee 158, 159, 165
Jefferson, T. 140
Jencks, C. 79
Jenkins, R. 45
Jenness, V. 103, 106, 117
Jewish community 78, 138, 163
Jewish Police Association 59
Johansen, A. 130, 132
Johnston, L. 137, 151
Jones, T. 127, 128, 147, 149

Keith, M. 11, 12, 18, 46, 76, 81, 90, 125, 126, 150, 151
Knight, Luke 5, 6
Knights, E. 62
Kwaku 166

Langmead-Jones, P. 68
Lawrence Report 1, 2, 3, 4, 8, 13, 14, 15, 16, 17, 18, 19, 20, 31, 34, 41, 43, 45, 53, 55, 56, 58, 61, 62, 70, 72, 74, 75, 80, 89, 96, 97,

99, 100, 106, 116, 119,
120, 121, 130, 133, 137,
138, 140–4, 145, 147,
153, 154, 155, 156, 159,
160, 161, 163, 164, 167
Lawrence, Doreen 5, 6, 159
Lawrence, Neville 5, 6
Lawrence, Stephen 1, 4–7,
43, 44, 61
Lea, J. 82, 126, 129
Leicester 127
Leigh, A. 51, 116, 133
Leinen, S. 27
Lesbian and Gay Police
Association 59
Liverpool 123
Loader, I. 125, 138, 139, 155,
157, 158, 162
Local government 74,
99–100, 122, 125, 126,
127, 128, 134, 154
Long, M. 161
Loveday, B. 66
Luthra, M. 73

Macpherson Report, see
Lawrence Report
Macpherson, Sir W. 6, 7, 8,
10, 34, 56, 80, 86, 116,
143
Maguire, M. 108
Mail on Sunday 165
Mandela, Nelson 5
Mark, R. 48
Marlow, A. 66
Maynard, W. 119
McLaughlin, E. 18, 55, 121,
125, 126, 130, 132, 134
Media 1, 2–3, 6, 12, 17, 23,
50, 51–2, 79, 81, 96, 122,
150, 155, 159, 164
Metropolitan Police 9, 15,
23, 24, 25, 32, 35, 36, 38,
42, 48, 49, 55, 58, 59, 63,
66, 78, 85, 88, 89, 92,
110, 111, 112, 120,
121–2, 124, 130, 143,
153, 155
Diversity Directorate 158
Operation Athena 154
Operation Swamp '81 82
Operation Trident 97

'Plus Programme' 139
'Protect and Respect' 37,
143
Racial and Violent Crime
Taskforce 112, 154
Special Patrol Group 80,
83
Metropolitan Police Act
1839 81
Metropolitan Police
Authority 28, 37, 120–1
Michael, David 24, 56, 58,
59
Miles, R. 12, 76, 79, 95
Miller, J. 84, 89, 90
Miller, S. 161
Minority ethnic
communities 16, 21, 23,
28, 38, 62, 65, 68, 69–70,
74, 78, 79, 83, 89, 120,
125, 126, 130, 138,
148–9, 153, 157, 166,
168
Mooney, J. 92
Moore, M.H. 149, 150
Morgan, R. 126
Morris, L. 79
Morsch, J. 102
Mulcahy, A. 125, 138, 139,
155, 157, 158, 162
Mulraney, S. 93
Multi-agency partnerships
17, 100, 127, 128, 135,
144
Murji, K. 134
Muslim Police Association
59
MVA 89, 90

National Council for Civil
Liberties 22
National Crime Squad 38
National Criminal
Intelligence Service 38
National Police Training 32
National Policing Plan 144,
150, 166
New South Wales 54, 98,
131
Newburn, T. 127, 128, 147,
149
Norris, Clifford 8

Norris, David 5, 6, 8
North America 53
Northern Ireland 37
Notting Hill 124
Nottingham 124, 127

O'Byrne, M. 154
Oakley, R. 64, 73
Observer 166
Ousely, Herman 7

PA News 10
Palmer, M. 161
Panzarella, R. 160
Patani, Anil 32
Pawson, R. 157
Pearson, G. 78, 81, 162
Pearson, Lee 4
Pettigrew, N. 91, 93, 159
Phillips, M. 102
Police
accountability 18, 84, 92,
93, 97, 120–136
attitudes and behaviour
of staff 15, 16, 28, 33,
39, 43, 44, 46–54, 57, 63,
71, 72–3, 92, 119, 133,
168
civilian staff 13, 16, 21, 28,
36, 61, 62, 66, 67–8, 74,
131
community and race
relations/diversity
training 13, 15–6, 38,
45, 47, 50, 57, 61–77,
147
community policing 51,
123, 137–8, 139, 144
community support
officers 68
complaints and discipline
3, 18, 45, 48, 49, 51, 57,
60, 74, 93, 120–36
consent 40–1, 42, 48, 120,
123, 139, 144
corruption 8, 41, 57, 130,
131, 160, 162
discretion 44, 84, 93
first-aid training 8, 61, 99
governance 18, 19, 93,
120–36, 138, 140, 143,
154, 157, 168

history 40, 41, 78–9, 81,
120, 138, 144
leadership and
management 7, 8, 11,
14, 32, 45, 50, 54, 55,
59–60, 67–8, 73, 74, 77,
98, 123–4, 134, 135, 140,
142, 144, 145, 155, 156,
158, 160, 167
legitimacy 40, 42, 48
occupational culture 15,
28, 30–1, 39, 43–60,
46–54, 72, 74, 75–6, 81,
94, 98, 131, 160, 168
pay 30
police research 44, 46, 52,
75, 85
private policing 137
problem-oriented
policing 51, 108, 116
public consultation/
liaison 18, 23–4, 28, 39,
50, 61, 99, 126–9, 149,
151, 154
racist abuse by police
staff 29
racist language 28–9, 30,
47, 54
recruitment and retention
of minority ethnic staff
14, 20–42, 44, 49, 56, 57,
74, 149, 159, 168
reform 15, 19, 36–7, 46,
54–8, 60, 62, 74, 121,
137, 138, 153, 154,
156–66, 168
special constables 21,
131
training 7, 32, 33, 43, 47,
49, 50, 54, 61–77, 93, 94,
147, 159
training staff 70–1
use of force 41, 80, 124,
162
women officers 28, 41, 48,
57
Police Act 1964 124, 140
Police and Criminal
Evidence Act 1984
16–7, 36, 50, 80, 83, 85,
86, 87, 92, 93, 94, 125–6,
129

Police and Magistrates
Court Act 1994 127, 134
Police authorities 20, 50, 88,
122, 124, 125, 128, 134
Police Complaints
Authority 18, 121,
129–31, 133
Police Complaints Board
129
Police Consultative
Committees 125–7
Police Federation 2, 58–9,
86, 155
Police Reform Act 2002 68,
121, 131, 134, 144
Police Review 28, 33, 37, 41,
55, 86, 143
Police services
Avon and Somerset 110,
111
Bedfordshire 35, 85, 110,
111
Birmingham City 23
Cambridgeshire 35, 110,
111
Cheshire 2, 110, 111
City of London 110, 111
Cleveland 110, 111, 112
Coventry City 23
Cumbria 110, 111
Derbyshire 110, 111
Devon and Cornwall 110,
111
Dorset 110, 111
Durham 110, 111
Dyfed Powys 110, 111
Essex 110, 111
Gloucestershire 36, 110,
111
Greater Manchester 2, 27,
28, 35, 55, 66, 85, 110,
111, 130, 154, 155
Gwent 110, 111
Hampshire 110, 111
Hertfordshire 35, 85, 110,
111
Humberside 110, 111
Kent 32, 110, 111
Lancashire 35, 85, 110,
111
Leicestershire 25, 36, 85,
86, 110, 111

Lincolnshire 110, 111, 112
Lothian and Borders 26
Merseyside 36, 57, 110,
111
Metropolitan Police, *see
separate entry*
Ministry of Defence
Police 129
National Crime Squad
129
National Criminal
Intelligence Squad 129
Norfolk 35, 110, 111
North Wales 2, 110, 111
North Yorkshire 110, 111
Northamptonshire 35,
110, 111
Northumbria 110, 111
Nottinghamshire 32, 35,
85, 110, 111, 123–4
Royal Parks Police 129
South Wales 110, 111, 112
South Yorkshire 110, 111
Staffordshire 110, 111
Suffolk 110, 111
Surrey 110, 111, 112
Sussex 110, 111
Thames Valley 35, 85,
110, 111
Warwickshire 110, 111
West Mercia 110, 111
West Midlands 3, 35, 85,
110, 111
West Yorkshire 28, 35, 85,
110, 111, 163
Wiltshire 110, 111
Police Training Council 64,
70
Policy Studies Institute 52
'Political correctness' 37, 46,
66, 86, 95, 157, 160, 162
Popkiss, Captain Arthur
123–4
Positive discrimination 27
Potter, K. 103
Prejudice 3, 9, 10, 11, 48–9,
67, 75, 76, 80, 81
Public trust and confidence
in the police 1, 7, 12, 19,
74, 84, 91, 125, 131, 140,
157, 159, 167

Race Relations (Amendment) Act 2000 33, 34, 36, 121, 154
Race Relations Act 1976 11, 27, 33–4
Racial discrimination 11, 32, 33
Racialization 13, 41, 48, 76, 78–80, 84, 154, 161–7, 169
Racially aggravated offences 17, 101–2, 108–9, 110, 112–3, 117
Racist violence and harassment 4, 18, 99–119, 124, 128, 159, 169
Police officers as perpetrators 2, 3, 29, 56, 125
Ramadhar, Ralph 23
Rastafarianism 28
Read, T. 119
Reiner, R. 41, 44, 46, 48, 50, 51, 52, 75, 92, 123, 138, 139, 144, 162
Reith, C. 41
Religion 105, 128, 146, 148, 154, 163
Roberts, Norwell 23, 24
Rose, G. 114, 116, 118
Rowe, M. 40, 41, 56, 66, 124, 138, 163
Royal Commission on Criminal Procedure 1979 82
Royal Commission on the Police 1962 22, 124

Saggar, S. 40
Salmon Report 155
Sampson, F. 83, 84
Saulsbury, W.E. 100
Savage, S. 125
Scarman Report 8, 11, 18, 21, 45, 49, 64, 74, 81, 82, 83, 129, 139, 153, 154, 155, 169

Scarman, Lord 11, 45, 74, 83, 125
Scientific Racism 10, 78–9
Scraton, P. 140
Scripture, A. E. 49
Senior Command Course 32
Sexuality 72, 105, 118, 128, 145–6, 148, 150
Sey, Ibrahim 133
Sharma, Satinda 32
Shearing, C. 160
Sherman, L.W. 40
Sibbit, R. 85, 86, 91
Sihera, Elaine 166
Sim, J. 81
Singh, G. 10
Singh, Surinder 32
Sivanandan, A. 74
Skolnick, J. 49, 75, 85
Small, C. 116
Smith, D.J. 29, 52
So Solid Crew 97
Social order and policing 48, 51–2, 141, 161–7
Sociology of 'race relations' 10
Solomos, J. 11, 45, 153, 162
South Africa 5, 164
Southgate, P. 63
Sparks, R. 150
Steedman, C. 122
Stephens, M. 124, 125
Stereotyping 2, 9, 10, 17, 39, 43, 44–5, 47, 48, 49, 51, 67, 75, 76, 80, 81, 83–4, 86, 90, 94, 96, 98, 133, 141, 148
Stone, V. 30, 31, 56, 91, 93, 159
Stop and search 10, 17, 33, 43, 44, 48, 68, 72, 78–99, 131, 159, 164
Storch, R.D. 48
Straw, Jack 7, 121
Street crime 16, 19, 48, 78, 82, 157, 162, 164, 166
Sunday Telegraph 164

Superintendents' Association 143

Tatchell, P. 105, 107, 146
Terrorism 102–3
The Secret Policeman 1, 12
The Times 23, 163
Thompson, E.P. 162
Thompson, G. 127
Tilley, N. 157
Travellers 146
Trojanowicz, R.C. 149, 150
Tuffin, R. 30, 31, 56

Underclass 78–9, 138
United States 10, 27, 39, 44, 51, 53, 79, 99, 102, 103, 106, 117, 119, 164
Urban unrest 41, 46, 81, 82, 91, 121, 124, 125, 153, 162

Vagrancy Act 1824 80, 82
Victims and victimisation 17, 38, 39, 48, 99, 104–5, 112, 114–6, 117, 119, 166
Villiers, P. 155, 160
Virdi, Girpul 60
Voting behaviour 39–40

Waddington, P.A.J. 15, 44, 52, 53, 90, 139
Walklate, S. 57
Watch Committees 122–4
Weber, Max 41
Westmarland, L. 57
Whitham, Dareen 4
Williams, C. 123
Wilmot, David 155
Witnesses 38, 132

Young, J. 82, 90, 92, 126, 129
Young, M. 57
Yusuf Daar, Mohammed 23

Zephaniah, Benjamin 25, 159